Blues for Lady Day

The Story of Billie Holiday

PAOLO PARISI

ONE PEACE BOOKS

INTRO

"Stormy Blues"

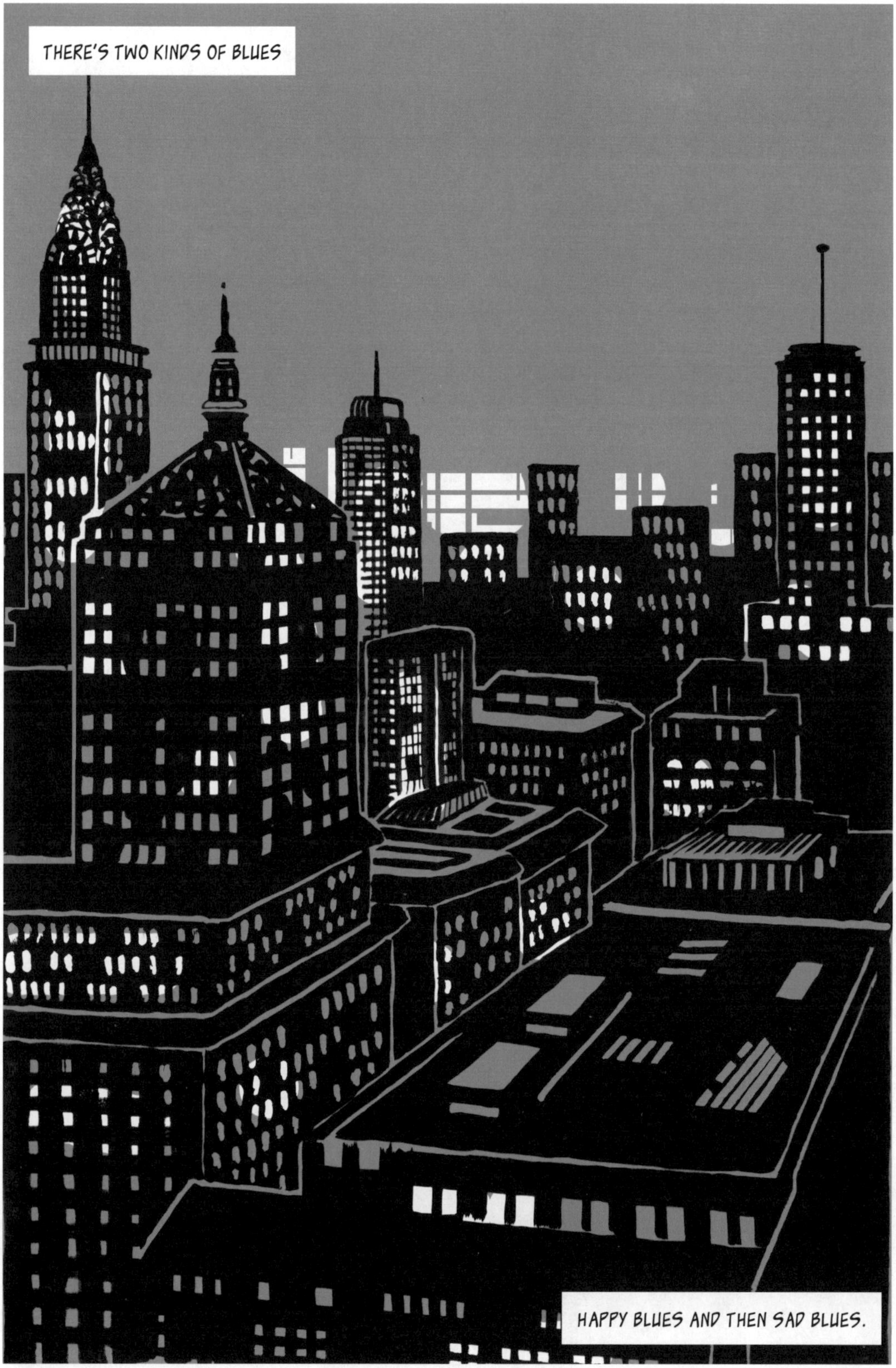
THERE'S TWO KINDS OF BLUES
HAPPY BLUES AND THEN SAD BLUES.

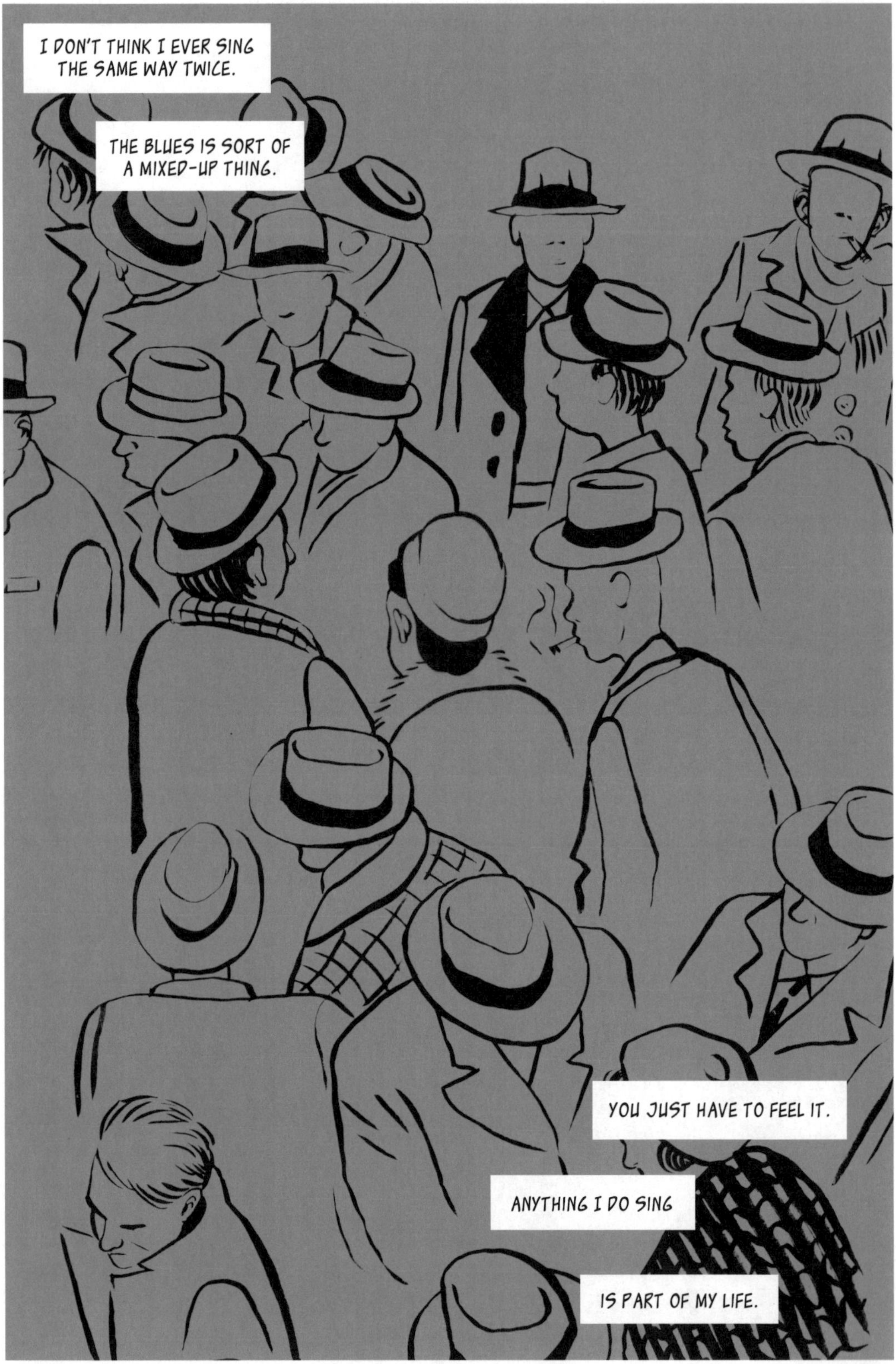
I DON'T THINK I EVER SING THE SAME WAY TWICE.
THE BLUES IS SORT OF A MIXED-UP THING.
YOU JUST HAVE TO FEEL IT.
ANYTHING I DO SING
IS PART OF MY LIFE.

BLUES FOR LADY DAY

"Me, Myself And I"

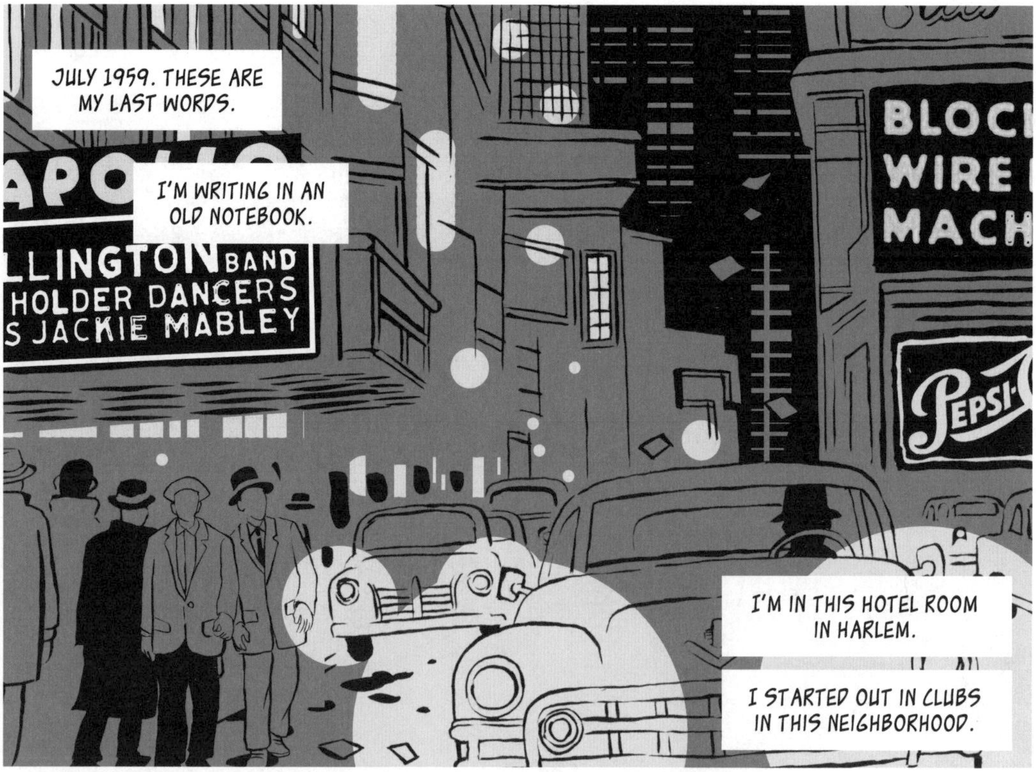
JULY 1959. THESE ARE MY LAST WORDS.
I'M WRITING IN AN OLD NOTEBOOK.
I'M IN THIS HOTEL ROOM IN HARLEM.
I STARTED OUT IN CLUBS IN THIS NEIGHBORHOOD.
APOLLO
LLINGTON BAND
HOLDER DANCERS
S JACKIE MABLEY
BLOC
WIRE
MACH
PEPSI-

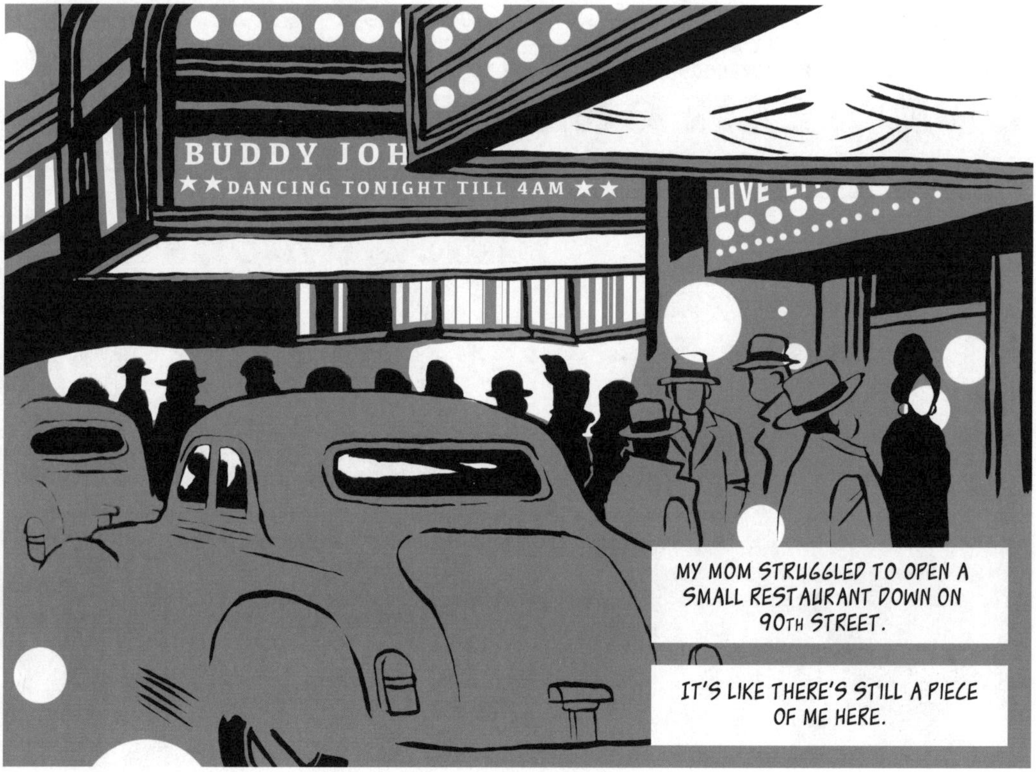
BUDDY JOH
★★DANCING TONIGHT TILL 4AM ★★
LIVE
MY MOM STRUGGLED TO OPEN A SMALL RESTAURANT DOWN ON 90TH STREET.
IT'S LIKE THERE'S STILL A PIECE OF ME HERE.

I WAS BORN IN PHILADELPHIA IN APRIL 1915. MY PARENTS WERE JUST KIDS AND LEFT ME TO BE RAISED BY MY GREAT GRANDMOTHER. SHE WAS 90 YEARS OLD AND HAD BEEN A SLAVE IN THE COTTON FIELDS. SHE COULDN'T READ OR WRITE, BUT KNEW THE WHOLE BIBLE BY HEART.

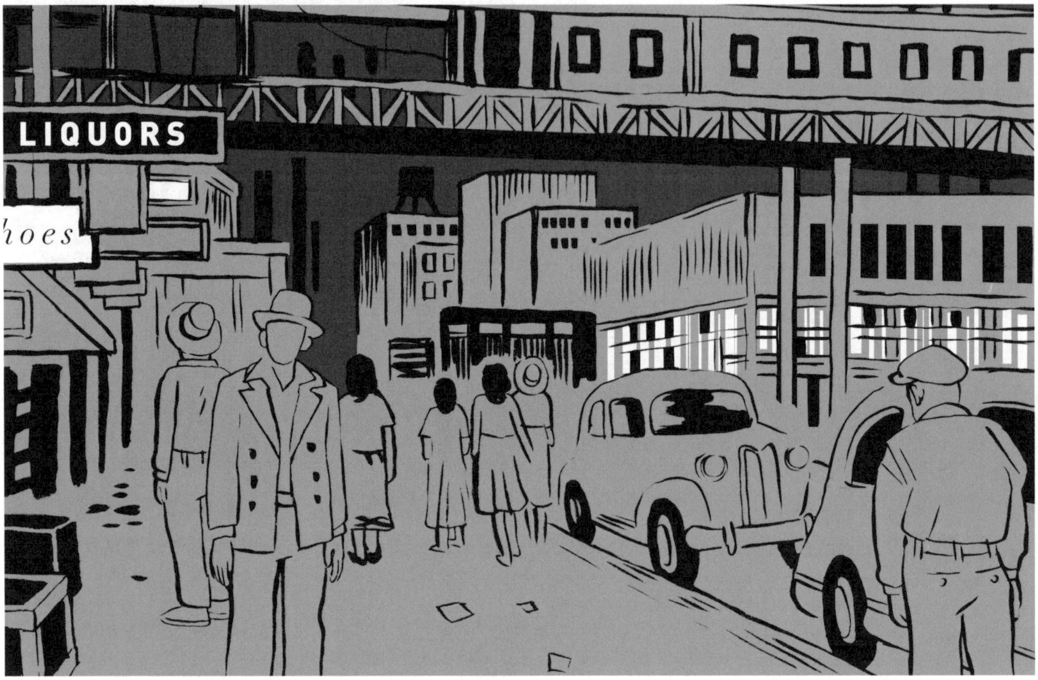
LIQUORS
hoes

BACK THEN, MY FATHER WAS A GUITAR PLAYER WITH FLETCHER HENDERSON'S ORCHESTRA. MY MOTHER HAD MOVED TO NEW YORK TO WORK AS A WAITRESS. I WAS REAL YOUNG, AND FOLLOWED HER TO THE BIG CITY. I STARTED WORKING IN A WHOREHOUSE. THE MONEY WAS GOOD, BUT I SOON GOT INTO TROUBLE.

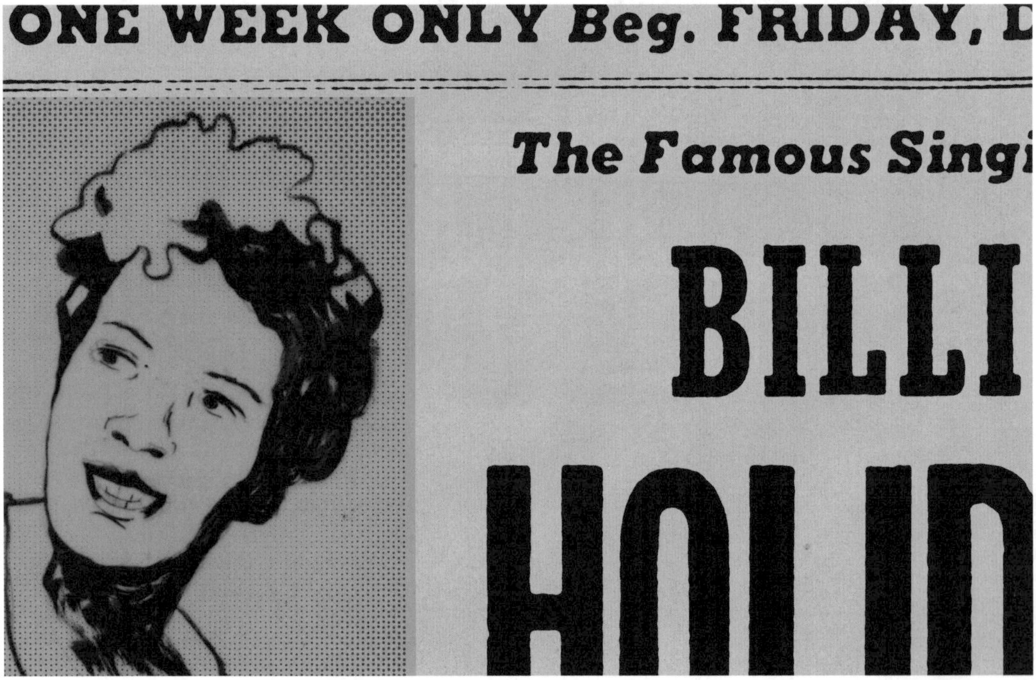
ONE WEEK ONLY Beg. FRIDAY,
The Famous Singi
BILLI
HOLID

I WAS JAILED FOR "PROSTITUTION" AND SERVED A FEW MONTHS AT WELFARE ISLAND ON THE EAST RIVER. WHEN I GOT OUT, MY MOTHER AND I GOT A SMALL APARTMENT TOGETHER IN HARLEM. THE AREA HAD A GREAT BUZZ. IT WAS FULL OF NIGHTCLUBS AND BARS WHICH OFFERED EVERY KIND OF ENTERTAINMENT.

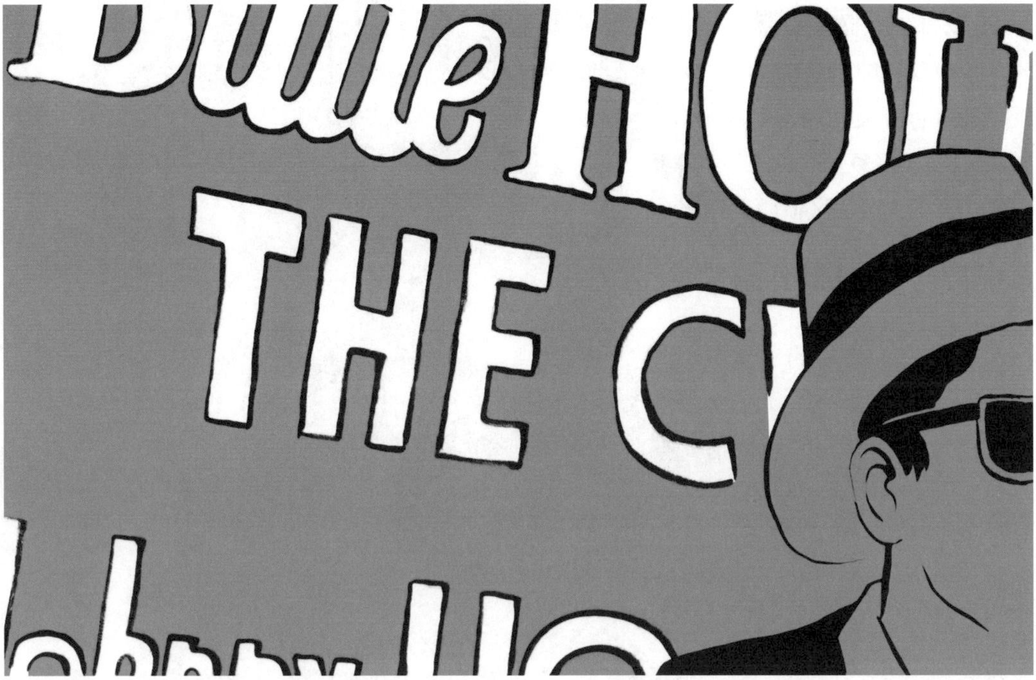

WE TOOK ONE DAY AT A TIME AND ANY JOB WAS GOOD TO HELP US GET BY. THEN ONE EVENING, PURELY BY CHANCE, I HAPPENED TO WALK INTO POD'S AND JERRY'S ON 7TH AVE. AND SOMEONE ASKED IF I COULD SING. IT WAS MY FIRST TIME, IT HAD NEVER CROSSED MY MIND TO GET UP ON STAGE. THAT'S WHEN MY CAREER AS A BLUES SINGER OFFICIALLY STARTED.

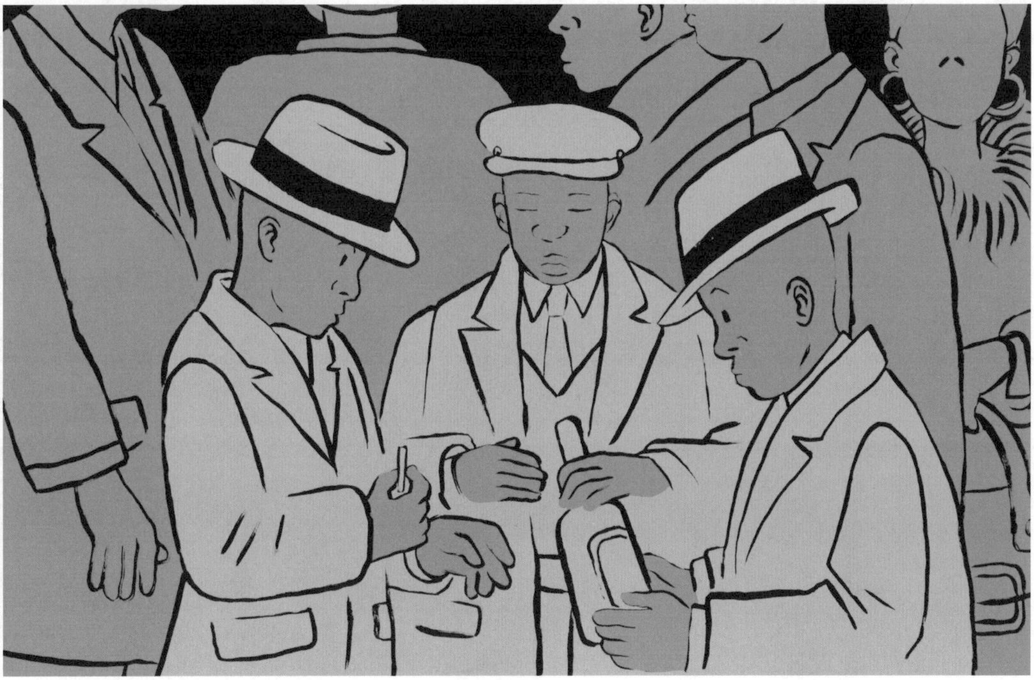

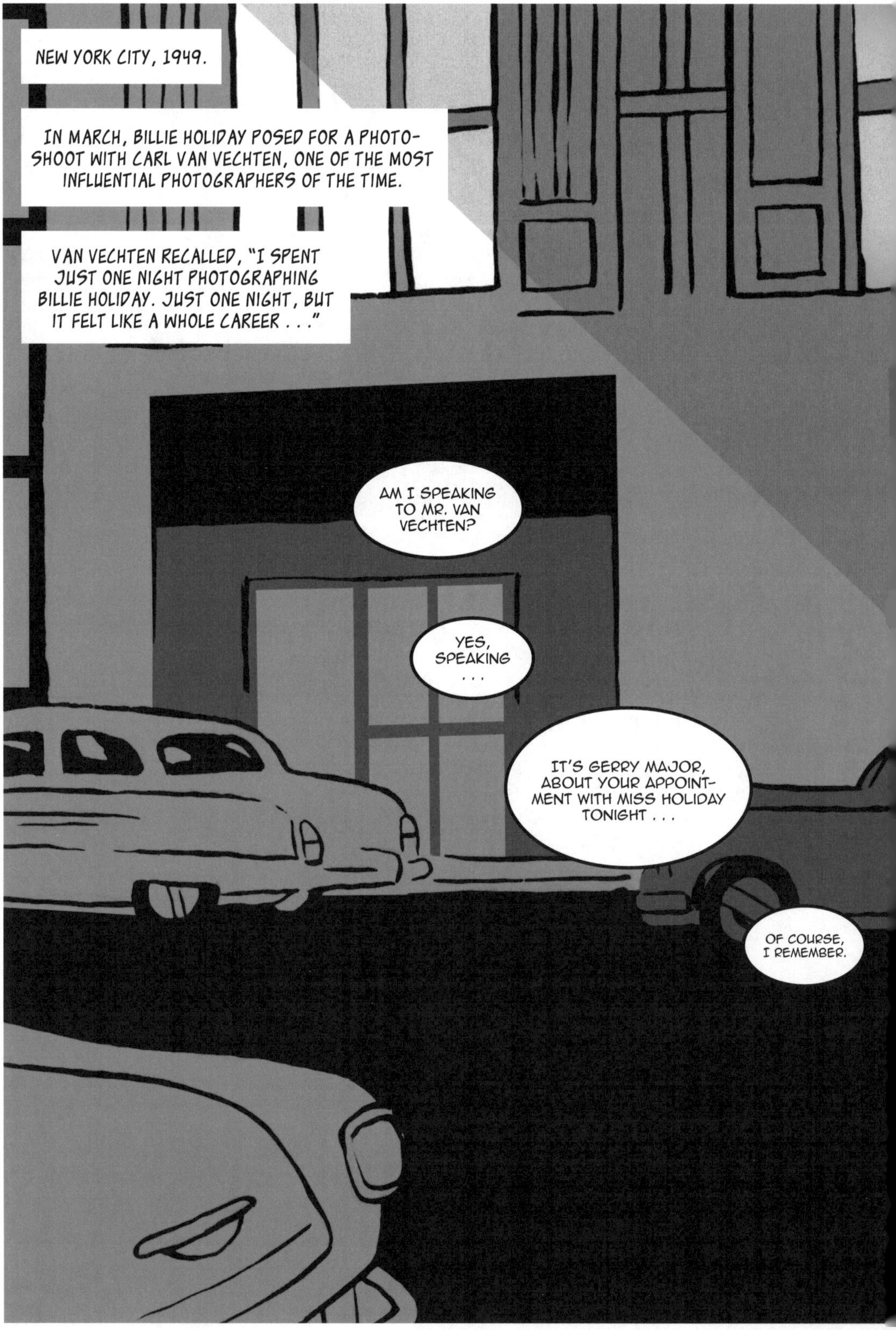
NEW YORK CITY, 1949.
IN MARCH, BILLIE HOLIDAY POSED FOR A PHOTO-SHOOT WITH CARL VAN VECHTEN, ONE OF THE MOST INFLUENTIAL PHOTOGRAPHERS OF THE TIME.
VAN VECHTEN RECALLED, "I SPENT JUST ONE NIGHT PHOTOGRAPHING BILLIE HOLIDAY. JUST ONE NIGHT, BUT IT FELT LIKE A WHOLE CAREER . . ."
AM I SPEAKING TO MR. VAN VECHTEN?
YES, SPEAKING . . .
IT'S GERRY MAJOR, ABOUT YOUR APPOINTMENT WITH MISS HOLIDAY TONIGHT . . .
OF COURSE, I REMEMBER.

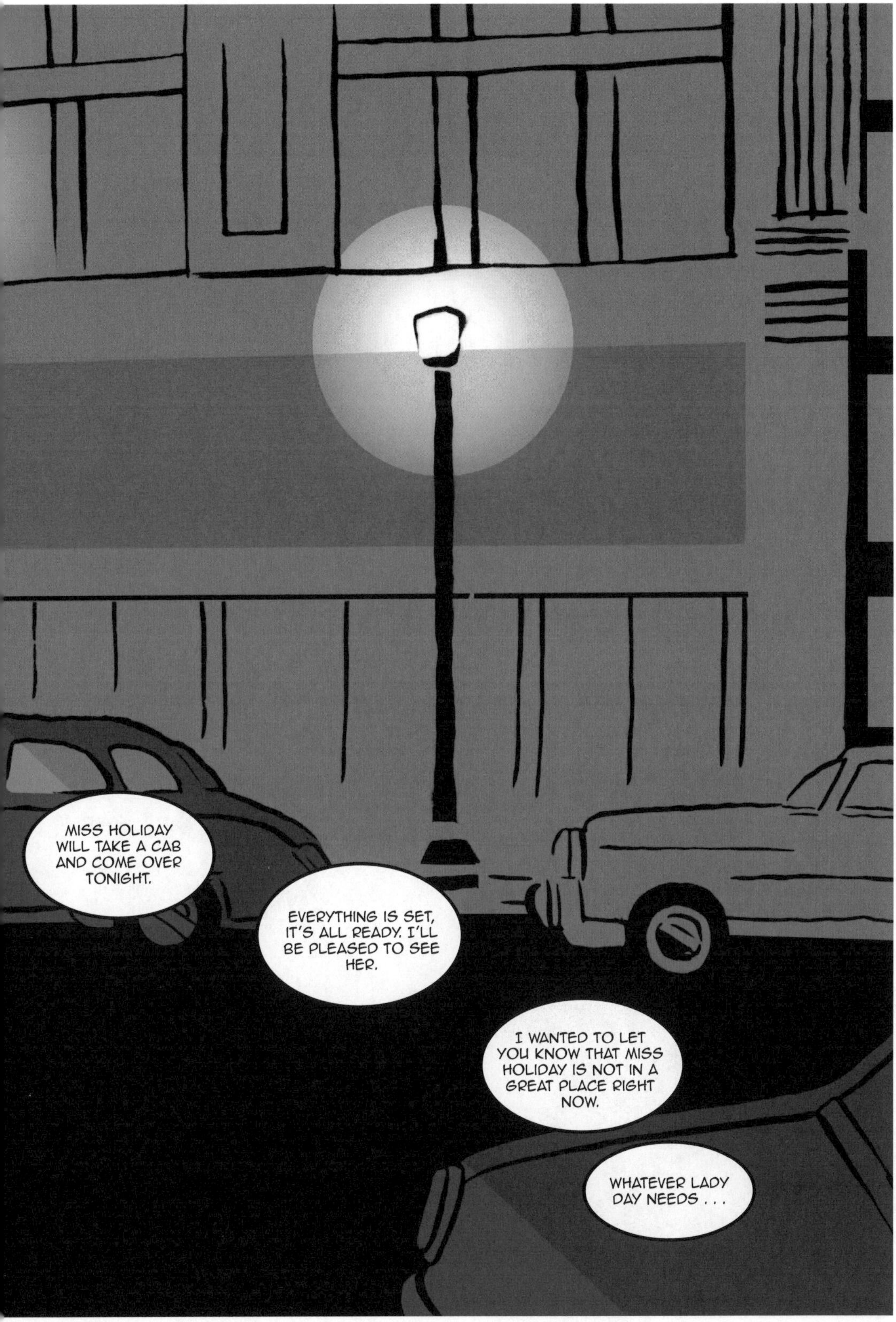
MISS HOLIDAY WILL TAKE A CAB AND COME OVER TONIGHT.
EVERYTHING IS SET, IT'S ALL READY. I'LL BE PLEASED TO SEE HER.
I WANTED TO LET YOU KNOW THAT MISS HOLIDAY IS NOT IN A GREAT PLACE RIGHT NOW.
WHATEVER LADY DAY NEEDS . . .

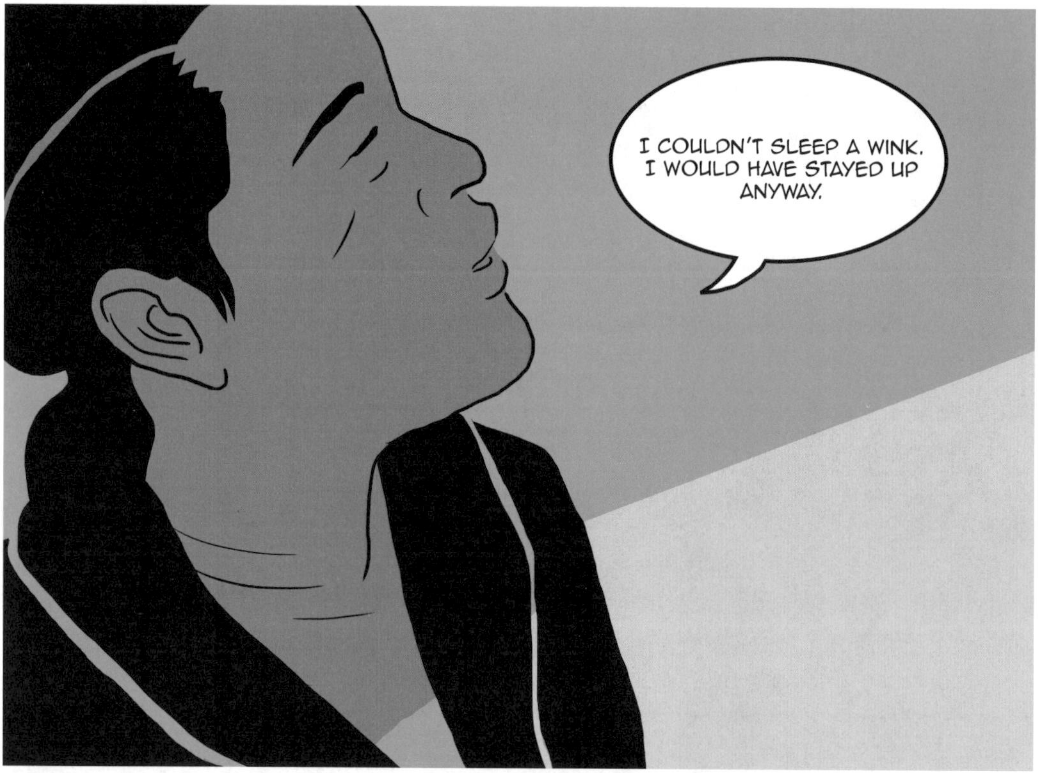
I COULDN'T SLEEP A WINK. I WOULD HAVE STAYED UP ANYWAY.

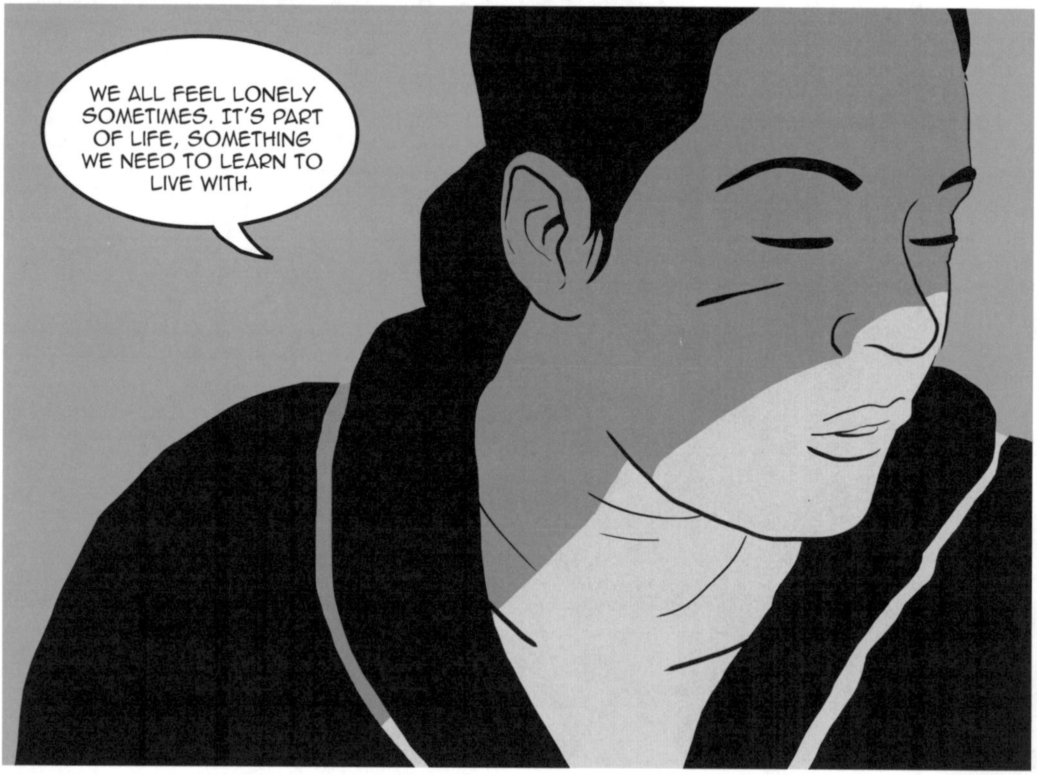
WE ALL FEEL LONELY SOMETIMES. IT'S PART OF LIFE, SOMETHING WE NEED TO LEARN TO LIVE WITH.

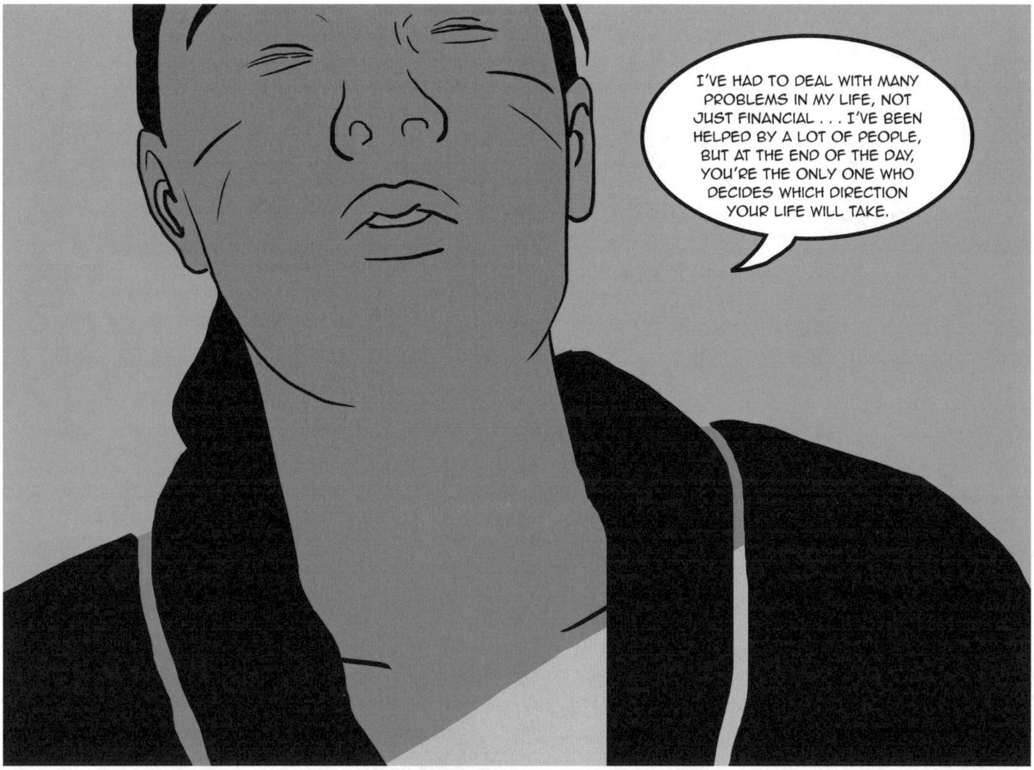
I'VE HAD TO DEAL WITH MANY PROBLEMS IN MY LIFE, NOT JUST FINANCIAL . . . I'VE BEEN HELPED BY A LOT OF PEOPLE, BUT AT THE END OF THE DAY, YOU'RE THE ONLY ONE WHO DECIDES WHICH DIRECTION YOUR LIFE WILL TAKE.

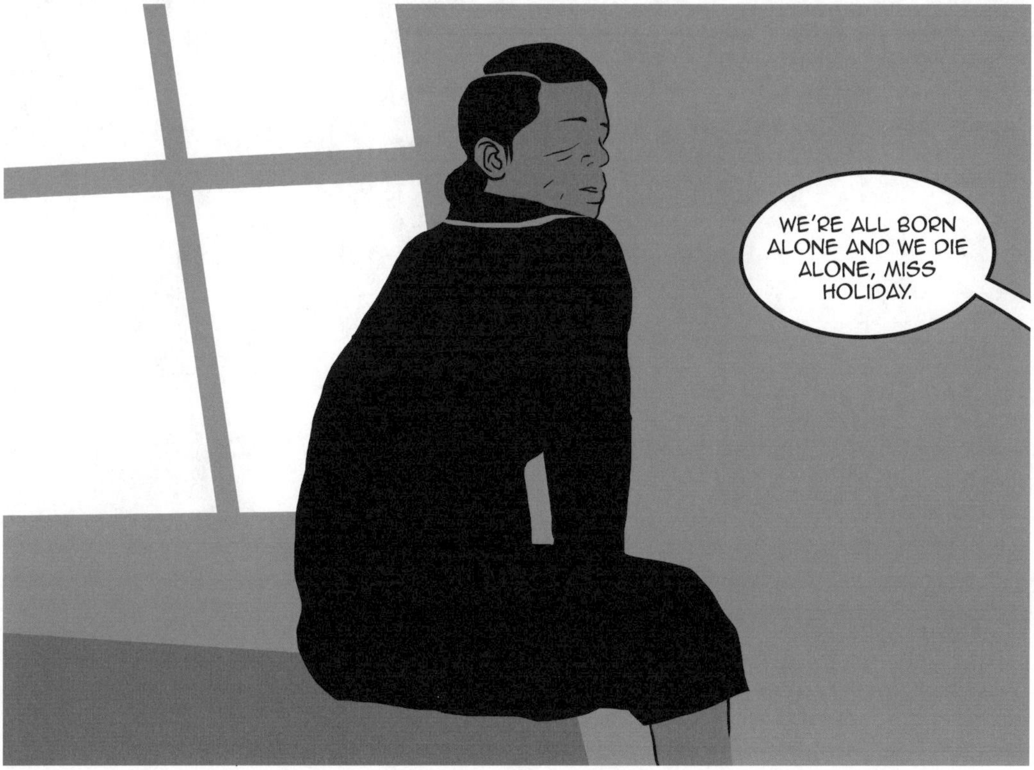
WE'RE ALL BORN ALONE AND WE DIE ALONE, MISS HOLIDAY.

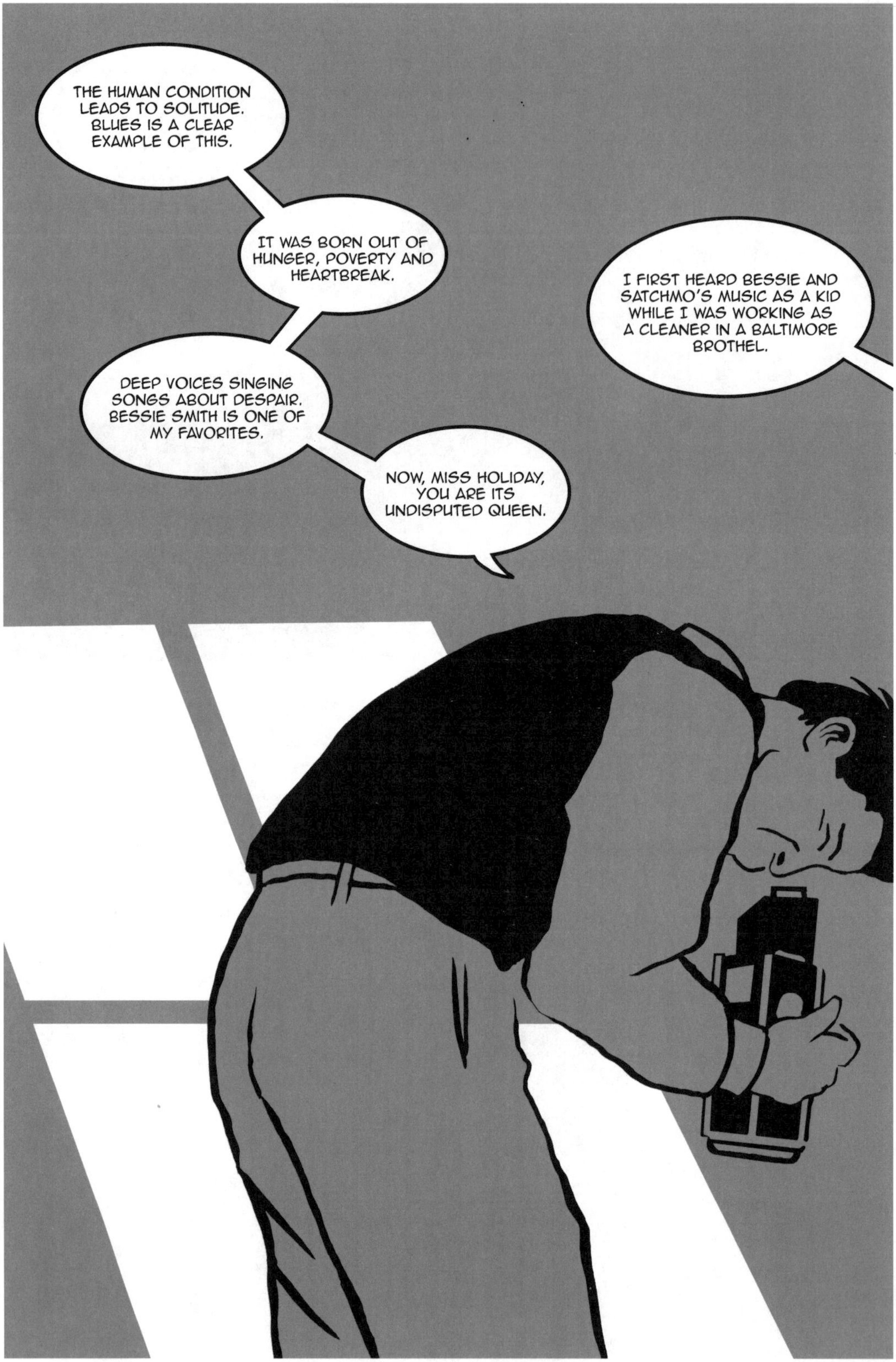
THE HUMAN CONDITION LEADS TO SOLITUDE. BLUES IS A CLEAR EXAMPLE OF THIS.
IT WAS BORN OUT OF HUNGER, POVERTY AND HEARTBREAK.
DEEP VOICES SINGING SONGS ABOUT DESPAIR. BESSIE SMITH IS ONE OF MY FAVORITES.
NOW, MISS HOLIDAY, YOU ARE ITS UNDISPUTED QUEEN.
I FIRST HEARD BESSIE AND SATCHMO'S MUSIC AS A KID WHILE I WAS WORKING AS A CLEANER IN A BALTIMORE BROTHEL.

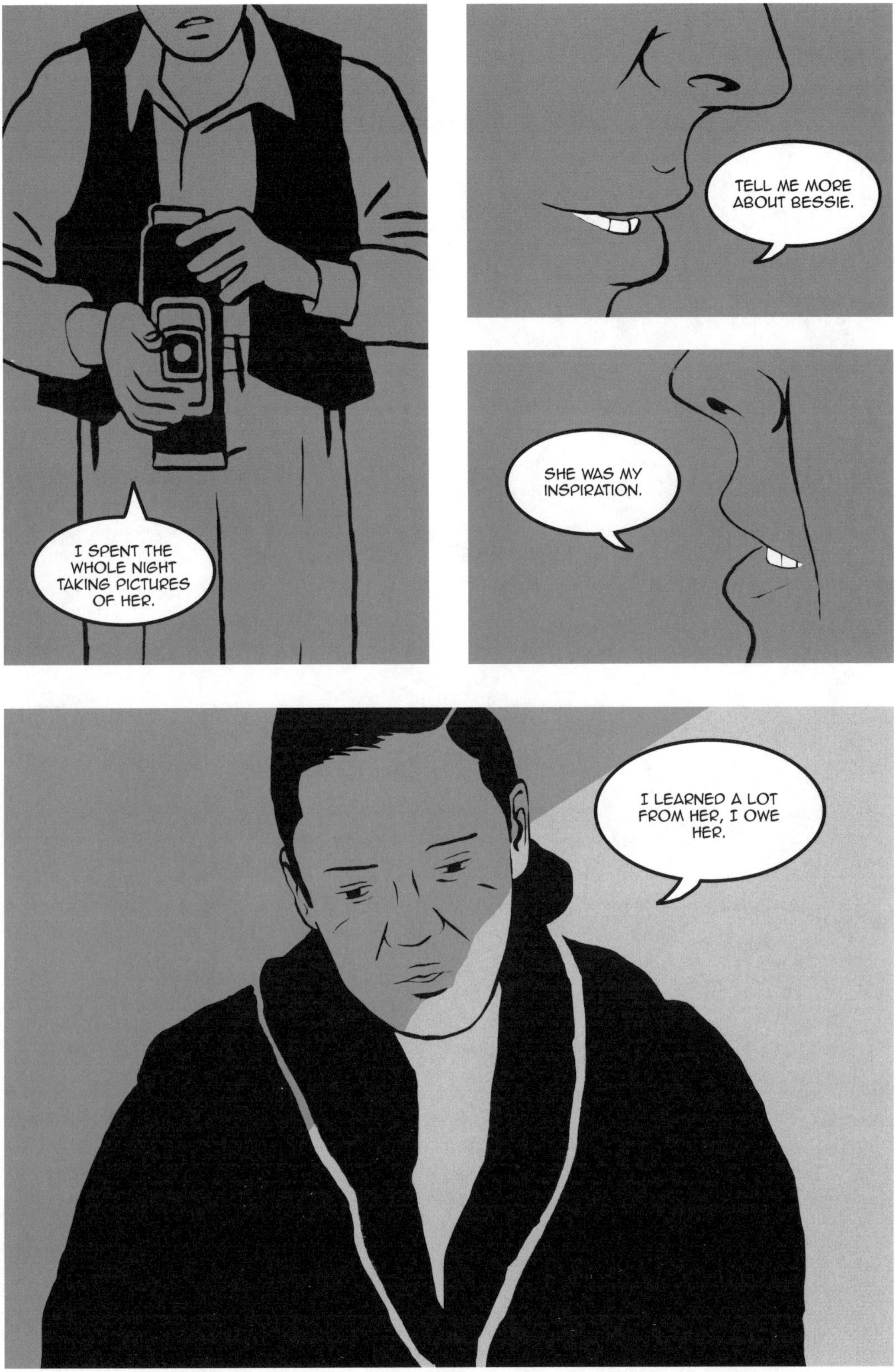
I SPENT THE WHOLE NIGHT TAKING PICTURES OF HER.
TELL ME MORE ABOUT BESSIE.
SHE WAS MY INSPIRATION.
I LEARNED A LOT FROM HER, I OWE HER.

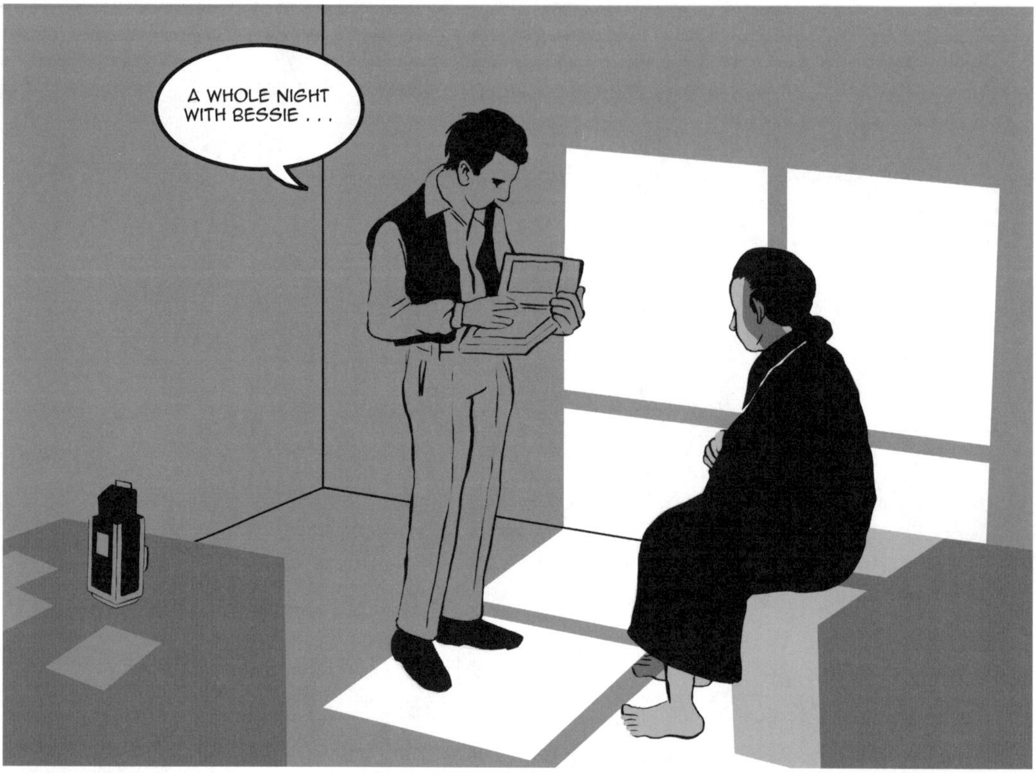
A WHOLE NIGHT WITH BESSIE . . .

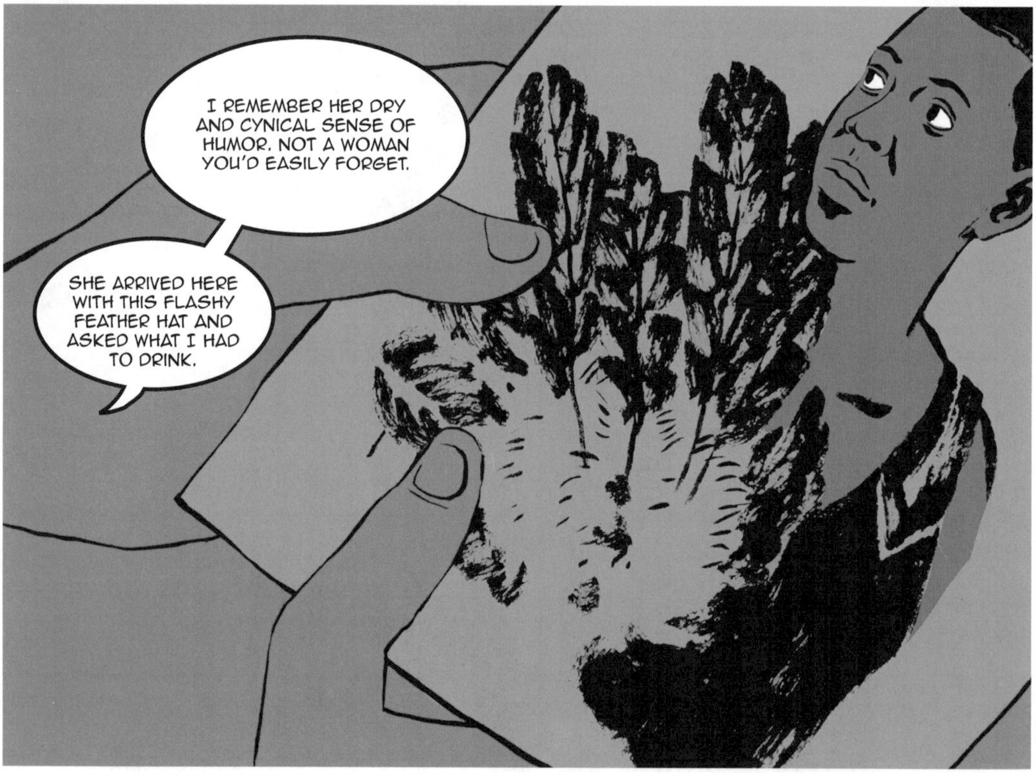
I REMEMBER HER DRY AND CYNICAL SENSE OF HUMOR. NOT A WOMAN YOU'D EASILY FORGET.
SHE ARRIVED HERE WITH THIS FLASHY FEATHER HAT AND ASKED WHAT I HAD TO DRINK.

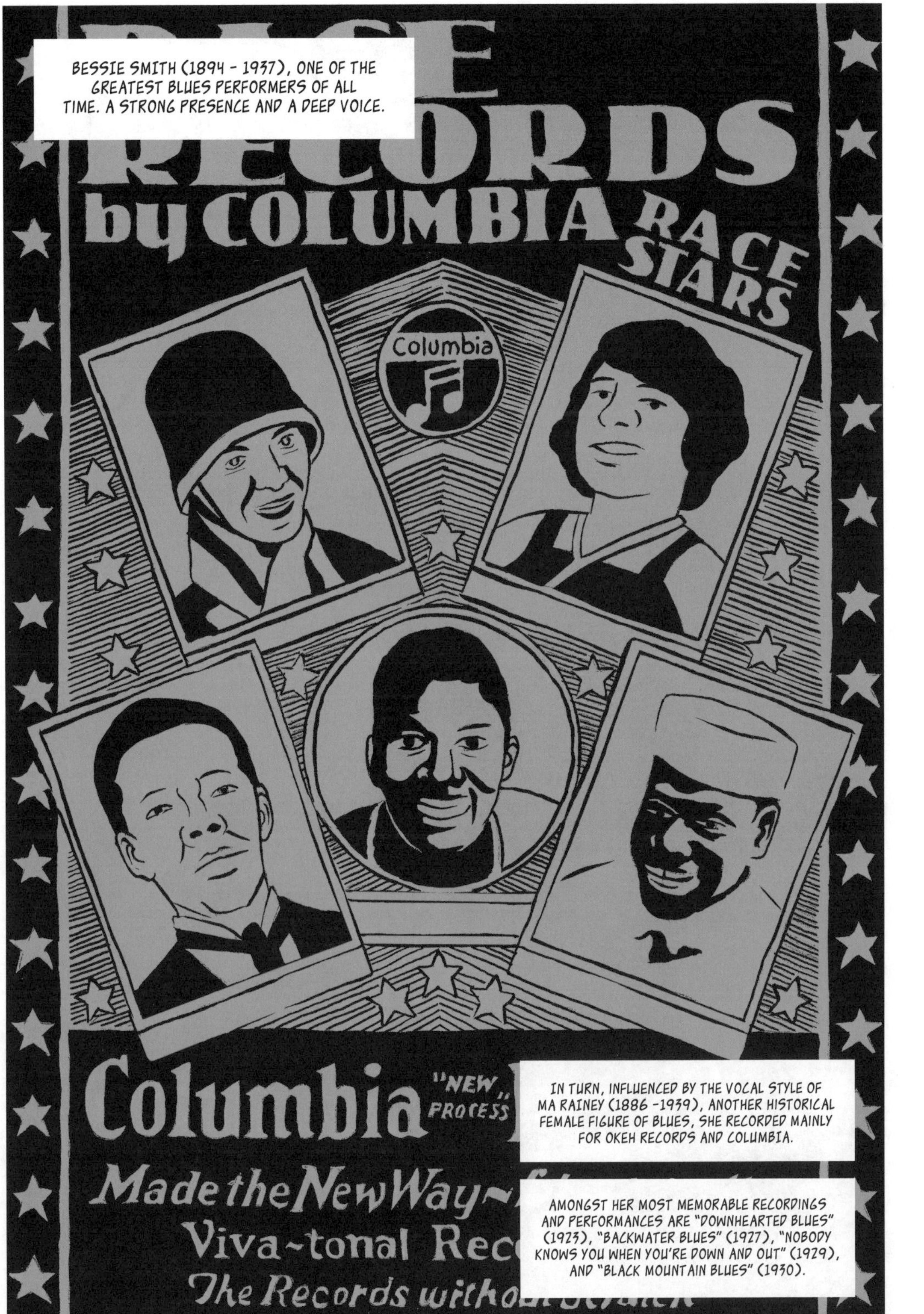
BESSIE SMITH (1894 - 1937), ONE OF THE GREATEST BLUES PERFORMERS OF ALL TIME. A STRONG PRESENCE AND A DEEP VOICE.
RECORDS
by COLUMBIA
RACE STARS
Columbia
Columbia
"NEW" PROCESS
Made the New Way~
Viva-tonal
The Records
IN TURN, INFLUENCED BY THE VOCAL STYLE OF MA RAINEY (1886 -1939), ANOTHER HISTORICAL FEMALE FIGURE OF BLUES, SHE RECORDED MAINLY FOR OKEH RECORDS AND COLUMBIA.
AMONGST HER MOST MEMORABLE RECORDINGS AND PERFORMANCES ARE "DOWNHEARTED BLUES" (1923), "BACKWATER BLUES" (1927), "NOBODY KNOWS YOU WHEN YOU'RE DOWN AND OUT" (1929), AND "BLACK MOUNTAIN BLUES" (1930).

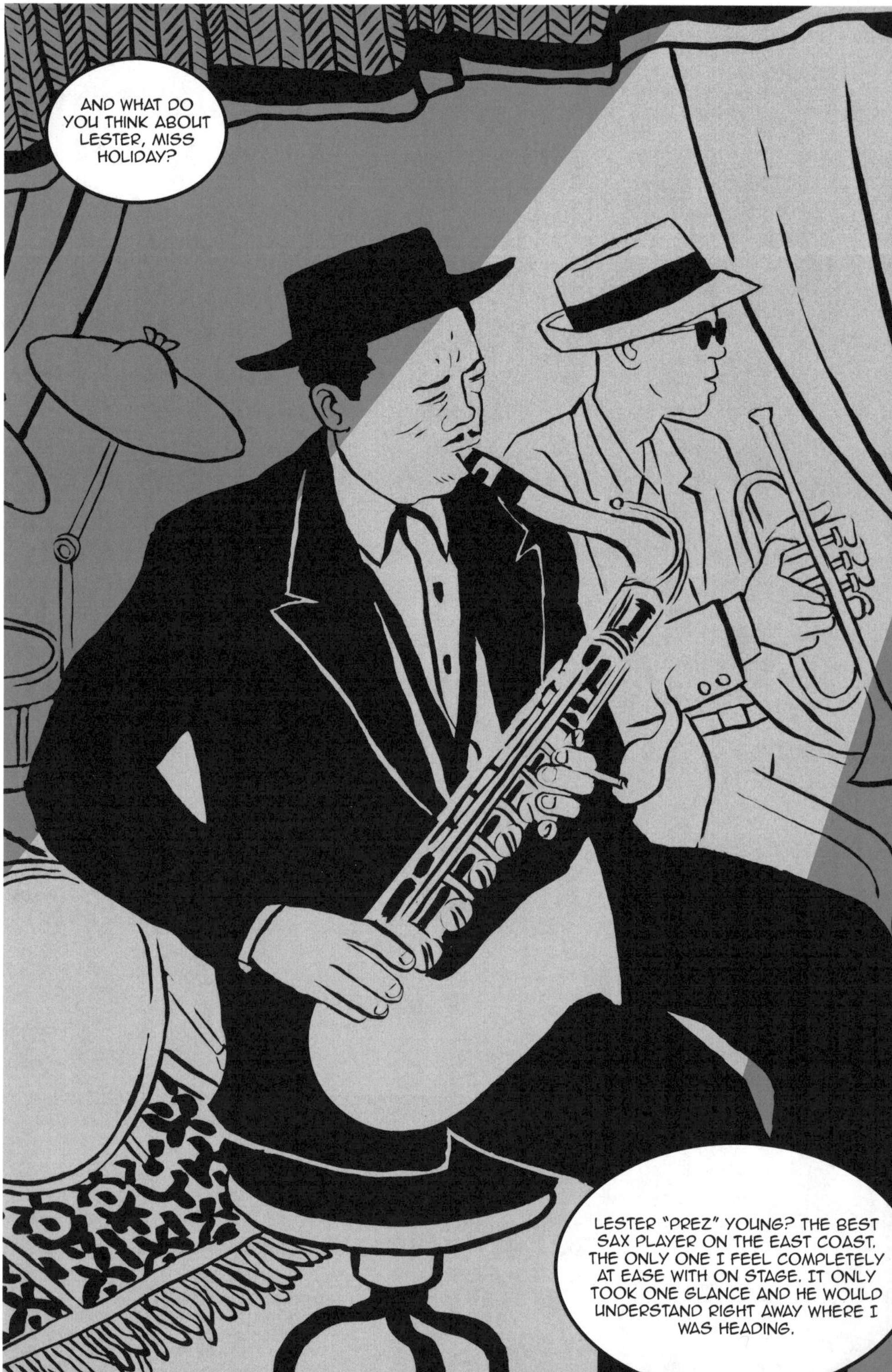
AND WHAT DO YOU THINK ABOUT LESTER, MISS HOLIDAY?
LESTER "PREZ" YOUNG? THE BEST SAX PLAYER ON THE EAST COAST. THE ONLY ONE I FEEL COMPLETELY AT EASE WITH ON STAGE. IT ONLY TOOK ONE GLANCE AND HE WOULD UNDERSTAND RIGHT AWAY WHERE I WAS HEADING.

I MET LESTER DURING ONE OF THOSE JAM SESSIONS WE USED TO HAVE AT SOMEONE'S HOUSE AT DAWN. AFTER WORK, WE'D ALL MEET UP AS SOON AS WE COULD AND CARRY ON IMPROVISING AND HAVING FUN UNTIL WE DROPPED.

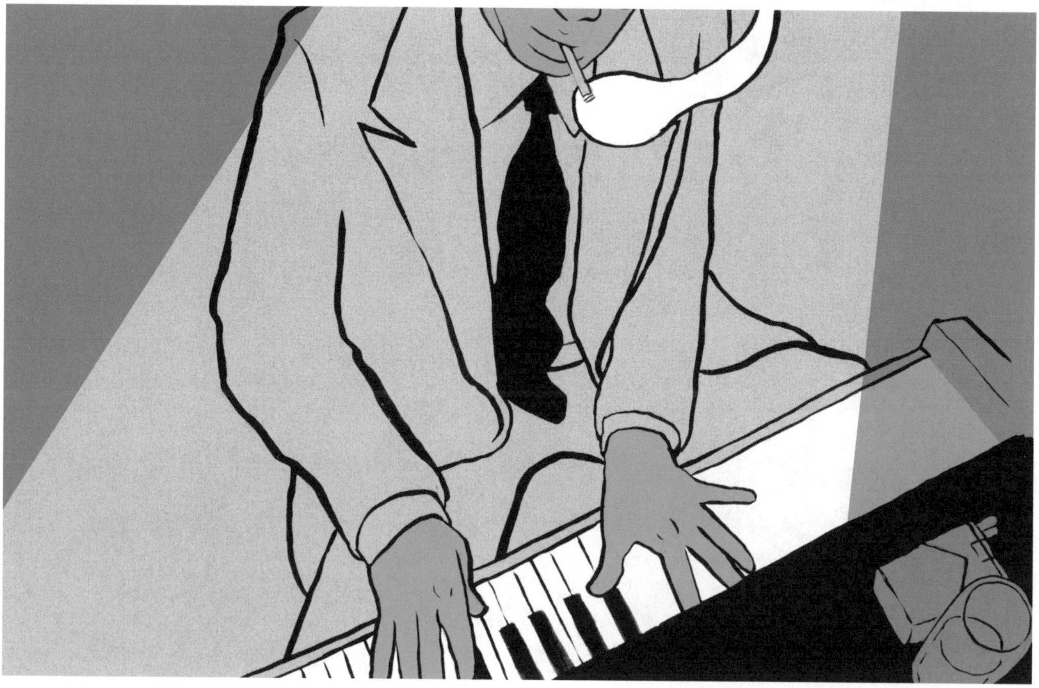

LESTER LOVED HOW I WOULD SING "BEHIND THE BEAT," SLOWING THE PACE. I WAS FASCINATED BY HIS CLEAN AND PRECISE TIMBRE. WE WERE MADE FOR ONE ANOTHER. FROM THEN ON, WE WERE INSEPARABLE AND I KNEW THAT, WHATEVER HAPPENED, HE WOULD BE THERE FOR ME.

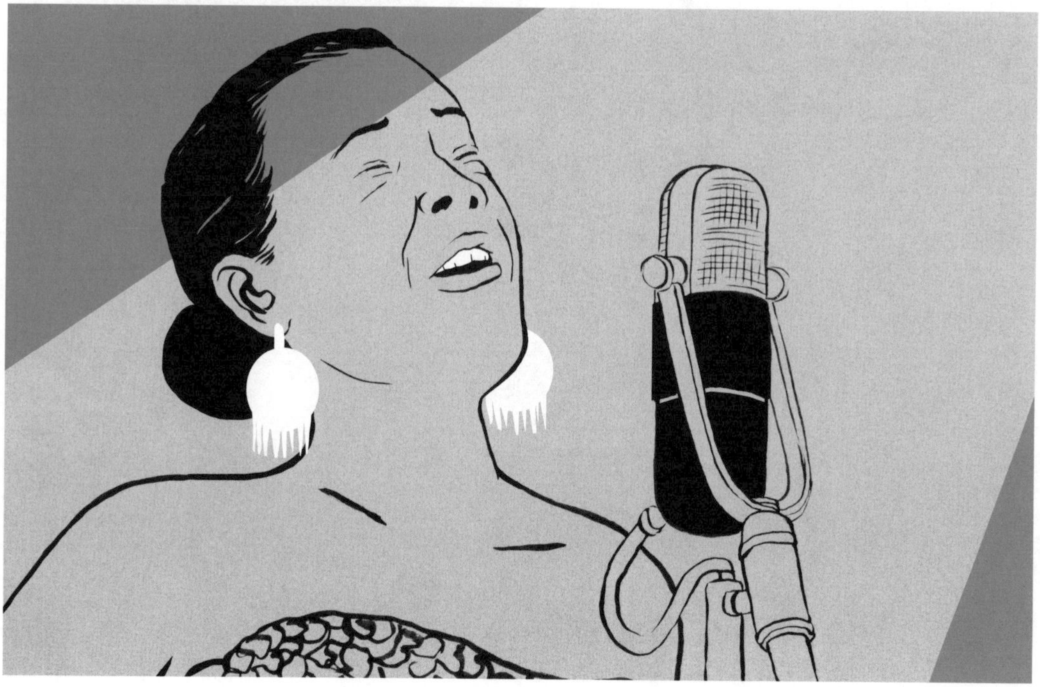

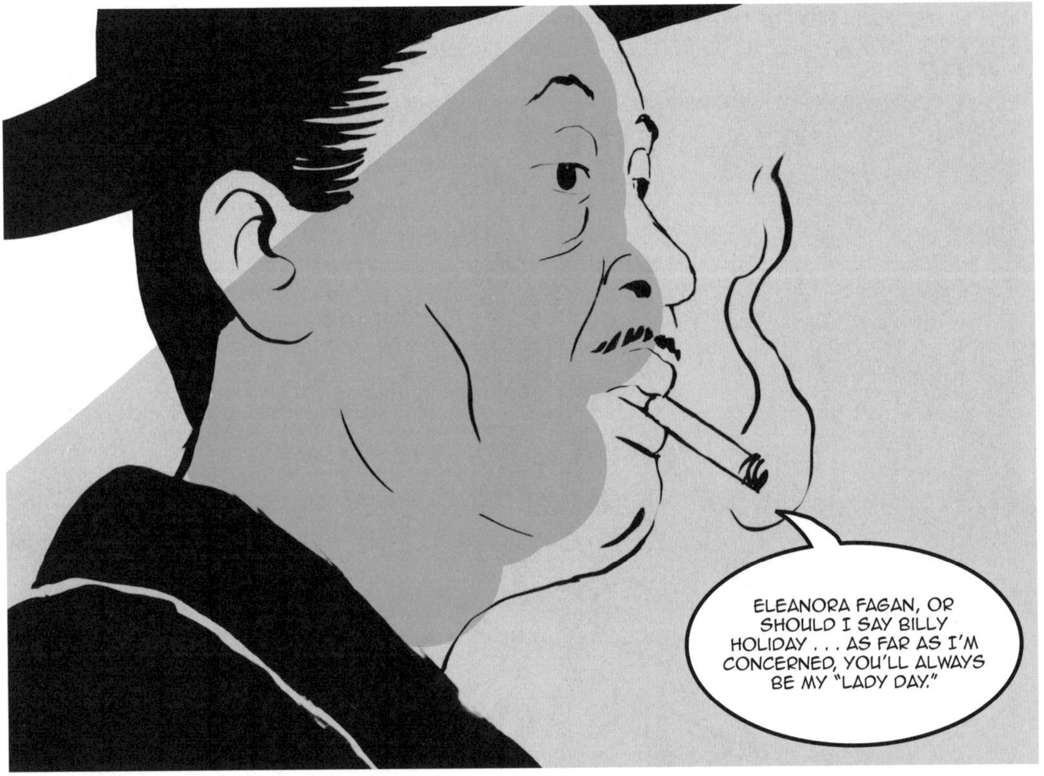
ELEANORA FAGAN, OR SHOULD I SAY BILLY HOLIDAY . . . AS FAR AS I'M CONCERNED, YOU'LL ALWAYS BE MY "LADY DAY."

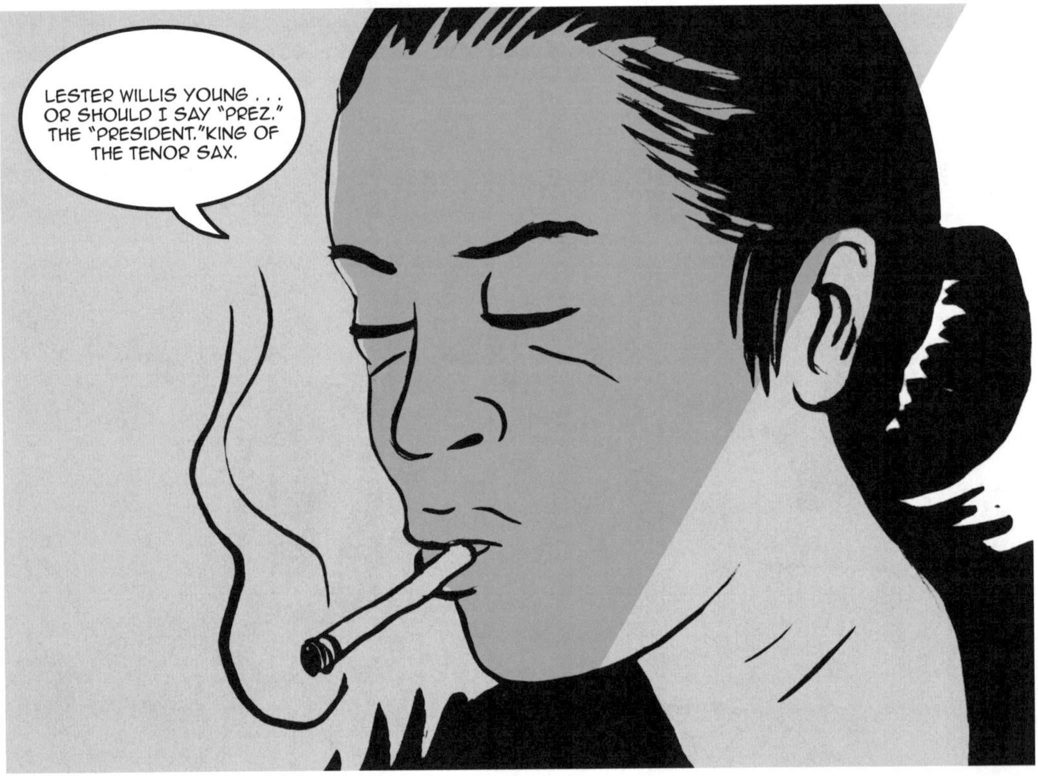
LESTER WILLIS YOUNG . . . OR SHOULD I SAY "PREZ." THE "PRESIDENT."KING OF THE TENOR SAX.

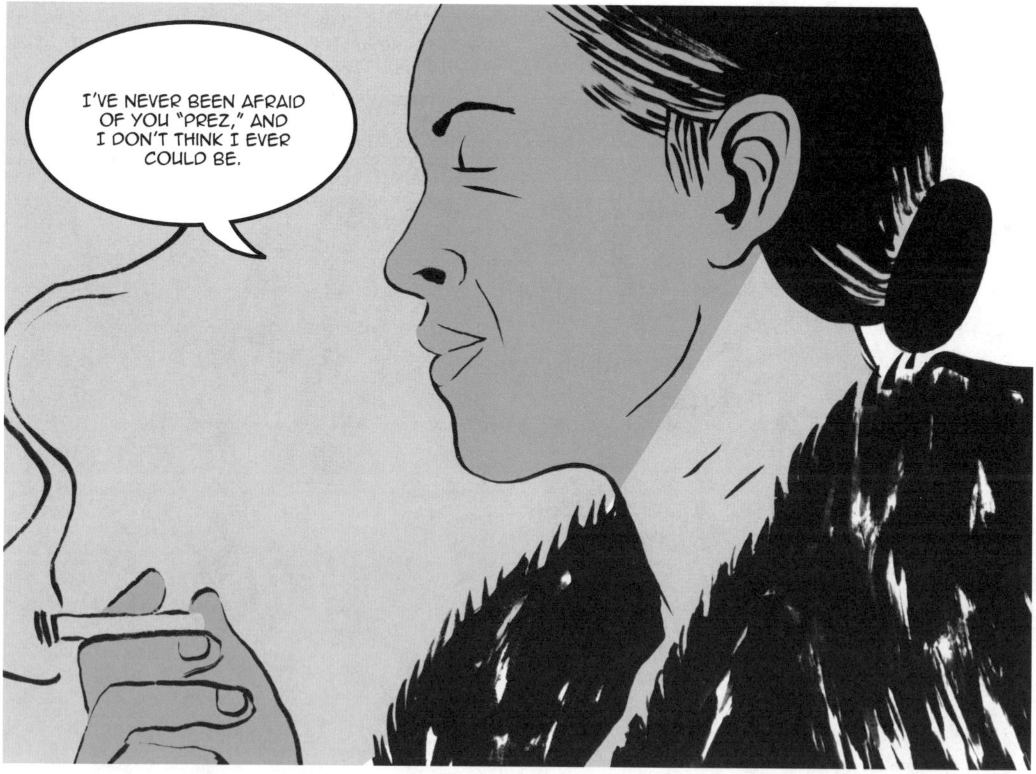
I'VE NEVER BEEN AFRAID OF YOU "PREZ," AND I DON'T THINK I EVER COULD BE.

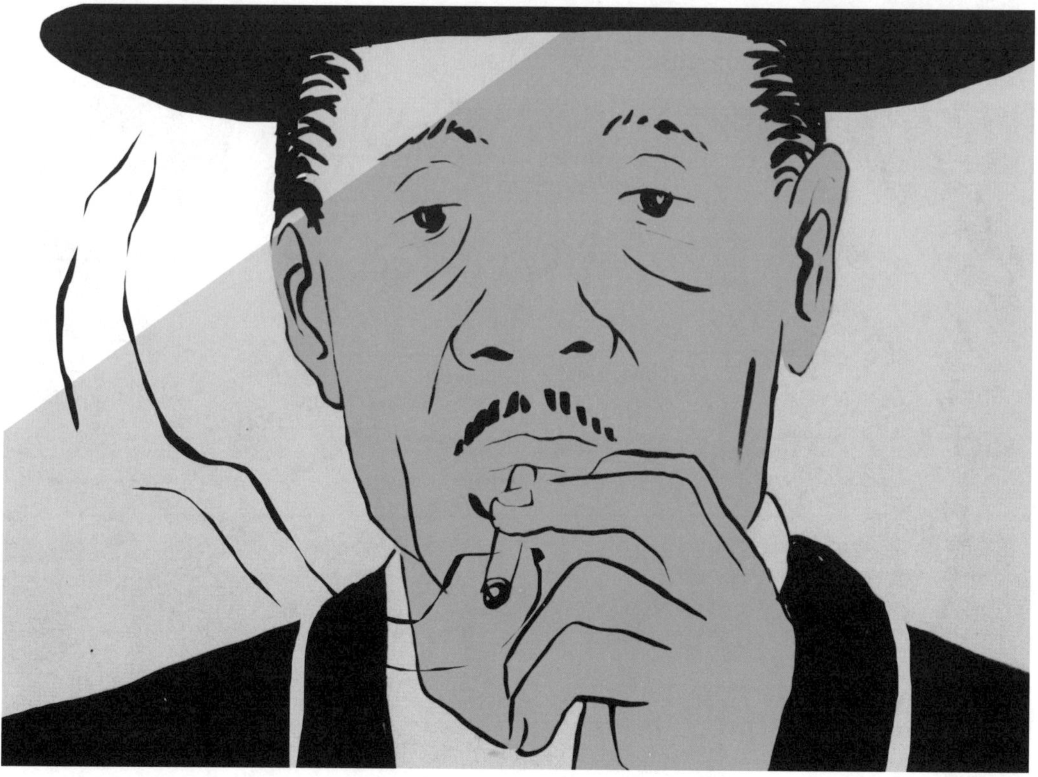

IT WAS 1937 WHEN I FIRST MET UP WITH COUNT BASIE'S BAND. WE STARTED A LONG, GRUELING TOUR, GOING FROM CITY TO CITY, FROM CLUB TO CLUB.

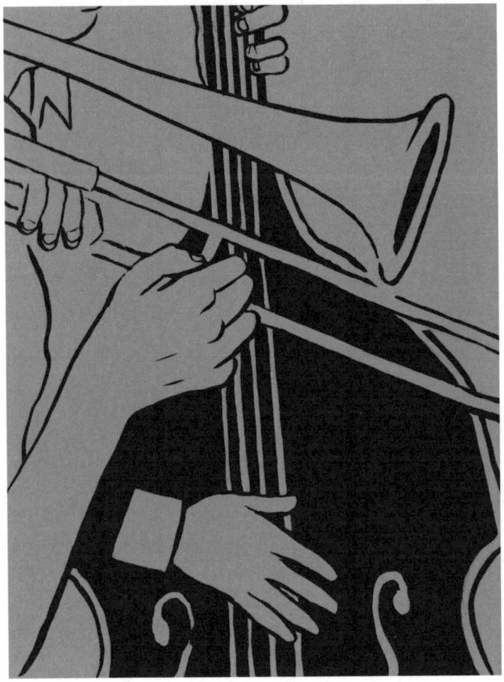

WE LIVED ON THE VERGE OF POVERTY, THE PAY WAS LOW AND MY ENTHUSIASM JUST WANED. COUNT WAS NOT PLEASED ABOUT THE SITUATION.

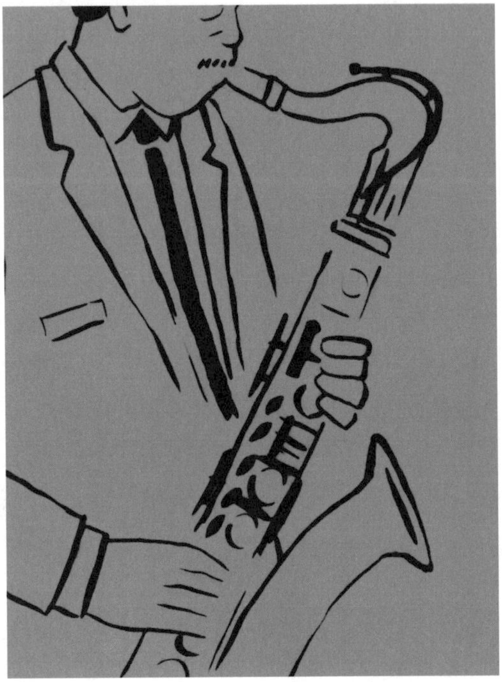

"IF YOU CARRY ON LIKE THIS," HE'D SAY, "WE'LL LOSE ALL OUR GIGS! IT'S LIKE YOU DON'T WANT TO PERFORM ANYMORE!" WE NEVER REALLY GOT ALONG, SO ONE DAY I QUIT.

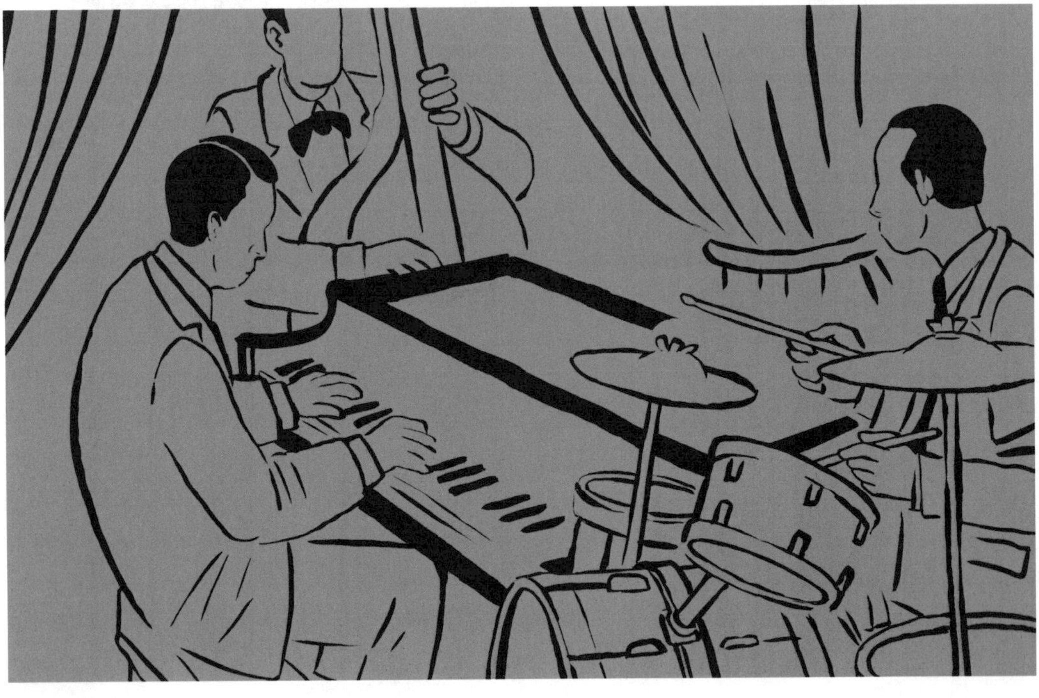

SOON AFTER, I STARTED WORKING WITH ARTIE SHAW AND HIS BAND. IT WAS THE FIRST TIME A WHITE ORCHESTRA WAS FRONTED BY A BLACK SINGER. HOWEVER, THERE WERE PROBLEMS. MOST TIMES, I HAD TO ENTER FROM A BLACKS ONLY ENTRANCE, OR HAD TO SLEEP AND EAT IN SEPARATE MOTELS.

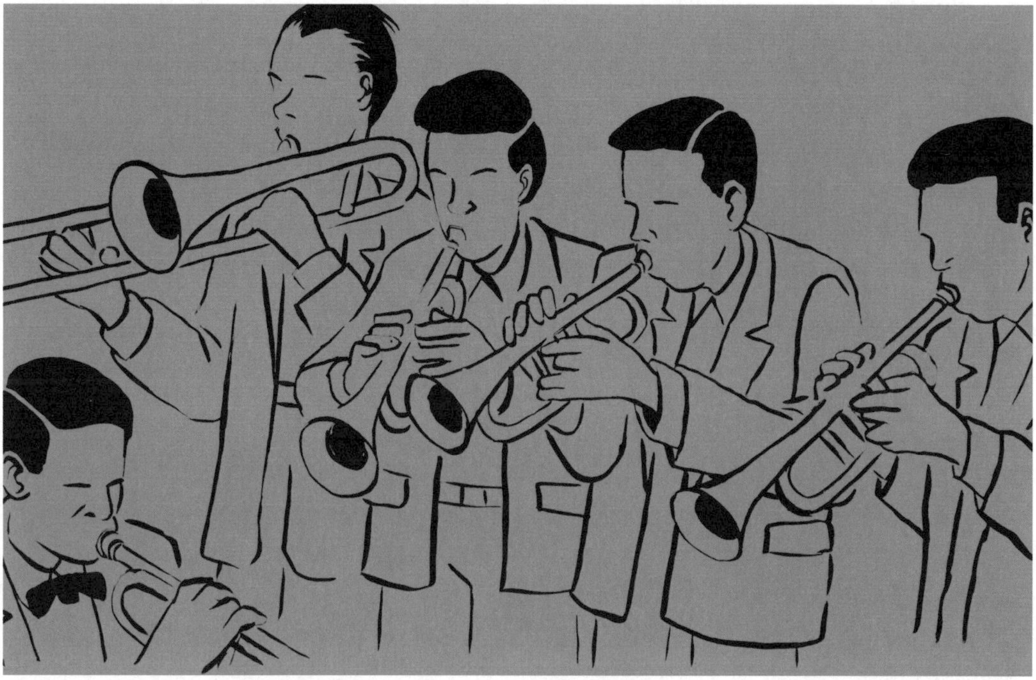

THESE EXPERIENCES TOUGHENED ME AND MADE ME MORE DETERMINED THAN EVER, ALTHOUGH IT WASN'T EASY TO COMPROMISE.

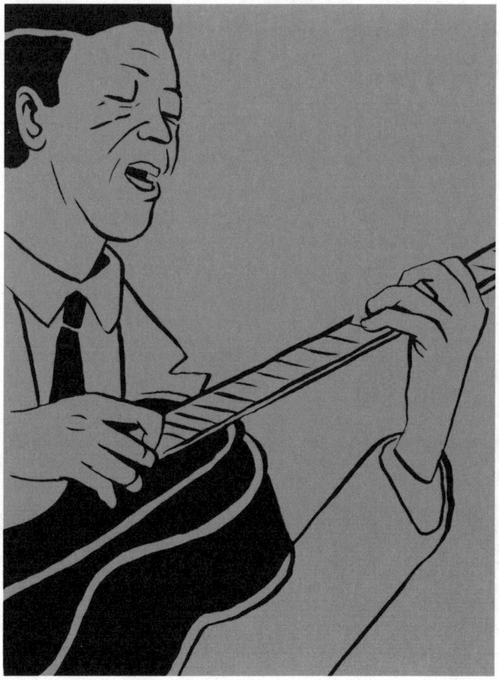

ARTIE UNDERSTOOD MY SITUATION PERFECTLY. HE WAS FROM A JEWISH FAMILY AND HAD EXPERIENCED DISCRIMINATION HIMSELF.

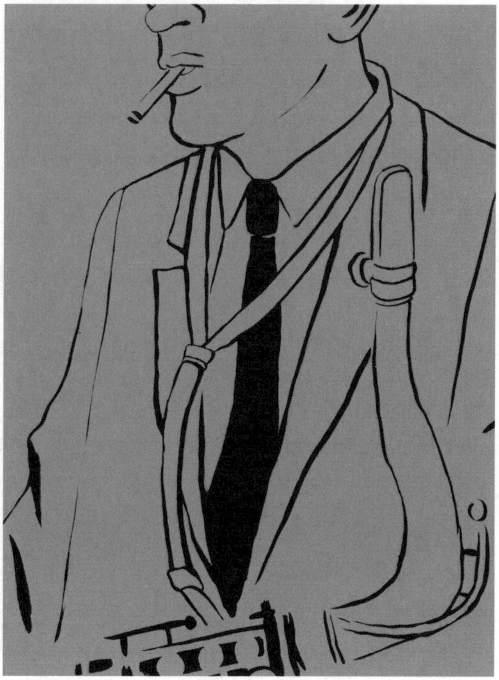

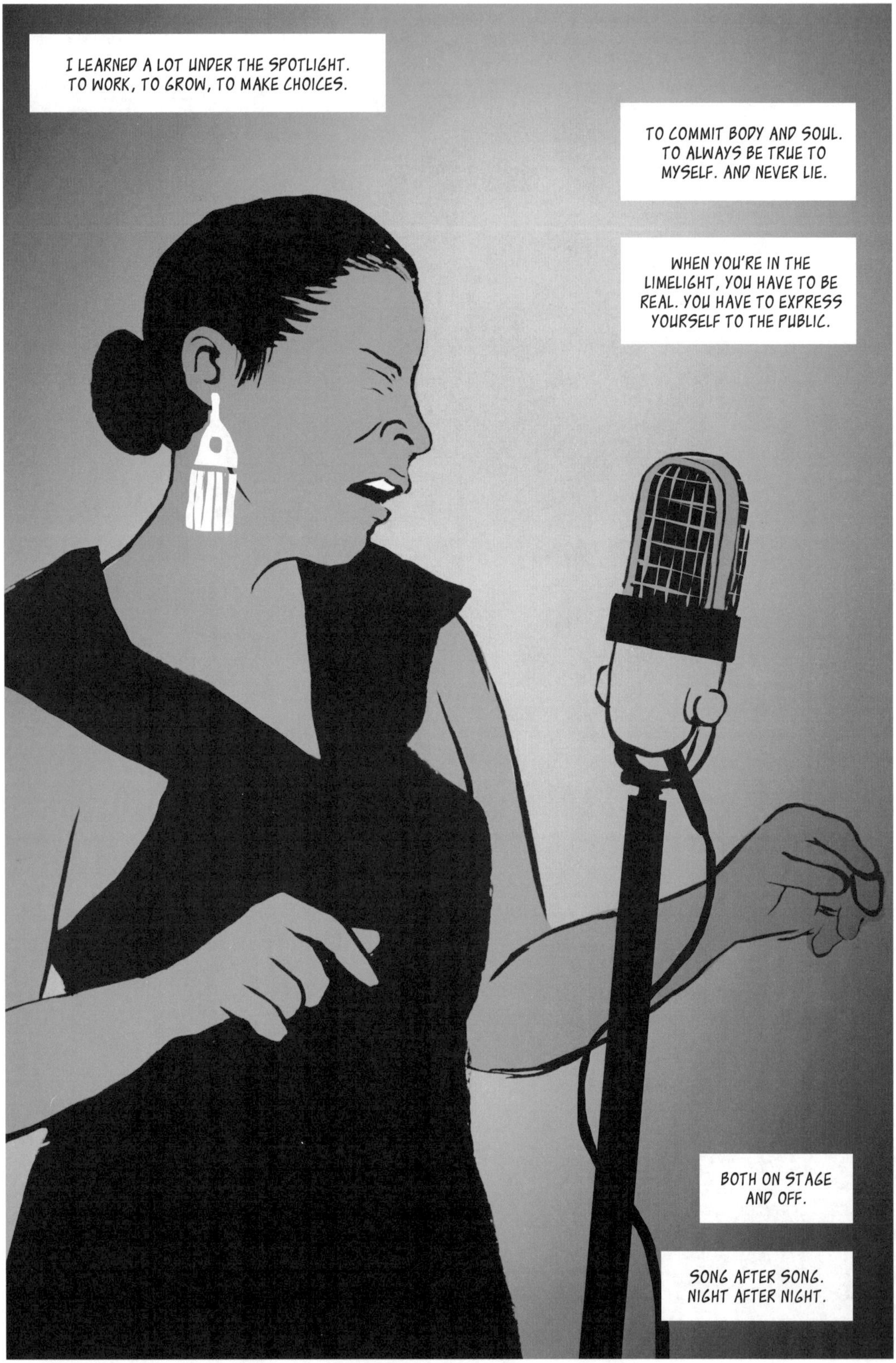
I LEARNED A LOT UNDER THE SPOTLIGHT. TO WORK, TO GROW, TO MAKE CHOICES.
TO COMMIT BODY AND SOUL. TO ALWAYS BE TRUE TO MYSELF. AND NEVER LIE.
WHEN YOU'RE IN THE LIMELIGHT, YOU HAVE TO BE REAL. YOU HAVE TO EXPRESS YOURSELF TO THE PUBLIC.
BOTH ON STAGE AND OFF.
SONG AFTER SONG. NIGHT AFTER NIGHT.

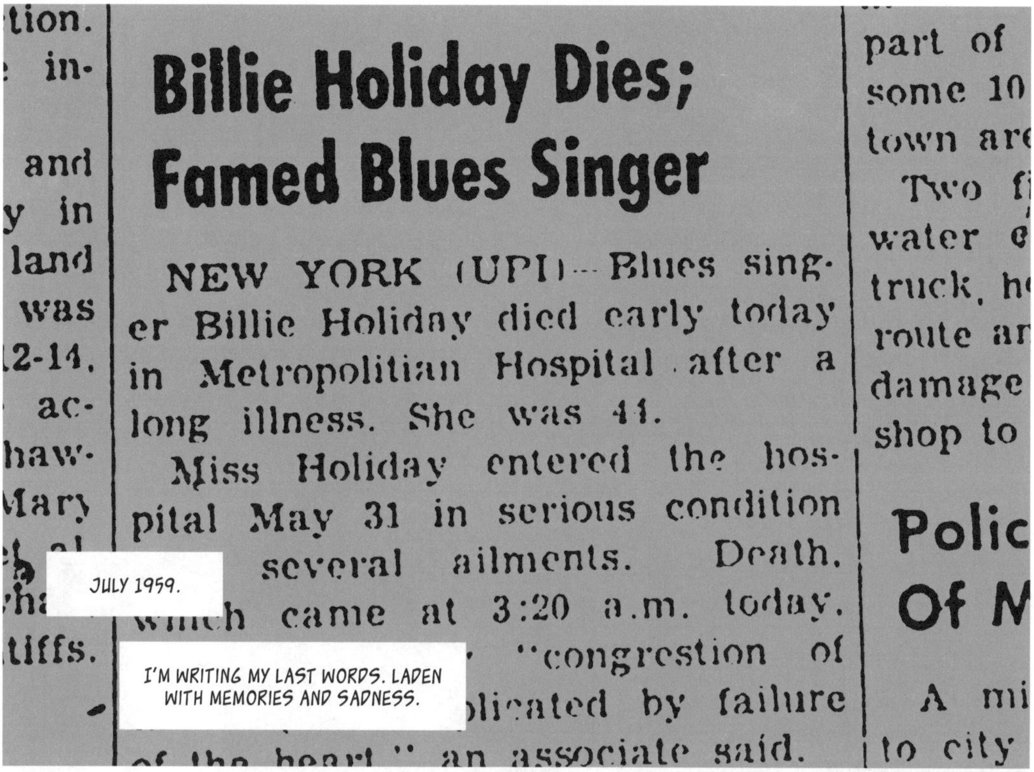

Billie Holiday Dies; Famed Blues Singer

NEW YORK (UPI)—Blues singer Billie Holiday died early today in Metropolitan Hospital after a long illness. She was 44.

Miss Holiday entered the hospital May 31 in serious condition ... several ailments. Death, which came at 3:20 a.m. today, ... "congrestion of ... plicated by failure of the heart," an associate said.

JULY 1959.
I'M WRITING MY LAST WORDS. LADEN WITH MEMORIES AND SADNESS.

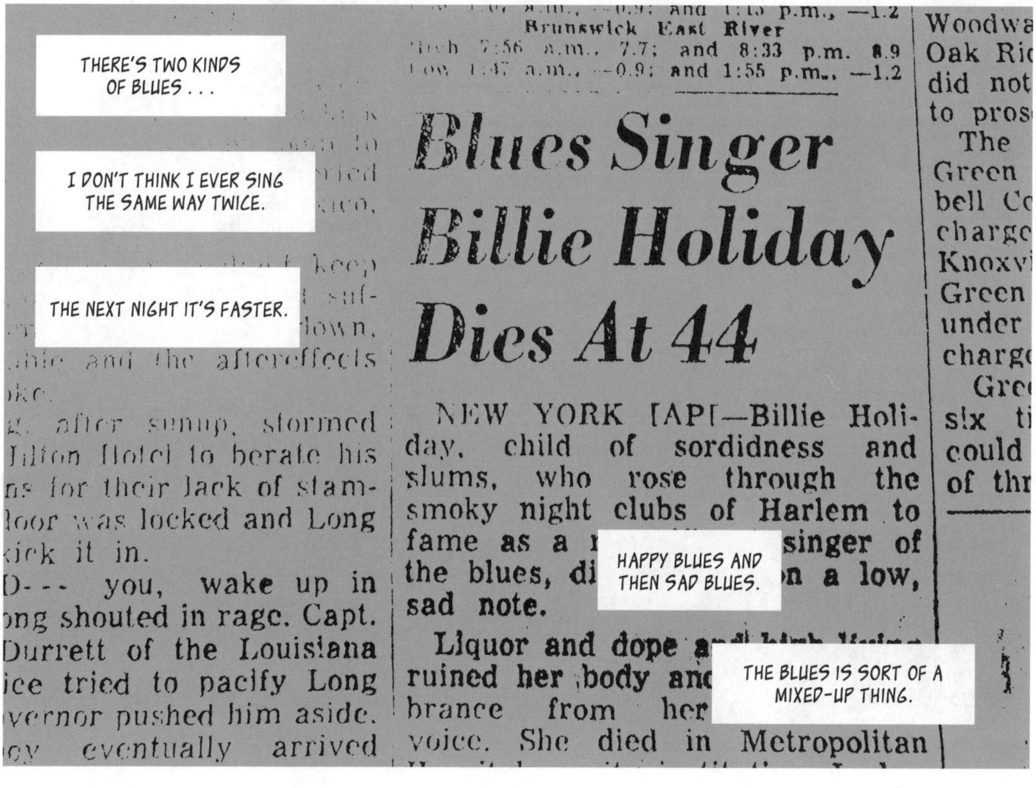

Brunswick East River
High 7:56 a.m., 7.7; and 8:33 p.m. 8.9
Low 1:47 a.m., —0.9; and 1:55 p.m., —1.2

Blues Singer Billie Holiday Dies At 44

NEW YORK [AP]—Billie Holiday, child of sordidness and slums, who rose through the smoky night clubs of Harlem to fame as a ... singer of the blues, di... n a low, sad note.

Liquor and dope a... ruined her body and ... brance from her ... voice. She died in Metropolitan

THERE'S TWO KINDS OF BLUES . . .
I DON'T THINK I EVER SING THE SAME WAY TWICE.
THE NEXT NIGHT IT'S FASTER.
HAPPY BLUES AND THEN SAD BLUES.
THE BLUES IS SORT OF A MIXED-UP THING.

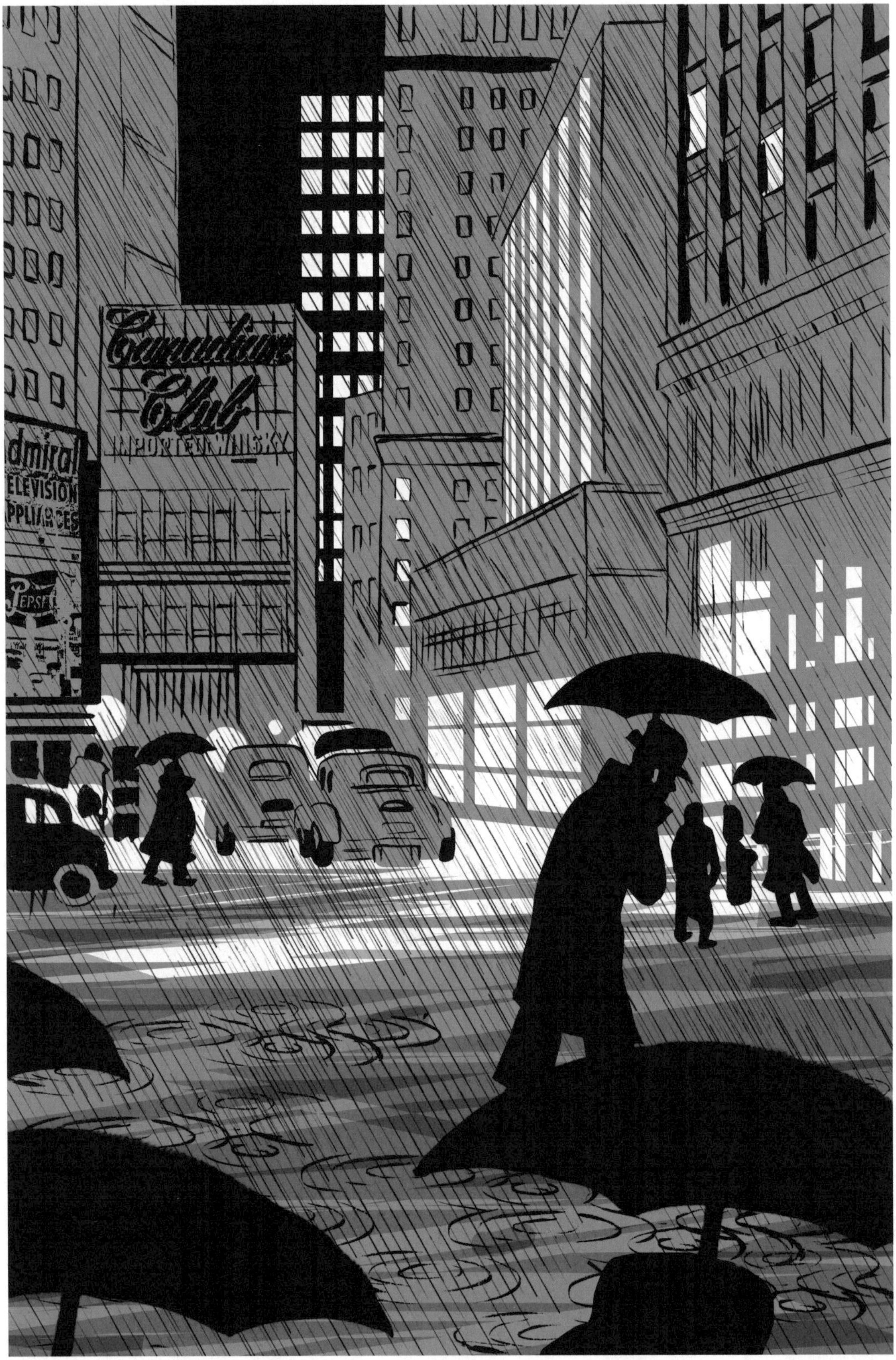
Canadian Club
IMPORTED WHISKY
dmiral
ELEVISION
PPLIANCES
Pepsi

"Body And Soul"

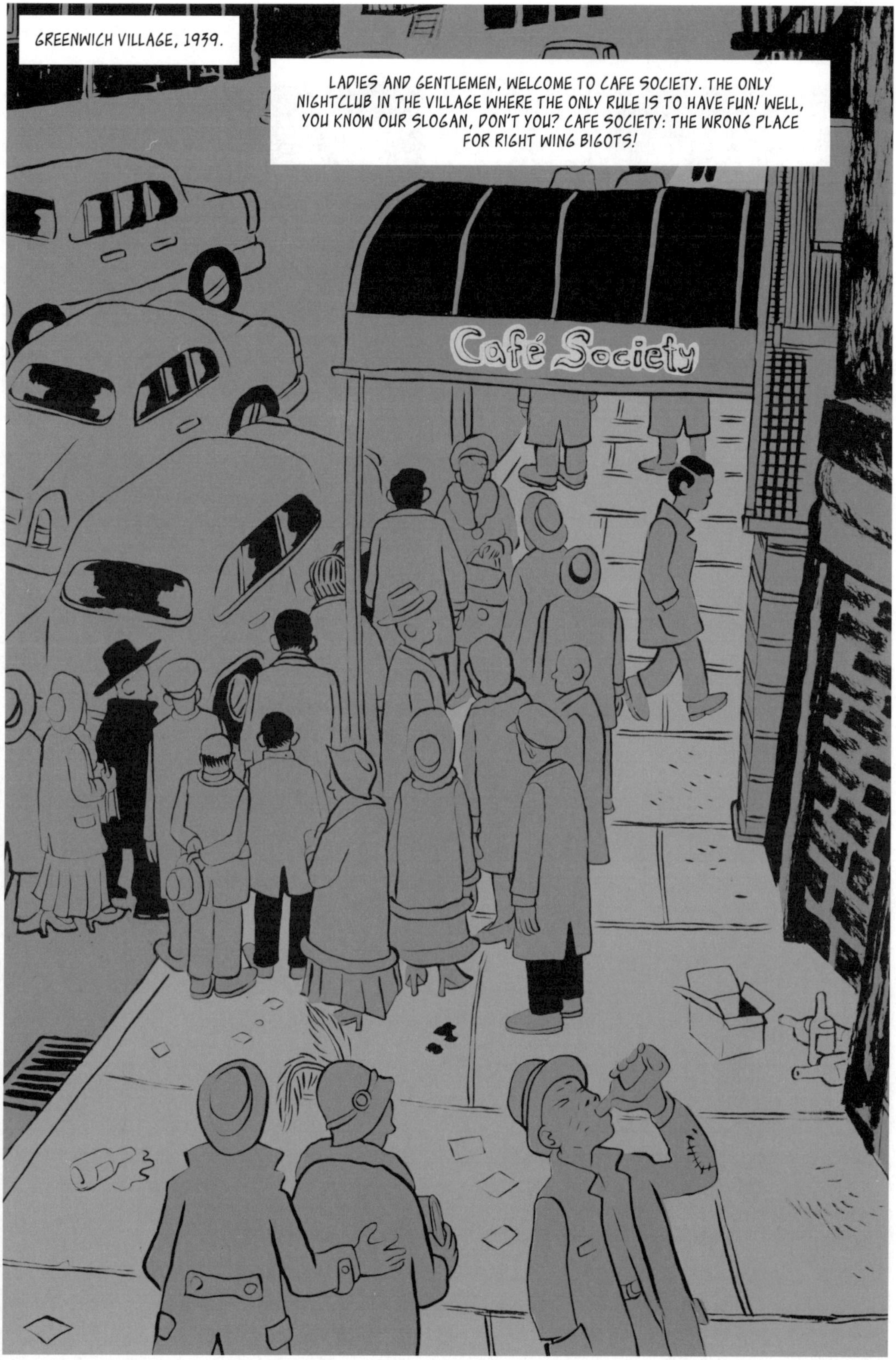
GREENWICH VILLAGE, 1939.
LADIES AND GENTLEMEN, WELCOME TO CAFE SOCIETY. THE ONLY NIGHTCLUB IN THE VILLAGE WHERE THE ONLY RULE IS TO HAVE FUN! WELL, YOU KNOW OUR SLOGAN, DON'T YOU? CAFE SOCIETY: THE WRONG PLACE FOR RIGHT WING BIGOTS!
Café Society

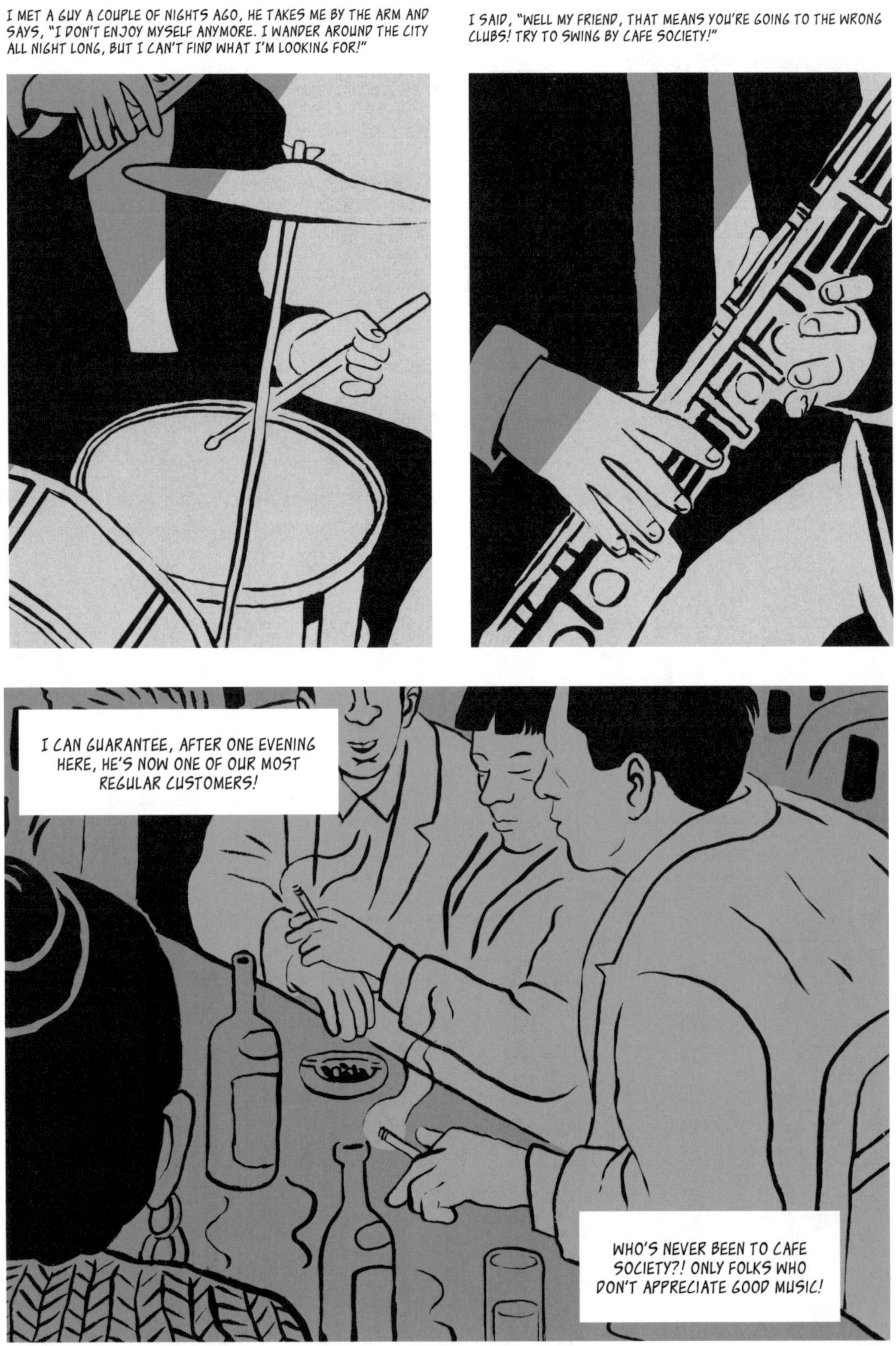
I MET A GUY A COUPLE OF NIGHTS AGO, HE TAKES ME BY THE ARM AND SAYS, "I DON'T ENJOY MYSELF ANYMORE. I WANDER AROUND THE CITY ALL NIGHT LONG, BUT I CAN'T FIND WHAT I'M LOOKING FOR!"
I SAID, "WELL MY FRIEND, THAT MEANS YOU'RE GOING TO THE WRONG CLUBS! TRY TO SWING BY CAFE SOCIETY!"
I CAN GUARANTEE, AFTER ONE EVENING HERE, HE'S NOW ONE OF OUR MOST REGULAR CUSTOMERS!
WHO'S NEVER BEEN TO CAFE SOCIETY?! ONLY FOLKS WHO DON'T APPRECIATE GOOD MUSIC!

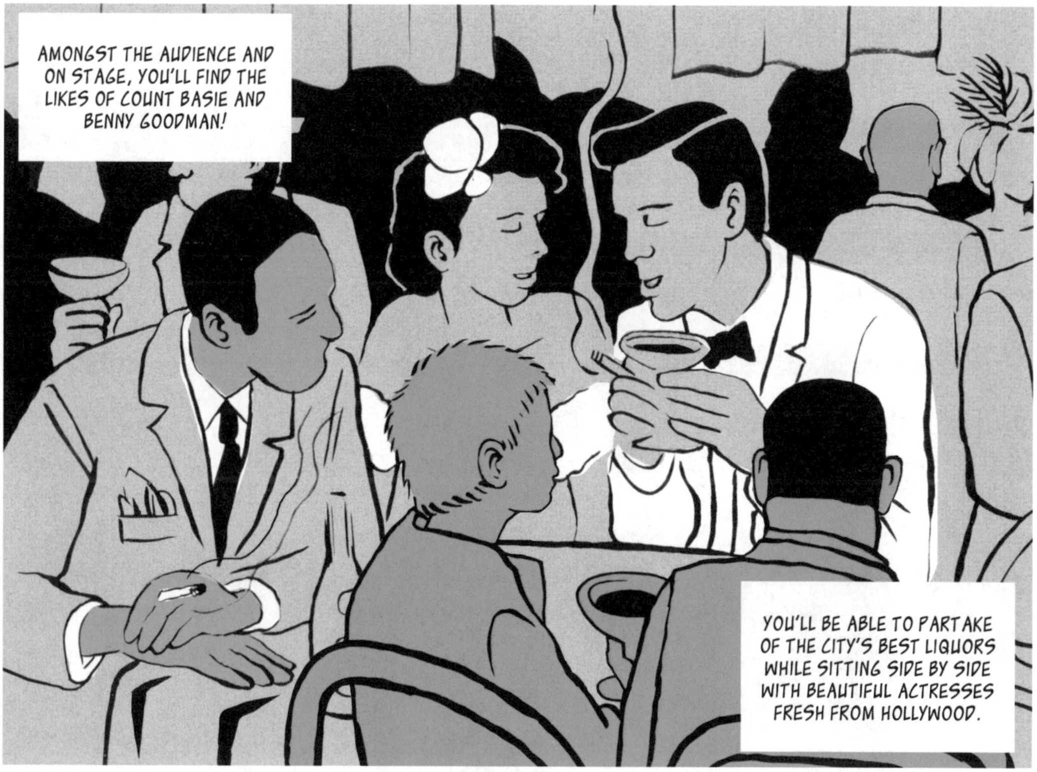
AMONGST THE AUDIENCE AND ON STAGE, YOU'LL FIND THE LIKES OF COUNT BASIE AND BENNY GOODMAN!
YOU'LL BE ABLE TO PARTAKE OF THE CITY'S BEST LIQUORS WHILE SITTING SIDE BY SIDE WITH BEAUTIFUL ACTRESSES FRESH FROM HOLLYWOOD.

NO COLOR BAR, NO DISCRIMINATION, NO LIMIT OR BANS.

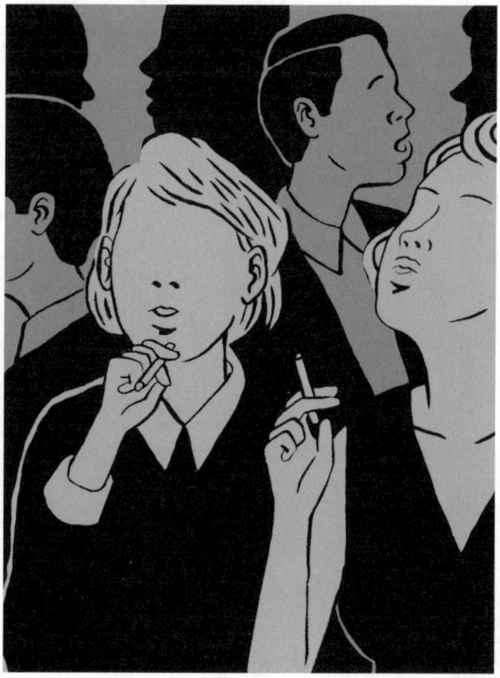

I CAN ASSURE YOU THAT TONIGHT IS YOUR NIGHT!

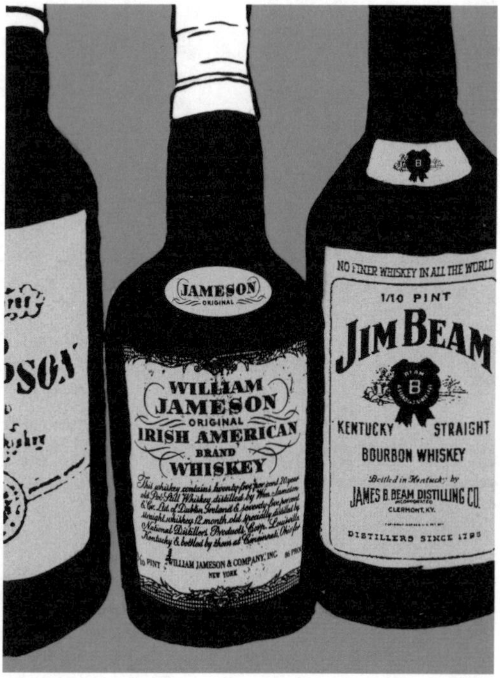
JAMESON
ORIGINAL
WILLIAM JAMESON
ORIGINAL
IRISH AMERICAN
BRAND
WHISKEY
NO FINER WHISKEY IN ALL THE WORLD
1/10 PINT
JIM BEAM
KENTUCKY STRAIGHT
BOURBON WHISKEY
Bottled in Kentucky by
JAMES B. BEAM DISTILLING CO.
CLERMONT, KY.
DISTILLERS SINCE 1795

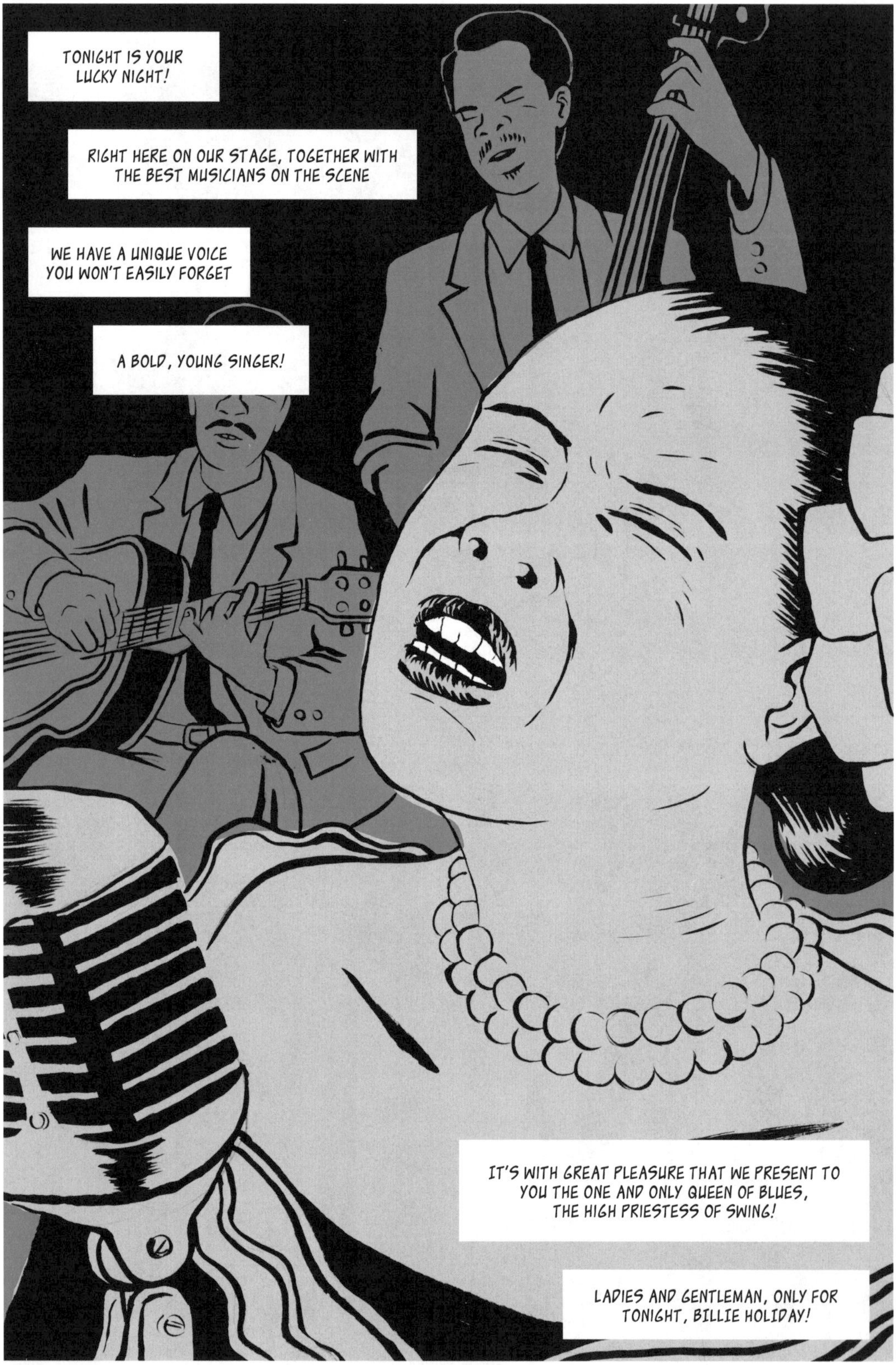
TONIGHT IS YOUR LUCKY NIGHT!
RIGHT HERE ON OUR STAGE, TOGETHER WITH THE BEST MUSICIANS ON THE SCENE
WE HAVE A UNIQUE VOICE YOU WON'T EASILY FORGET
A BOLD, YOUNG SINGER!
IT'S WITH GREAT PLEASURE THAT WE PRESENT TO YOU THE ONE AND ONLY QUEEN OF BLUES, THE HIGH PRIESTESS OF SWING!
LADIES AND GENTLEMAN, ONLY FOR TONIGHT, BILLIE HOLIDAY!

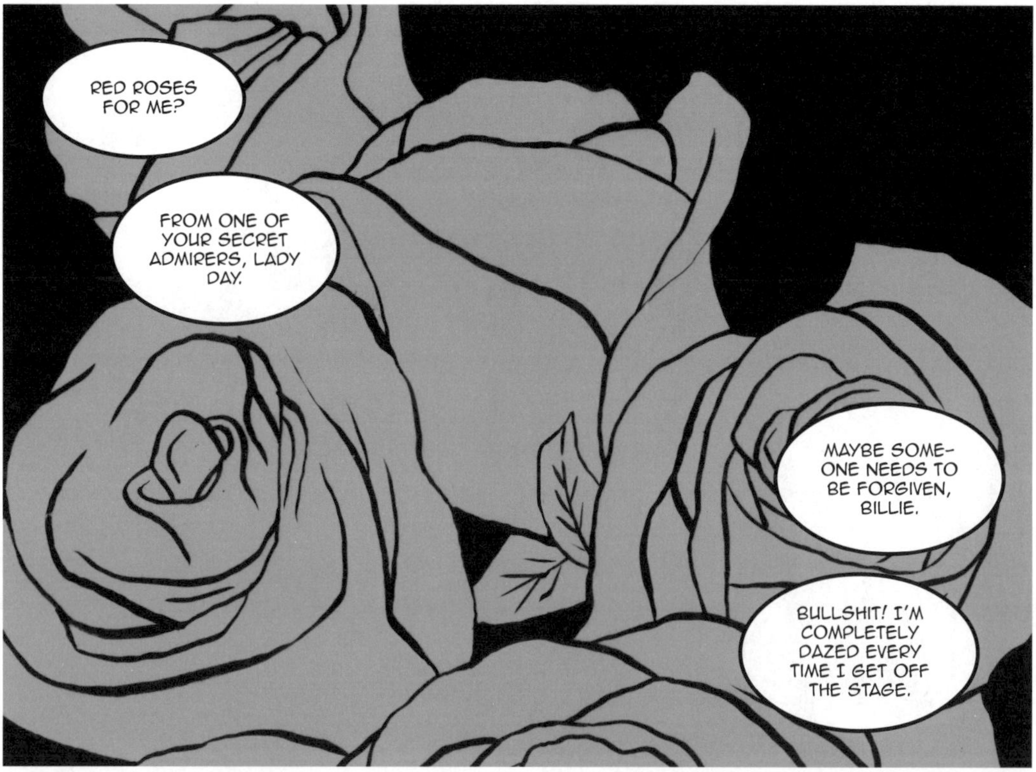
RED ROSES FOR ME?
FROM ONE OF YOUR SECRET ADMIRERS, LADY DAY.
MAYBE SOME-ONE NEEDS TO BE FORGIVEN, BILLIE.
BULLSHIT! I'M COMPLETELY DAZED EVERY TIME I GET OFF THE STAGE.

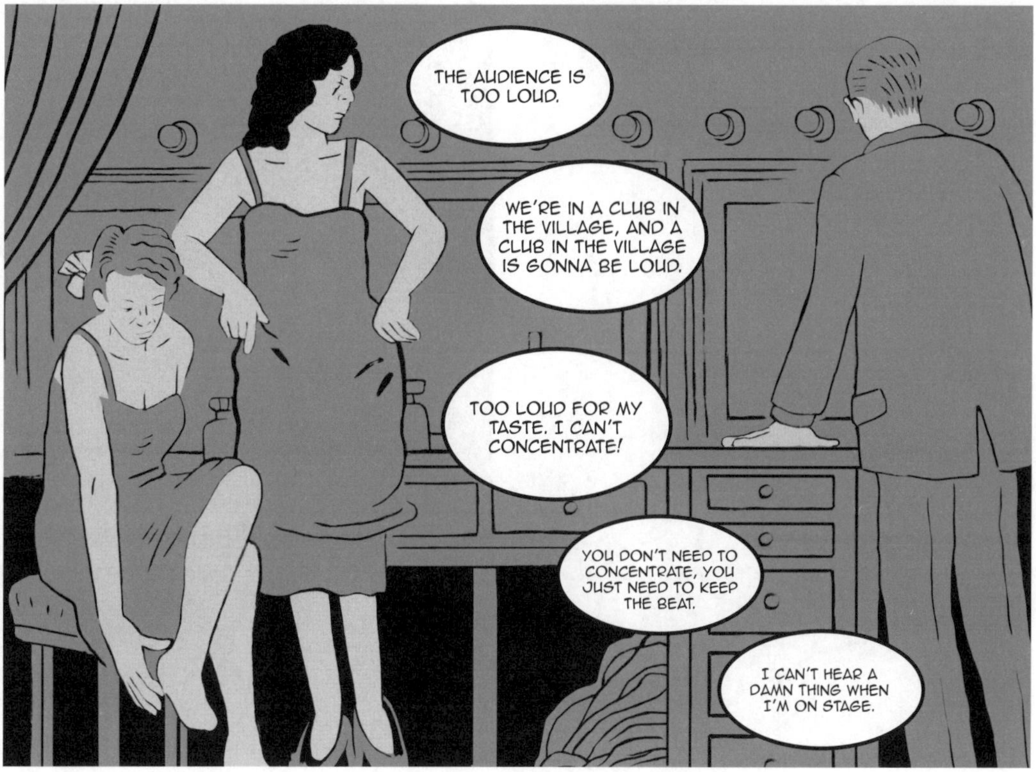
THE AUDIENCE IS TOO LOUD.
WE'RE IN A CLUB IN THE VILLAGE, AND A CLUB IN THE VILLAGE IS GONNA BE LOUD.
TOO LOUD FOR MY TASTE. I CAN'T CONCENTRATE!
YOU DON'T NEED TO CONCENTRATE, YOU JUST NEED TO KEEP THE BEAT.
I CAN'T HEAR A DAMN THING WHEN I'M ON STAGE.

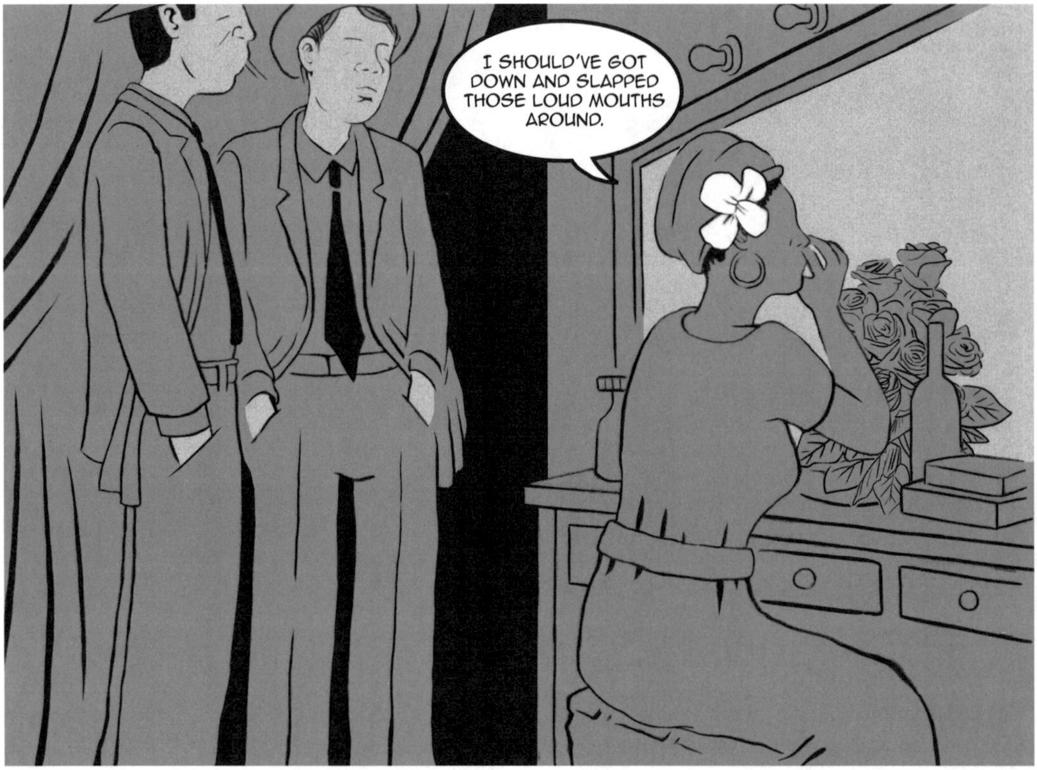
I SHOULD'VE GOT DOWN AND SLAPPED THOSE LOUD MOUTHS AROUND.

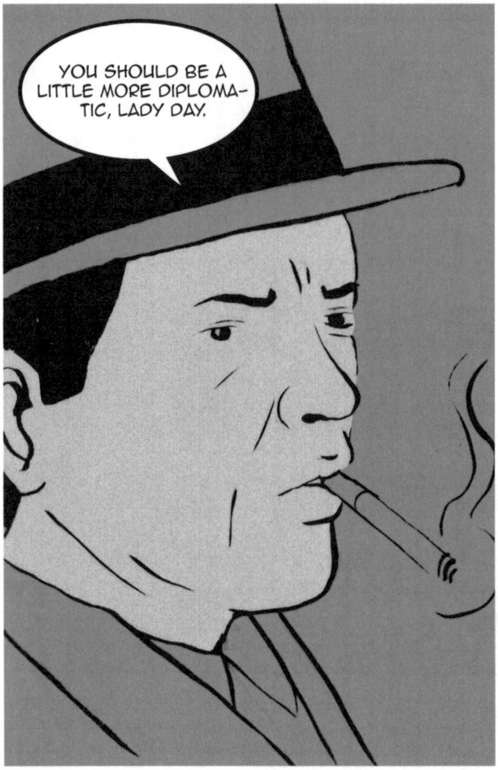
YOU SHOULD BE A LITTLE MORE DIPLOMA-TIC, LADY DAY.

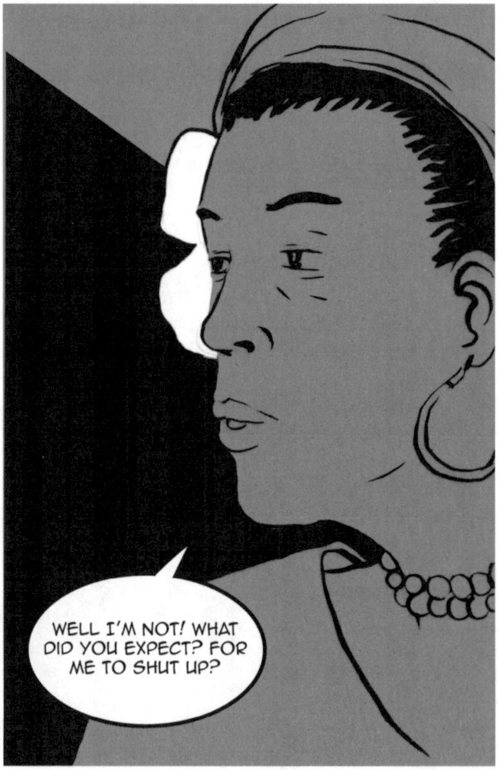
WELL I'M NOT! WHAT DID YOU EXPECT? FOR ME TO SHUT UP?

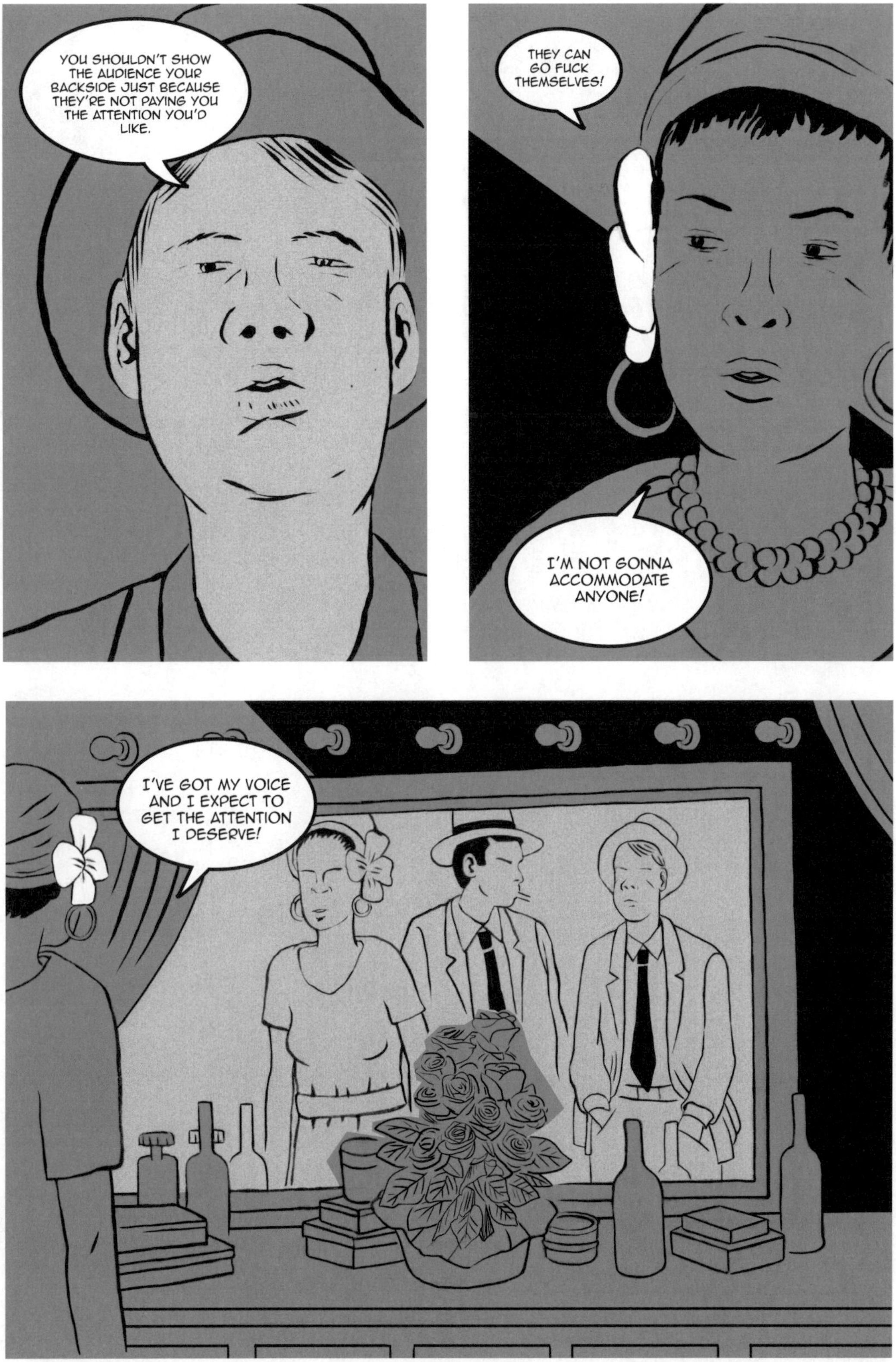
YOU SHOULDN'T SHOW THE AUDIENCE YOUR BACKSIDE JUST BECAUSE THEY'RE NOT PAYING YOU THE ATTENTION YOU'D LIKE.
THEY CAN GO FUCK THEMSELVES!
I'M NOT GONNA ACCOMMODATE ANYONE!
I'VE GOT MY VOICE AND I EXPECT TO GET THE ATTENTION I DESERVE!

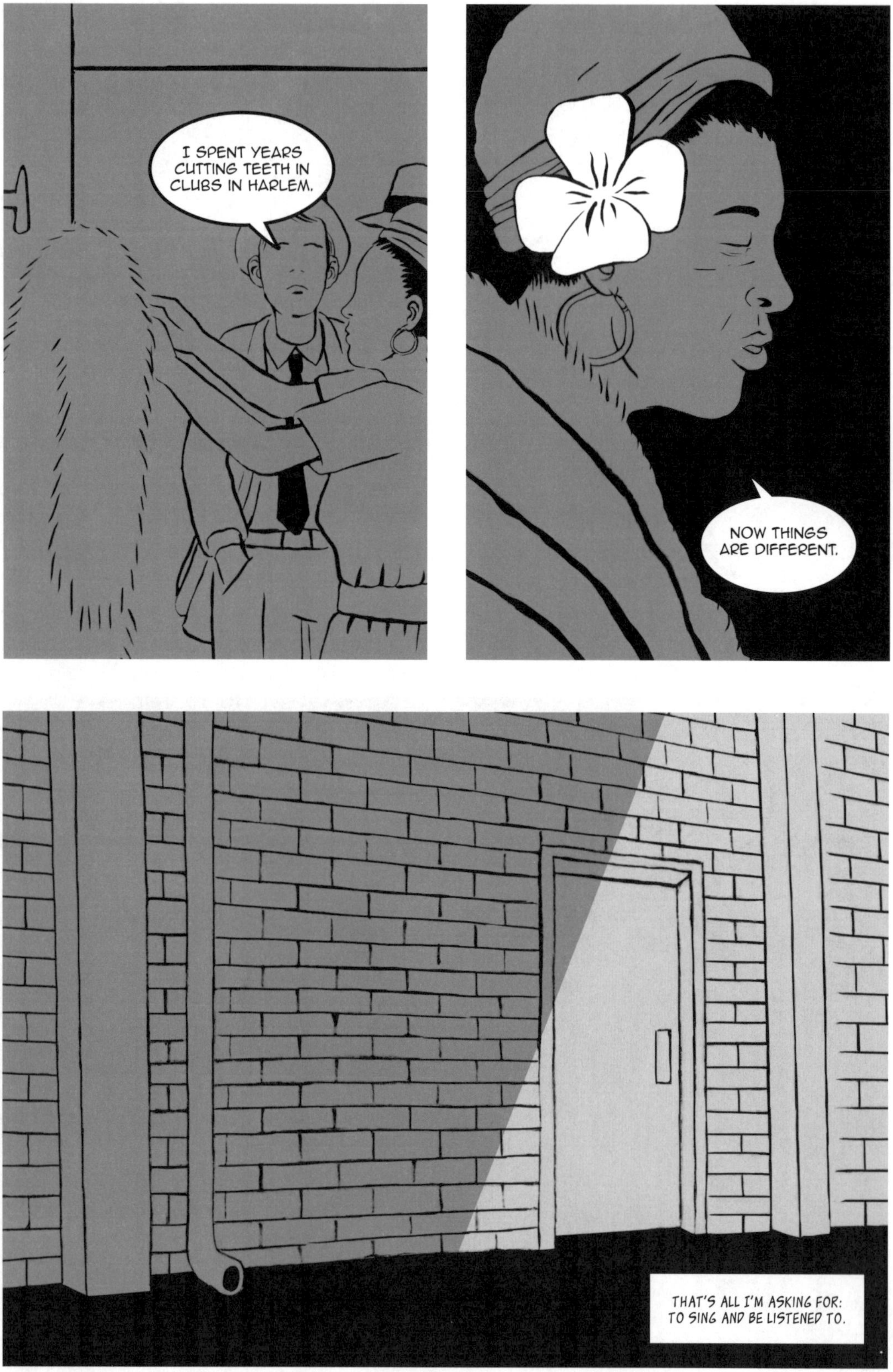
I SPENT YEARS CUTTING TEETH IN CLUBS IN HARLEM.
NOW THINGS ARE DIFFERENT.
THAT'S ALL I'M ASKING FOR: TO SING AND BE LISTENED TO.

"Strange Fruit"

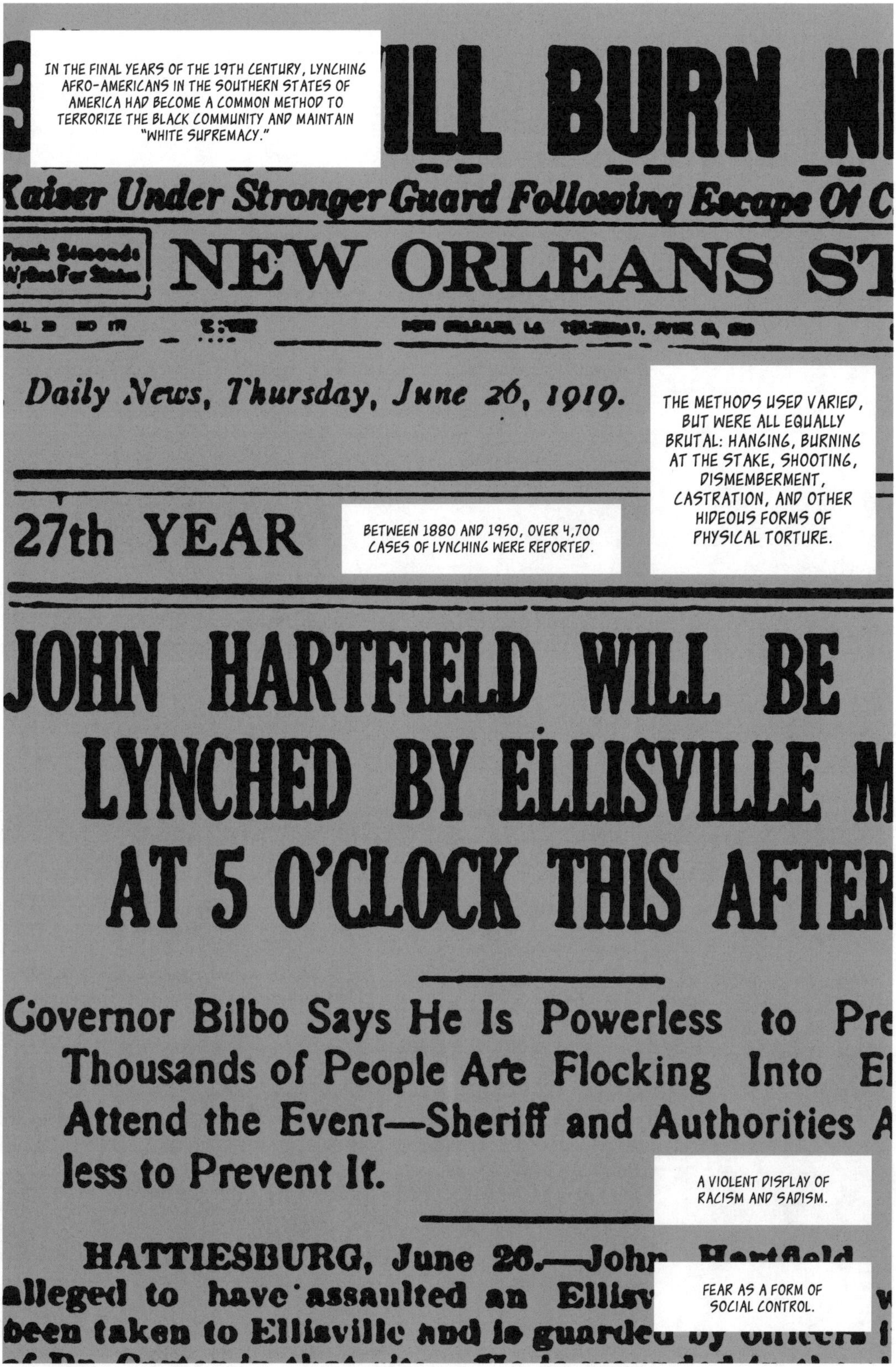
IN THE FINAL YEARS OF THE 19TH CENTURY, LYNCHING AFRO-AMERICANS IN THE SOUTHERN STATES OF AMERICA HAD BECOME A COMMON METHOD TO TERRORIZE THE BLACK COMMUNITY AND MAINTAIN "WHITE SUPREMACY."
ILL BURN N
Kaiser Under Stronger Guard Following Escape Of C
NEW ORLEANS ST
Daily News, Thursday, June 26, 1919.
THE METHODS USED VARIED, BUT WERE ALL EQUALLY BRUTAL: HANGING, BURNING AT THE STAKE, SHOOTING, DISMEMBERMENT, CASTRATION, AND OTHER HIDEOUS FORMS OF PHYSICAL TORTURE.
27th YEAR
BETWEEN 1880 AND 1950, OVER 4,700 CASES OF LYNCHING WERE REPORTED.
JOHN HARTFIELD WILL BE
LYNCHED BY ELLISVILLE M
AT 5 O'CLOCK THIS AFTER
Governor Bilbo Says He Is Powerless to Pre
Thousands of People Are Flocking Into El
Attend the Event—Sheriff and Authorities A
less to Prevent It.
A VIOLENT DISPLAY OF RACISM AND SADISM.
HATTIESBURG, June 26.—John
alleged to have assaulted an Ellisv
been taken to Ellisville and is guarded by
FEAR AS A FORM OF SOCIAL CONTROL.

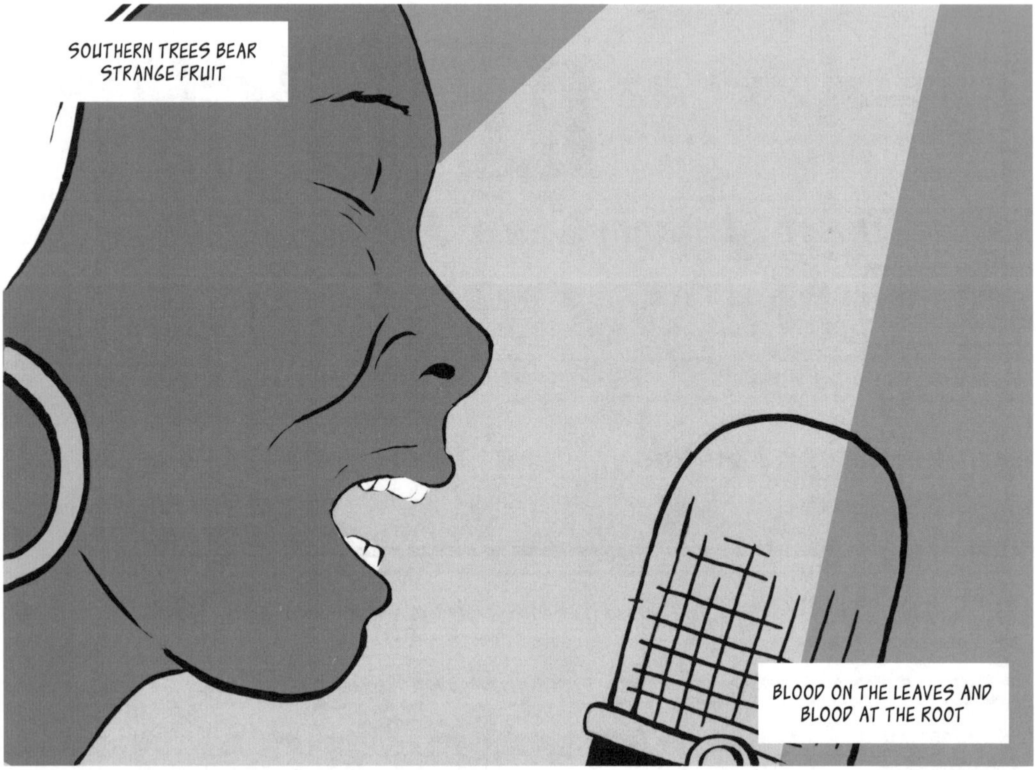
SOUTHERN TREES BEAR STRANGE FRUIT
BLOOD ON THE LEAVES AND BLOOD AT THE ROOT

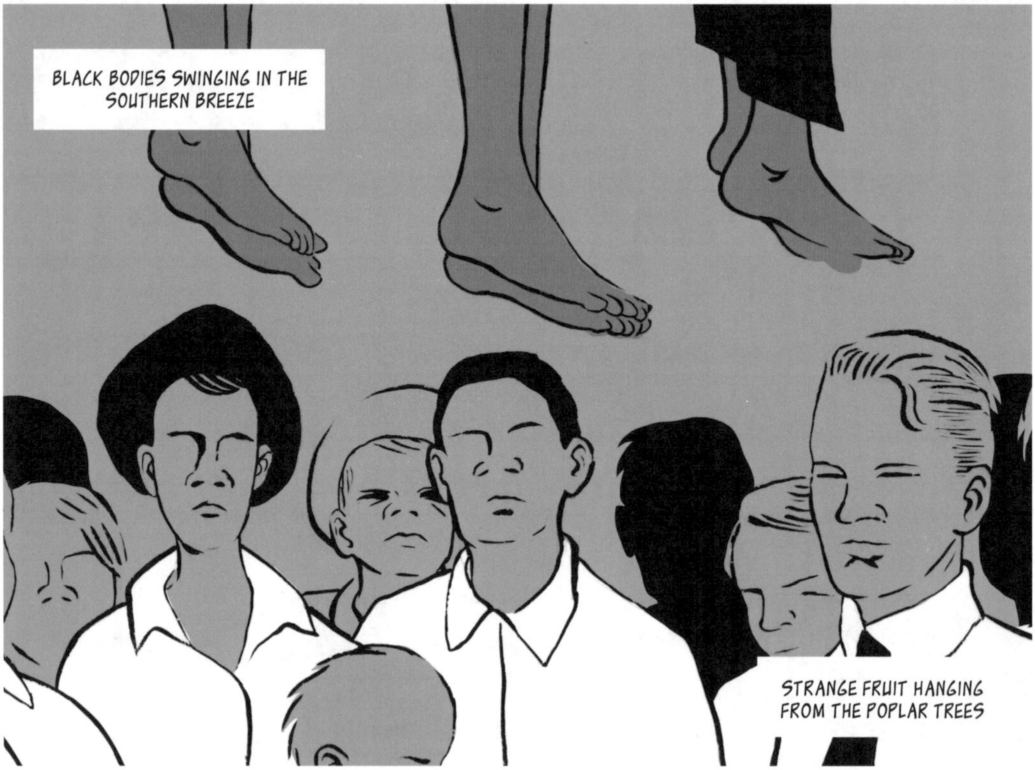
BLACK BODIES SWINGING IN THE SOUTHERN BREEZE
STRANGE FRUIT HANGING FROM THE POPLAR TREES

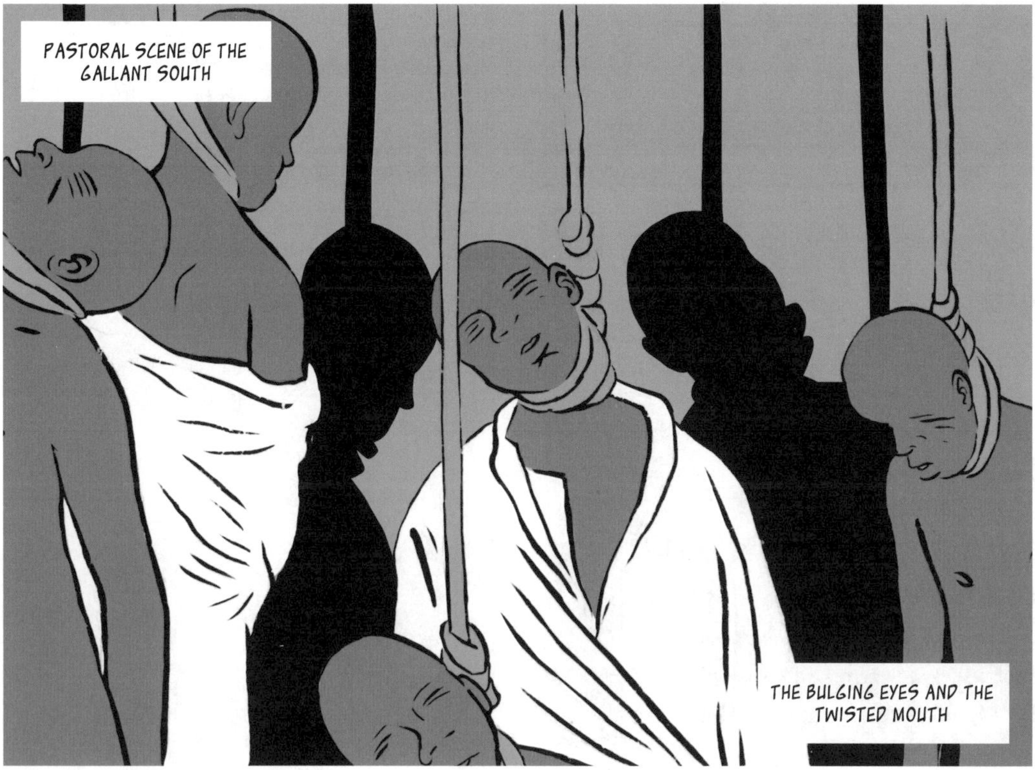
PASTORAL SCENE OF THE GALLANT SOUTH
THE BULGING EYES AND THE TWISTED MOUTH

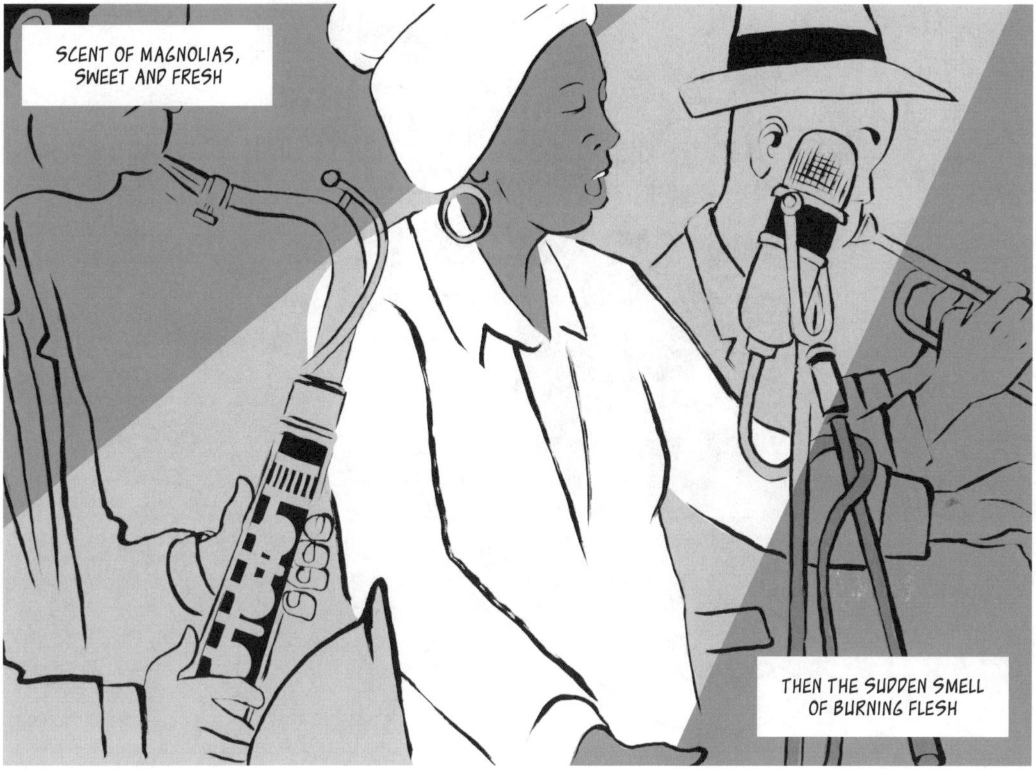
SCENT OF MAGNOLIAS, SWEET AND FRESH
THEN THE SUDDEN SMELL OF BURNING FLESH

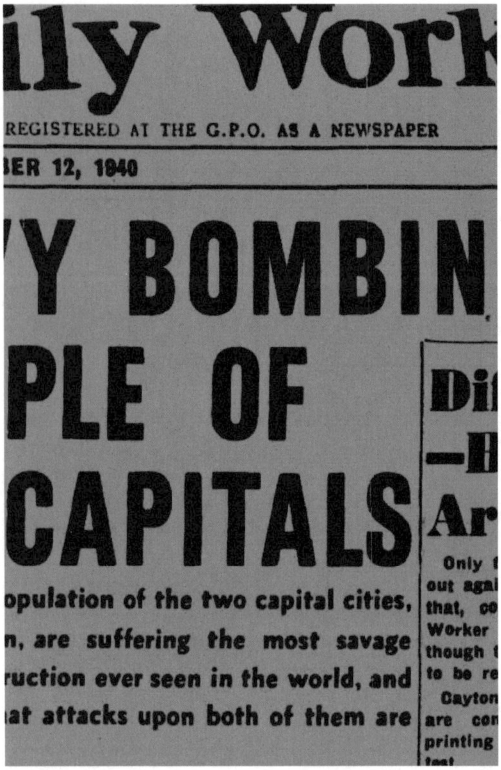
ily Work
REGISTERED AT THE G.P.O. AS A NEWSPAPER
BER 12, 1940
Y BOMBIN
PLE OF
CAPITALS
opulation of the two capital cities,
n, are suffering the most savage
ruction ever seen in the world, and
at attacks upon both of them are
Di
—B
Ar
Only
out agai
that, co
Worker
though
to be re
Cayton
are con
printing

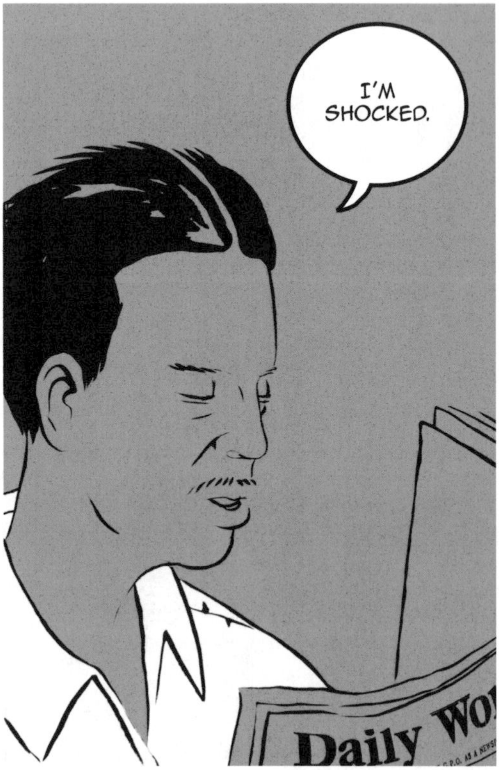
I'M SHOCKED.
Daily Wor

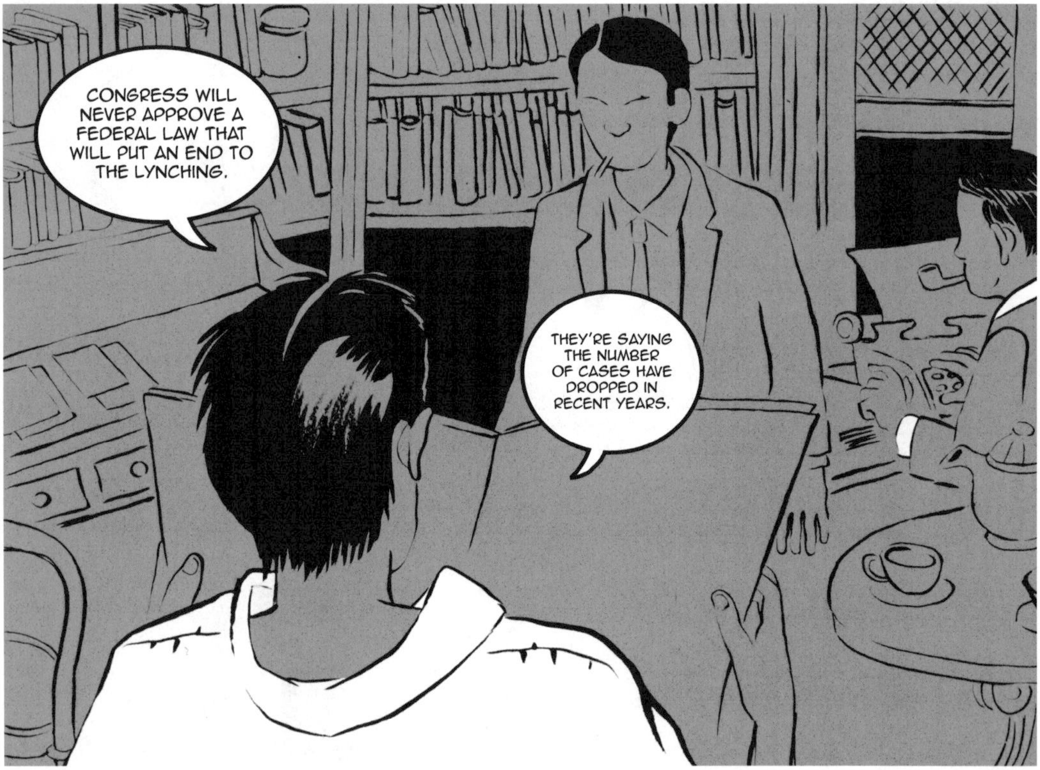
CONGRESS WILL NEVER APPROVE A FEDERAL LAW THAT WILL PUT AN END TO THE LYNCHING.
THEY'RE SAYING THE NUMBER OF CASES HAVE DROPPED IN RECENT YEARS.

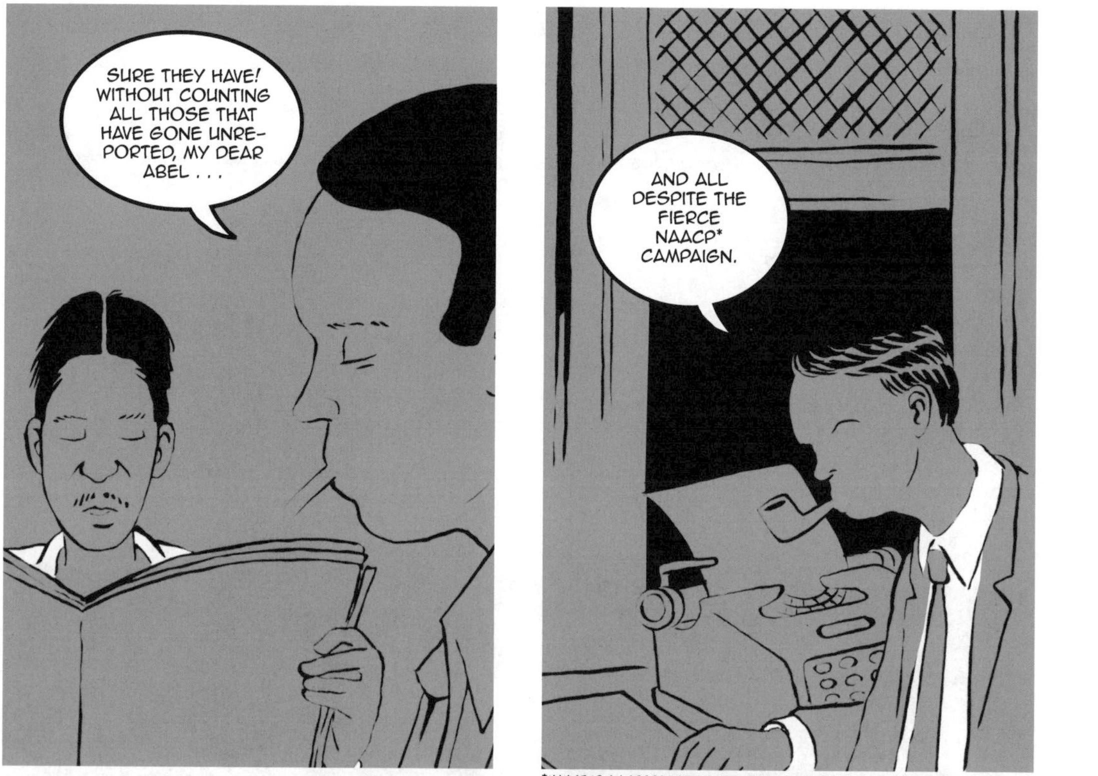
SURE THEY HAVE! WITHOUT COUNTING ALL THOSE THAT HAVE GONE UNRE-PORTED, MY DEAR ABEL . . .
AND ALL DESPITE THE FIERCE NAACP* CAMPAIGN.

*NAACP IS AN ABBREVIATION OF THE NATIONAL ASSOCIATION FOR THE ADVANCEMENT OF COLORED PEOPLE.

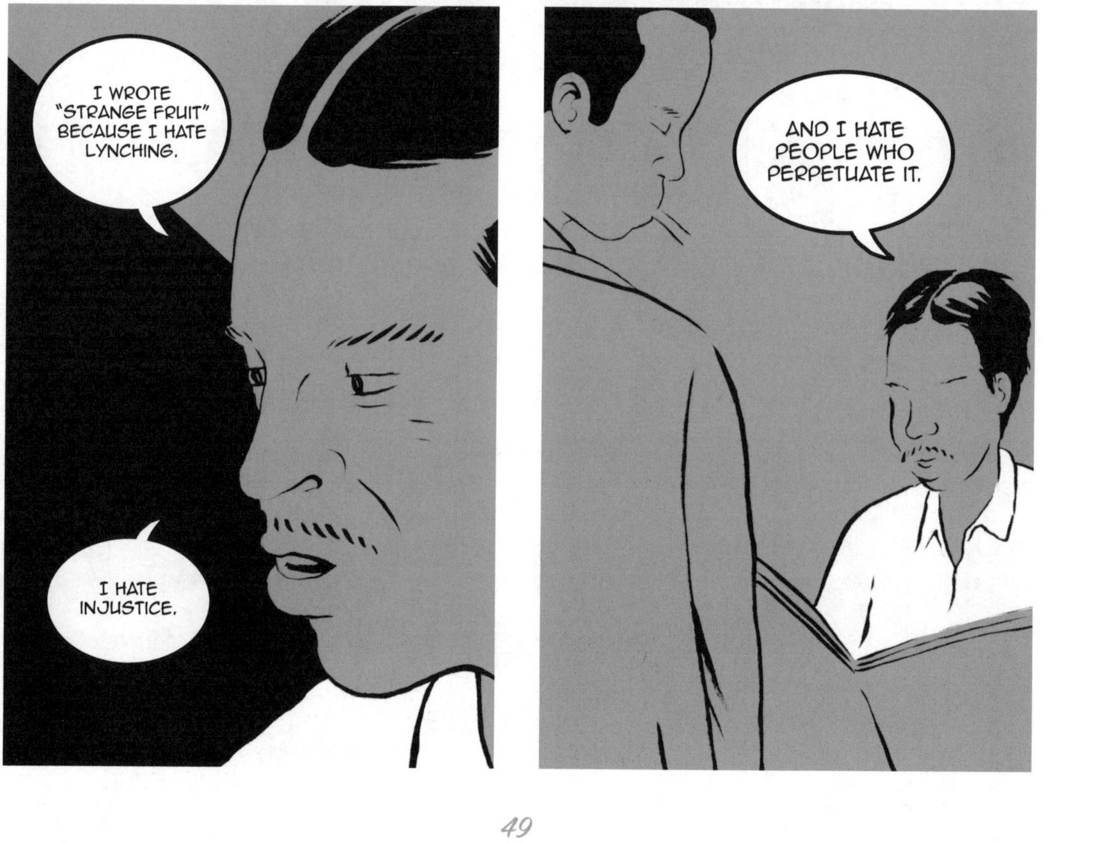
I WROTE "STRANGE FRUIT" BECAUSE I HATE LYNCHING.
I HATE INJUSTICE.
AND I HATE PEOPLE WHO PERPETUATE IT.

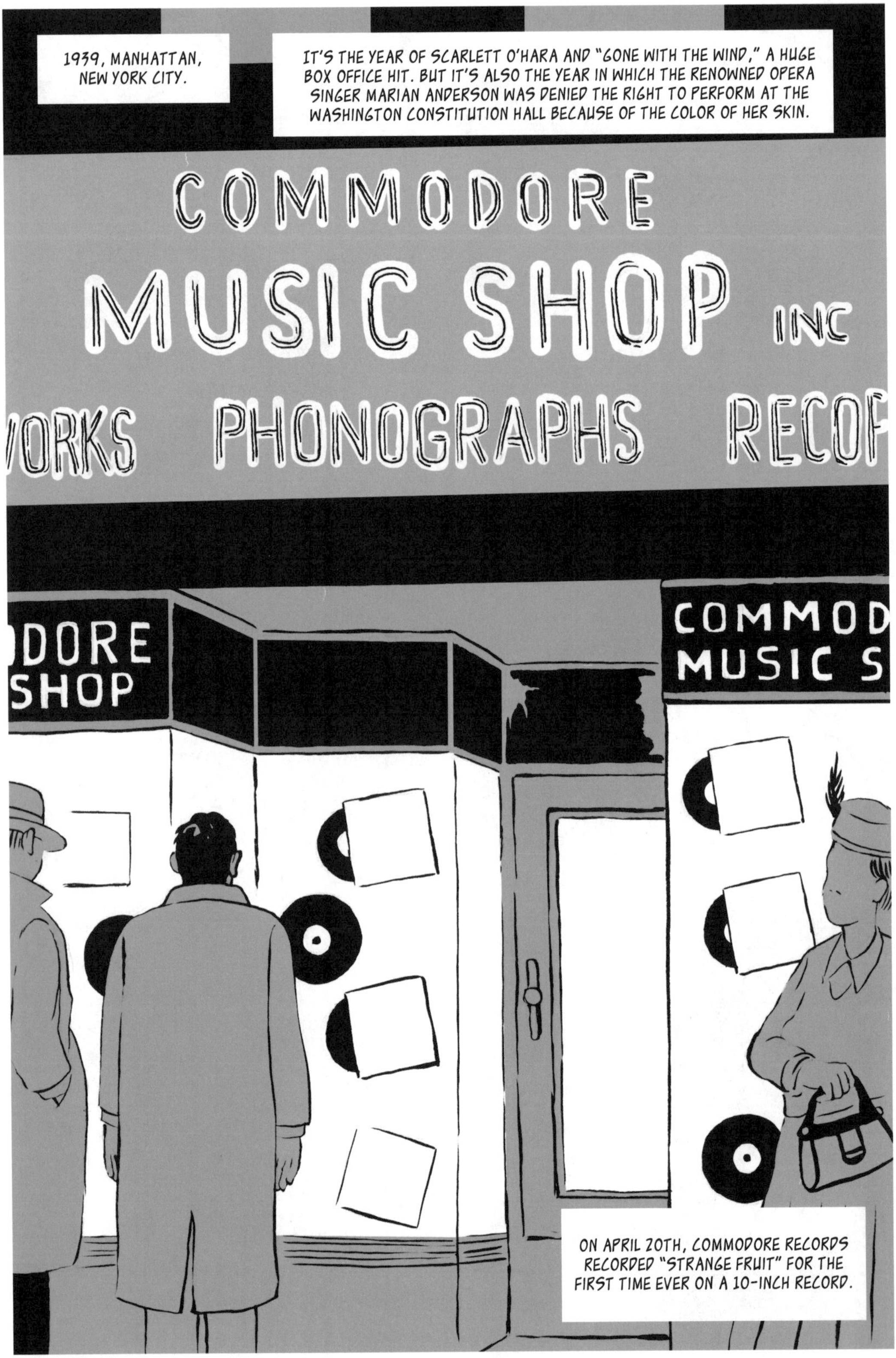
1939, MANHATTAN, NEW YORK CITY.
IT'S THE YEAR OF SCARLETT O'HARA AND "GONE WITH THE WIND," A HUGE BOX OFFICE HIT. BUT IT'S ALSO THE YEAR IN WHICH THE RENOWNED OPERA SINGER MARIAN ANDERSON WAS DENIED THE RIGHT TO PERFORM AT THE WASHINGTON CONSTITUTION HALL BECAUSE OF THE COLOR OF HER SKIN.
COMMODORE
MUSIC SHOP INC
ORKS PHONOGRAPHS RECOR
DORE SHOP
COMMOD MUSIC S
ON APRIL 20TH, COMMODORE RECORDS RECORDED "STRANGE FRUIT" FOR THE FIRST TIME EVER ON A 10-INCH RECORD.

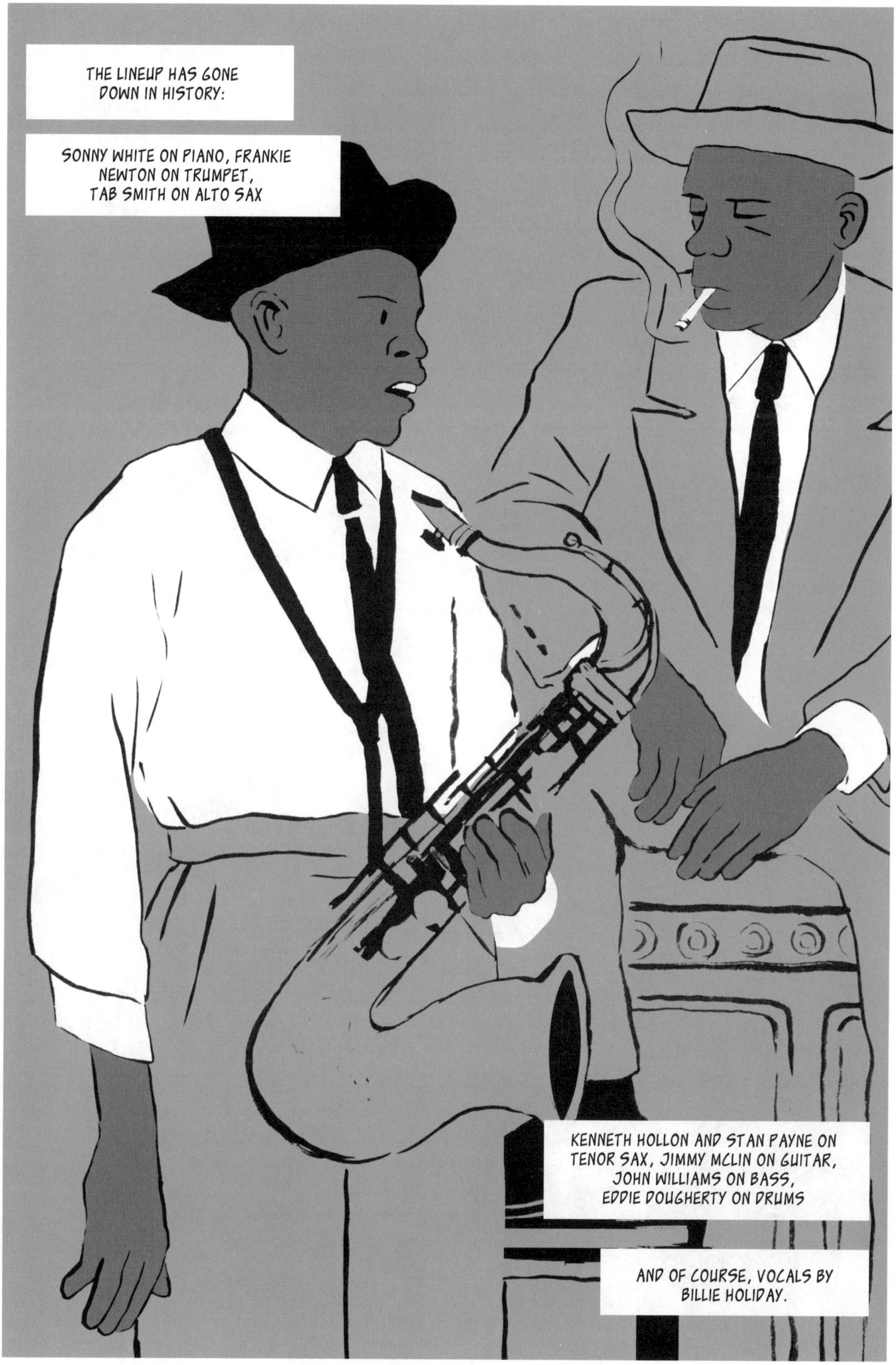
THE LINEUP HAS GONE DOWN IN HISTORY:
SONNY WHITE ON PIANO, FRANKIE NEWTON ON TRUMPET, TAB SMITH ON ALTO SAX
KENNETH HOLLON AND STAN PAYNE ON TENOR SAX, JIMMY MCLIN ON GUITAR, JOHN WILLIAMS ON BASS, EDDIE DOUGHERTY ON DRUMS
AND OF COURSE, VOCALS BY BILLIE HOLIDAY.

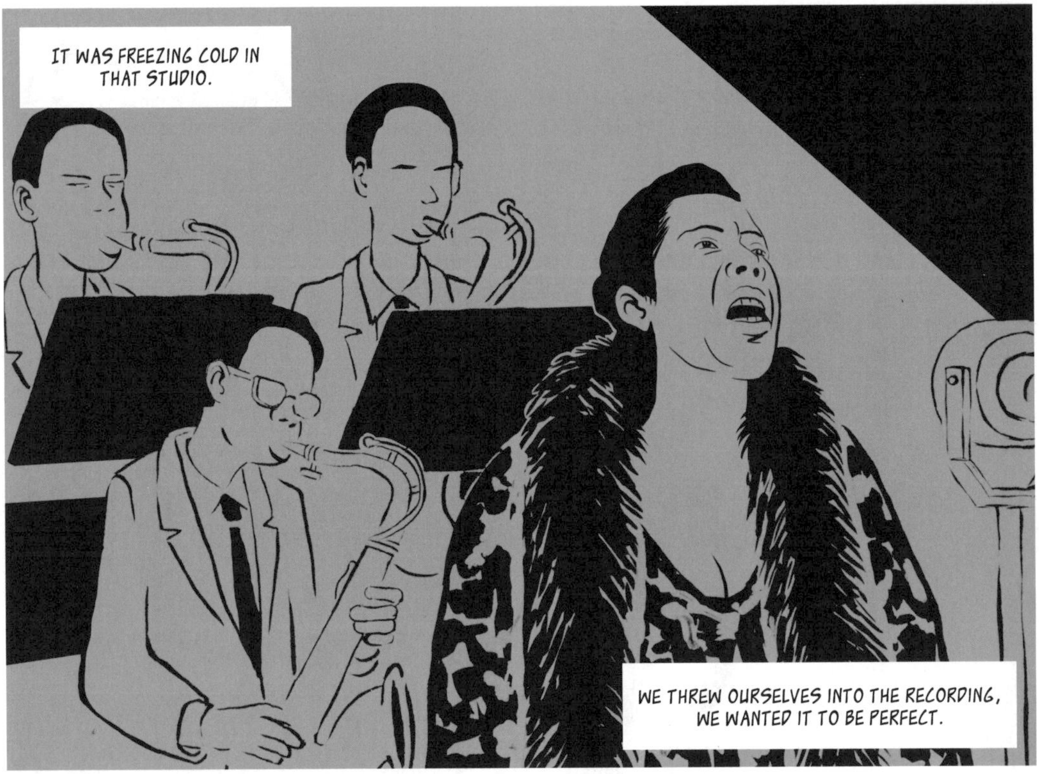
IT WAS FREEZING COLD IN THAT STUDIO.
WE THREW OURSELVES INTO THE RECORDING, WE WANTED IT TO BE PERFECT.

FRANKIE DID HIS TRUMPET INTRO. SILENCE FELL, THE REST CAME NATURALLY.

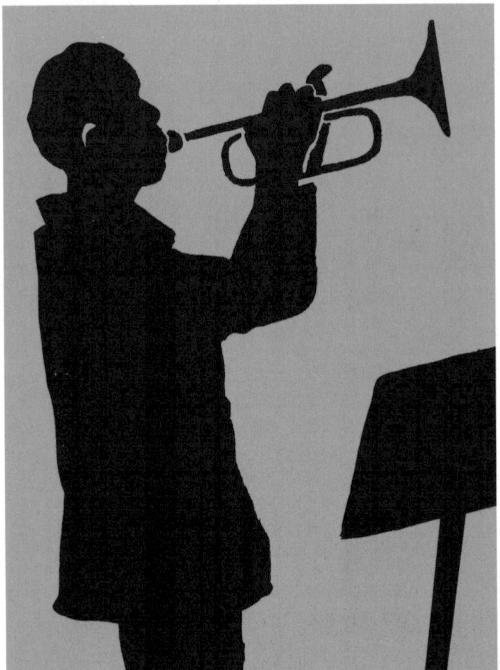

I REMEMBER THE FIRST TIME THEY SUGGESTED I SING THE SONG. SONNY WHITE WAS WITH ME.

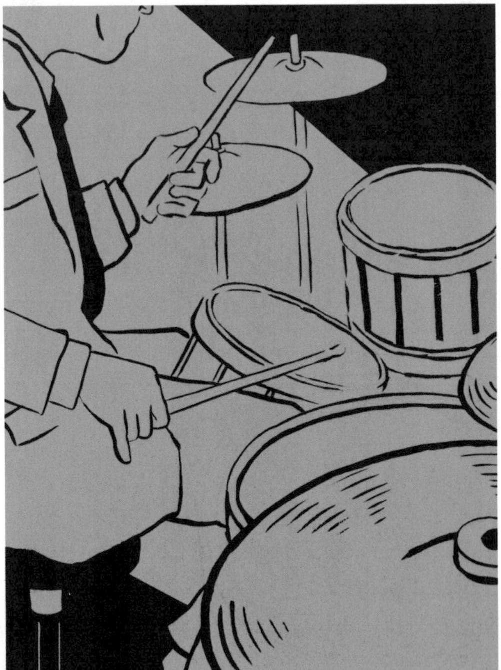

THIS GUY CALLED ABEL MEEROPOL SHOWED UP, HE WAS A TEACHER AND AN ACTIVIST IN THE AMERICAN COMMUNIST PARTY.

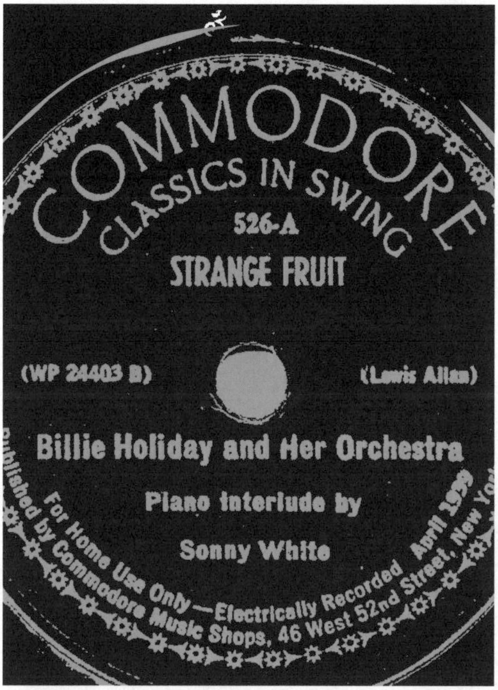
COMMODORE
CLASSICS IN SWING
526-A
STRANGE FRUIT
(WP 24403 B)
(Lewis Allan)
Billie Holiday and Her Orchestra
Piano interlude by
Sonny White
For Home Use Only—Electrically Recorded April 1939
Published by Commodore Music Shops, 46 West 52nd Street, New York

HE WANTED ME TO SING A POEM HE'D WRITTEN ABOUT LYNCHING IN THE DEEP SOUTH.

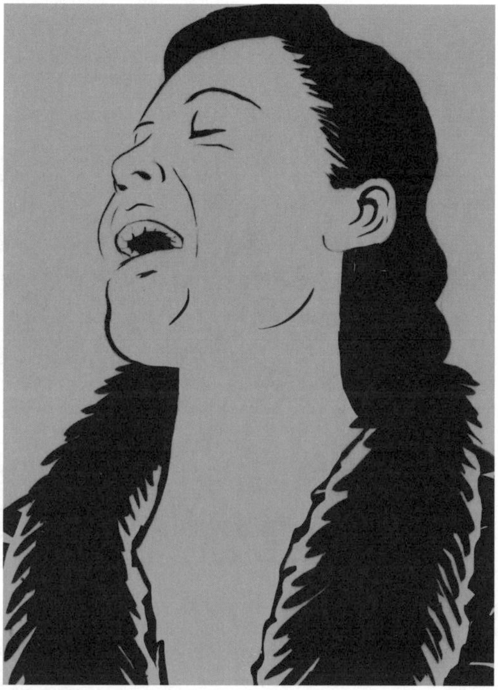

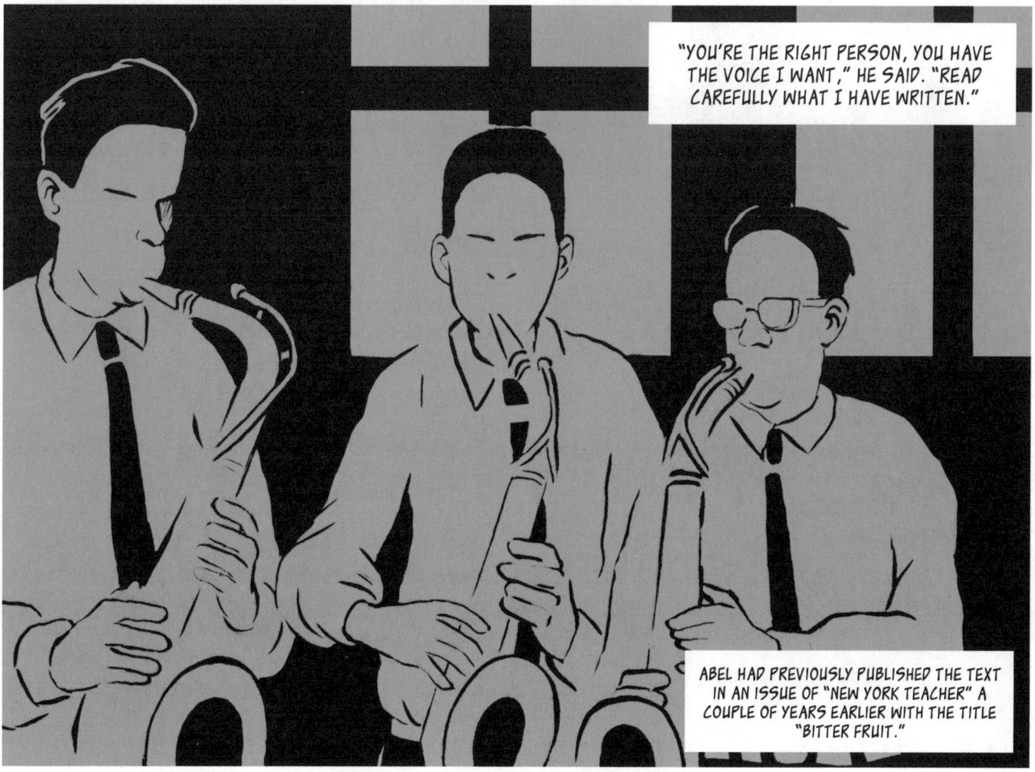
"YOU'RE THE RIGHT PERSON, YOU HAVE THE VOICE I WANT," HE SAID. "READ CAREFULLY WHAT I HAVE WRITTEN."
ABEL HAD PREVIOUSLY PUBLISHED THE TEXT IN AN ISSUE OF "NEW YORK TEACHER" A COUPLE OF YEARS EARLIER WITH THE TITLE "BITTER FRUIT."

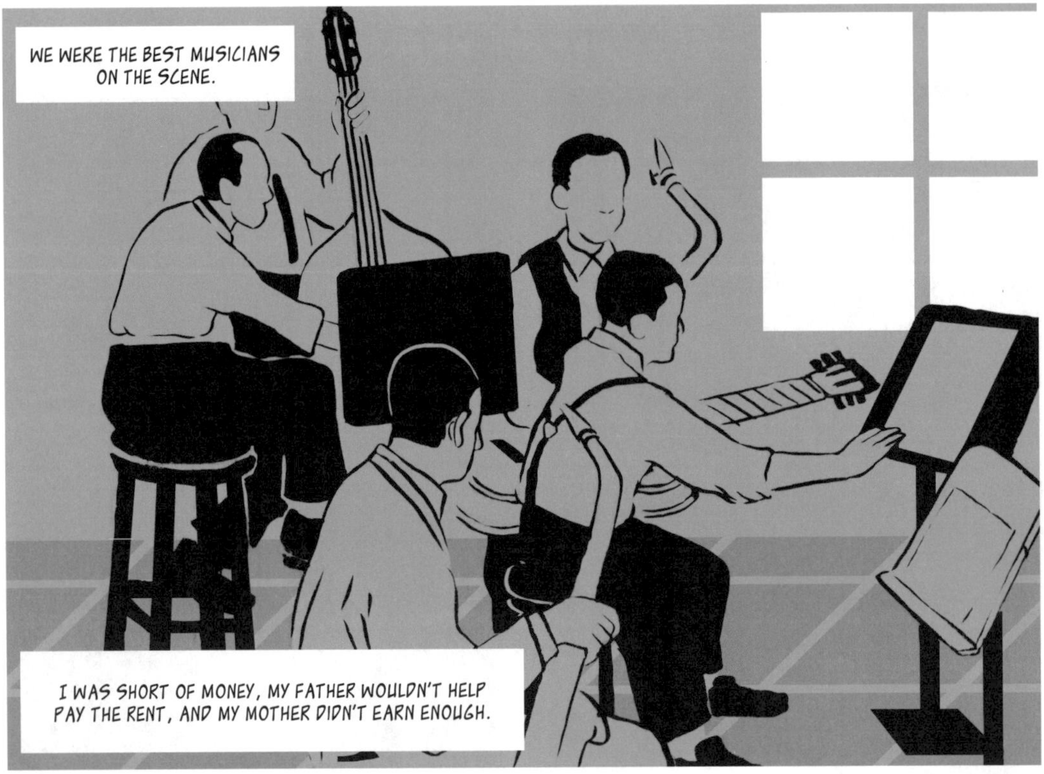
WE WERE THE BEST MUSICIANS ON THE SCENE.
I WAS SHORT OF MONEY, MY FATHER WOULDN'T HELP PAY THE RENT, AND MY MOTHER DIDN'T EARN ENOUGH.

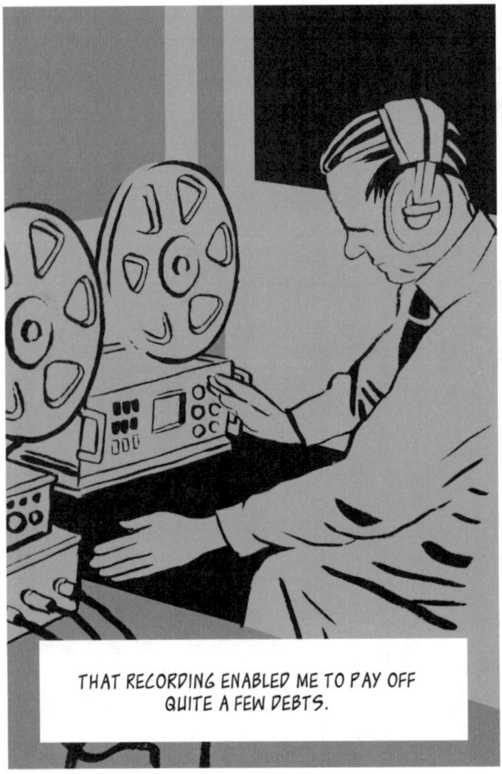
THAT RECORDING ENABLED ME TO PAY OFF QUITE A FEW DEBTS.

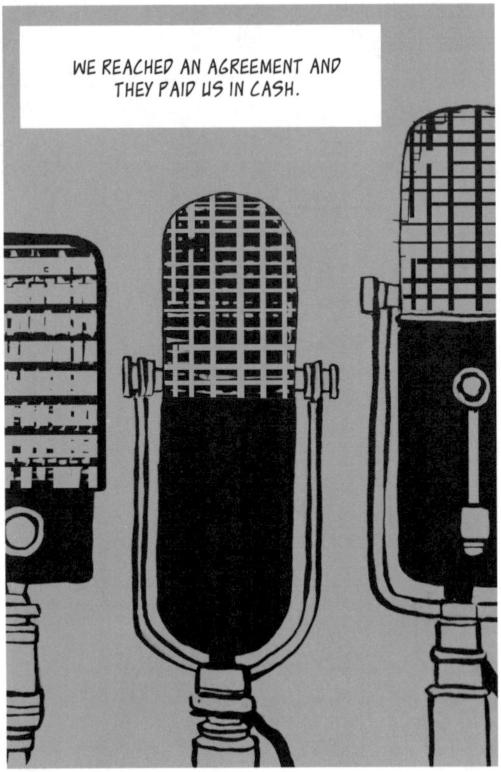
WE REACHED AN AGREEMENT AND THEY PAID US IN CASH.

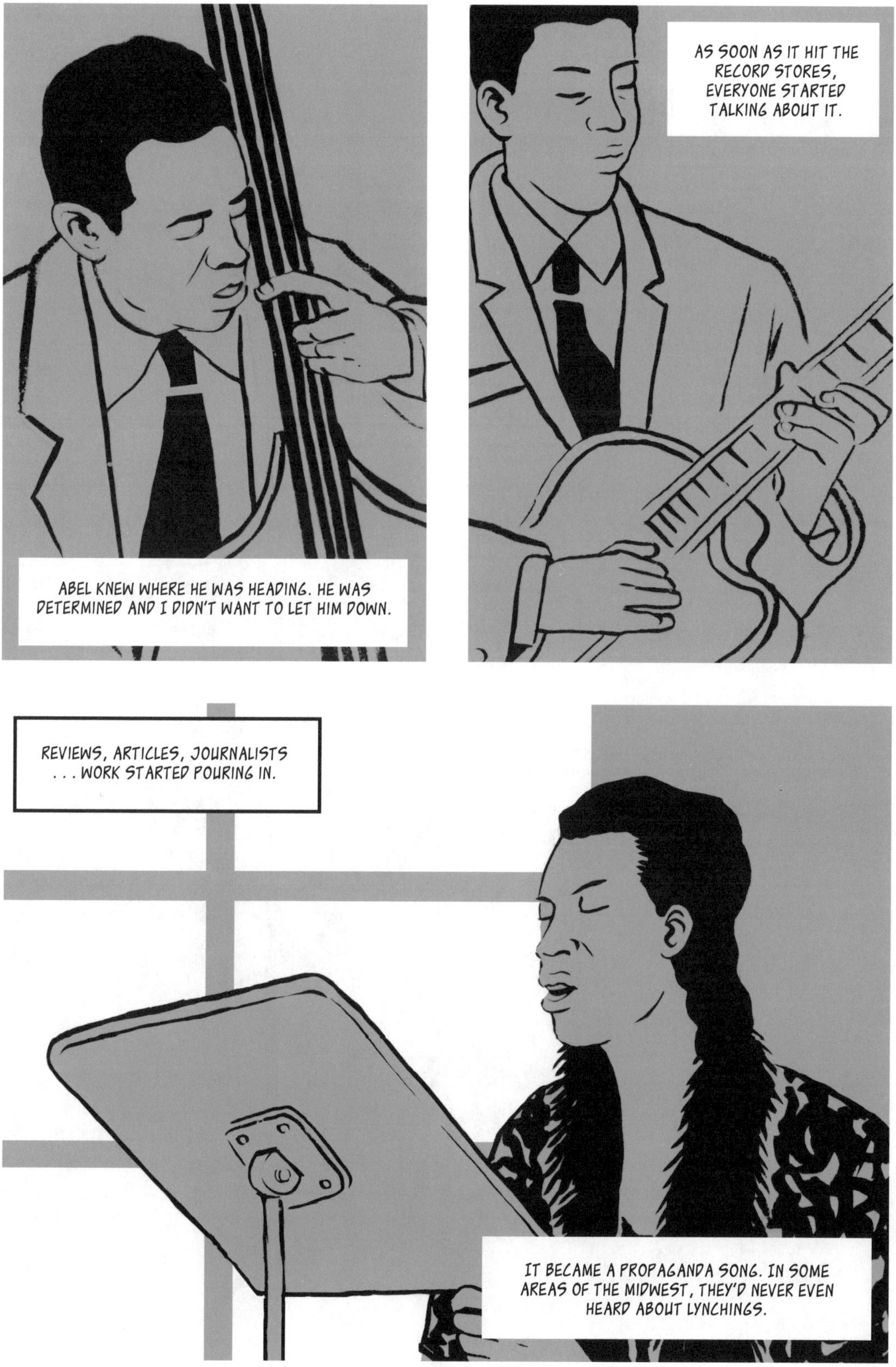
ABEL KNEW WHERE HE WAS HEADING. HE WAS DETERMINED AND I DIDN'T WANT TO LET HIM DOWN.
AS SOON AS IT HIT THE RECORD STORES, EVERYONE STARTED TALKING ABOUT IT.
REVIEWS, ARTICLES, JOURNALISTS . . . WORK STARTED POURING IN.
IT BECAME A PROPAGANDA SONG. IN SOME AREAS OF THE MIDWEST, THEY'D NEVER EVEN HEARD ABOUT LYNCHINGS.

THE FIRST TIME WE PLAYED IT LIVE, THE PREDOMINATELY WHITE AUDIENCE WAS LEFT SPEECHLESS.

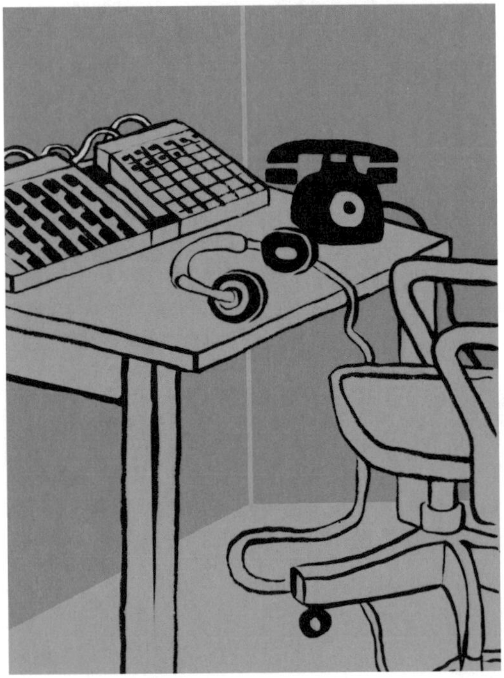

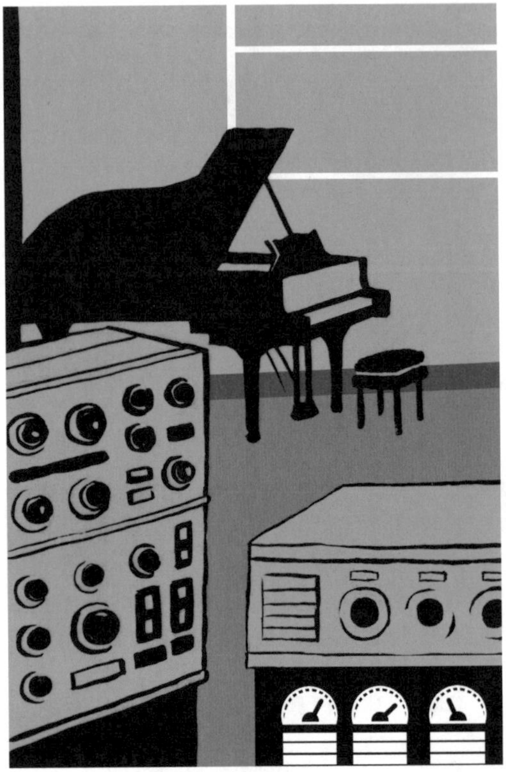

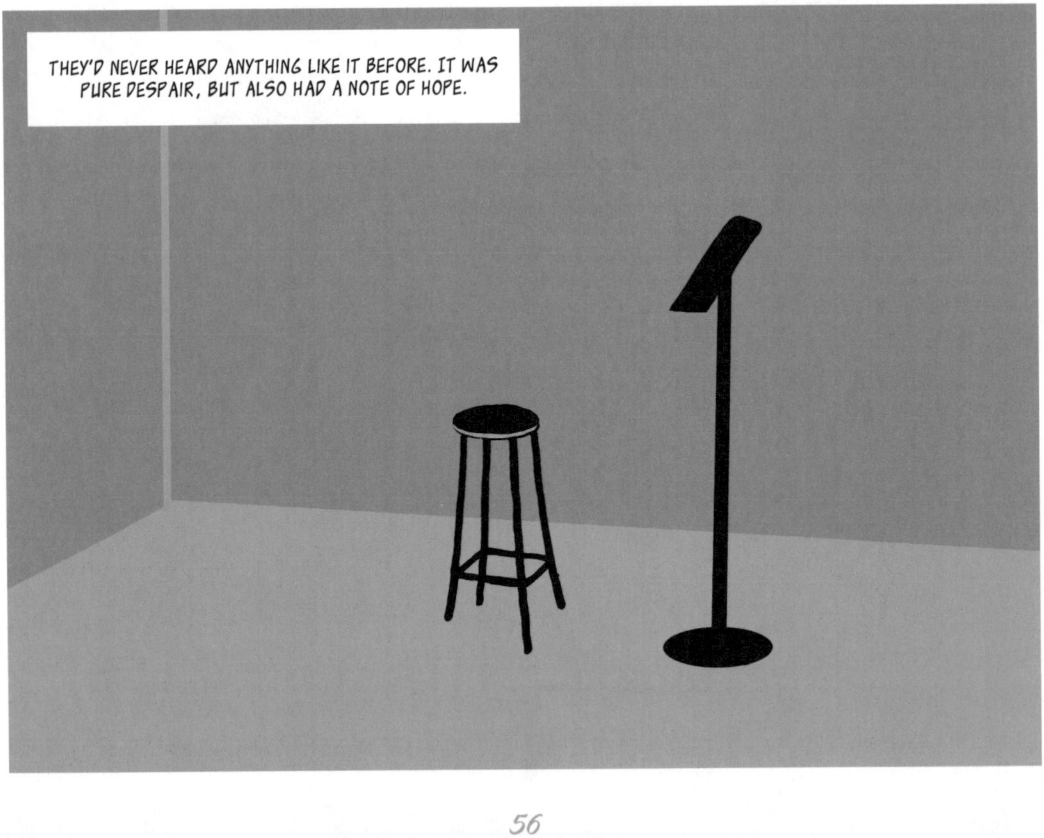
THEY'D NEVER HEARD ANYTHING LIKE IT BEFORE. IT WAS PURE DESPAIR, BUT ALSO HAD A NOTE OF HOPE.

"Love Me Or Leave Me"

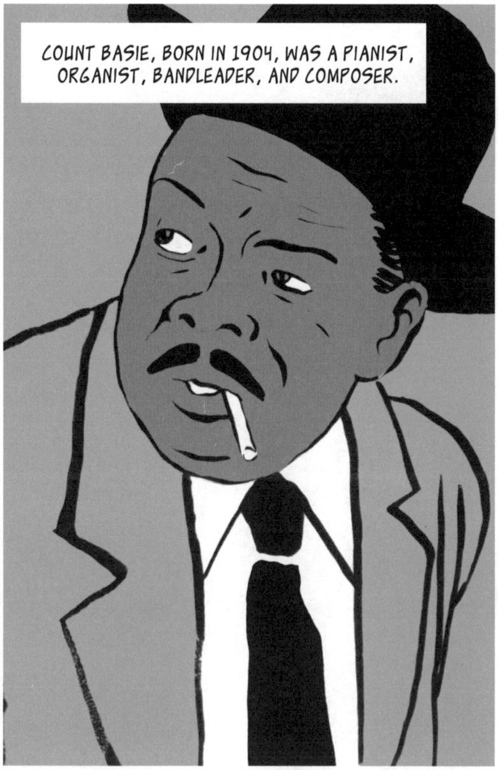
COUNT BASIE, BORN IN 1904, WAS A PIANIST, ORGANIST, BANDLEADER, AND COMPOSER.

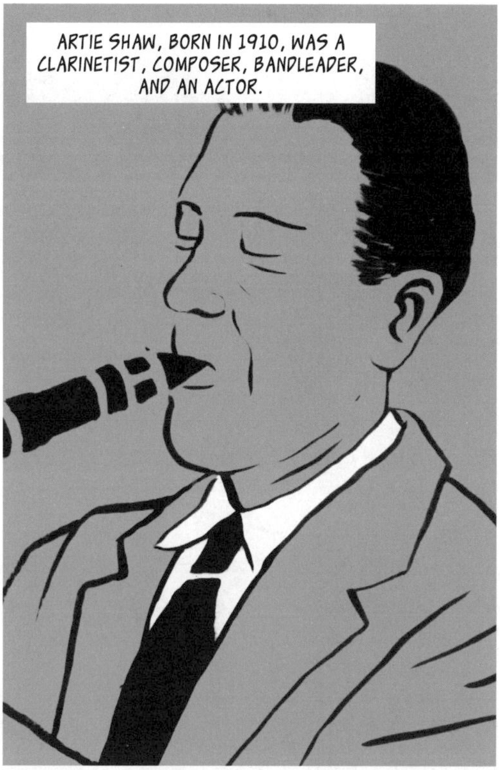
ARTIE SHAW, BORN IN 1910, WAS A CLARINETIST, COMPOSER, BANDLEADER, AND AN ACTOR.

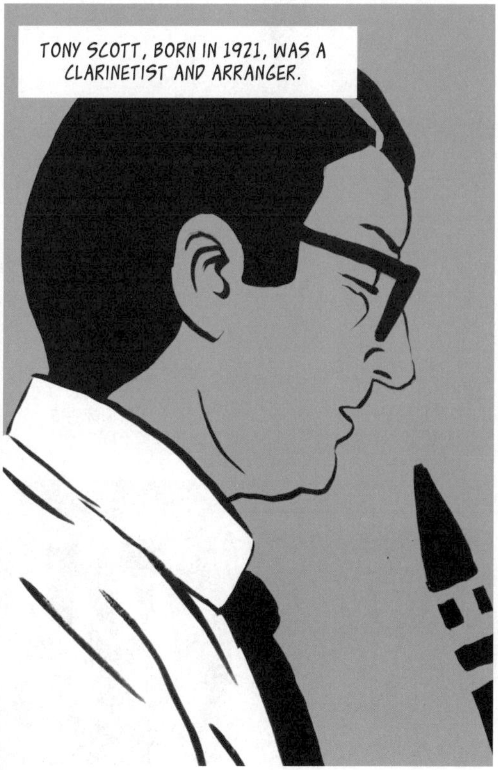
TONY SCOTT, BORN IN 1921, WAS A CLARINETIST AND ARRANGER.

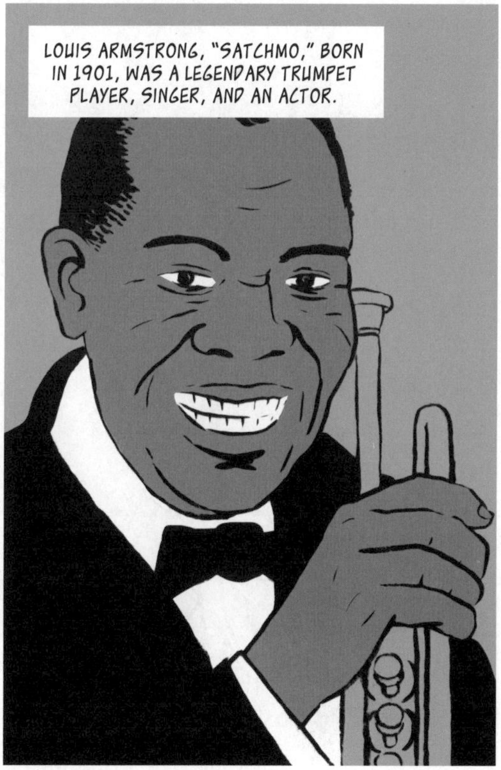
LOUIS ARMSTRONG, "SATCHMO," BORN IN 1901, WAS A LEGENDARY TRUMPET PLAYER, SINGER, AND AN ACTOR.

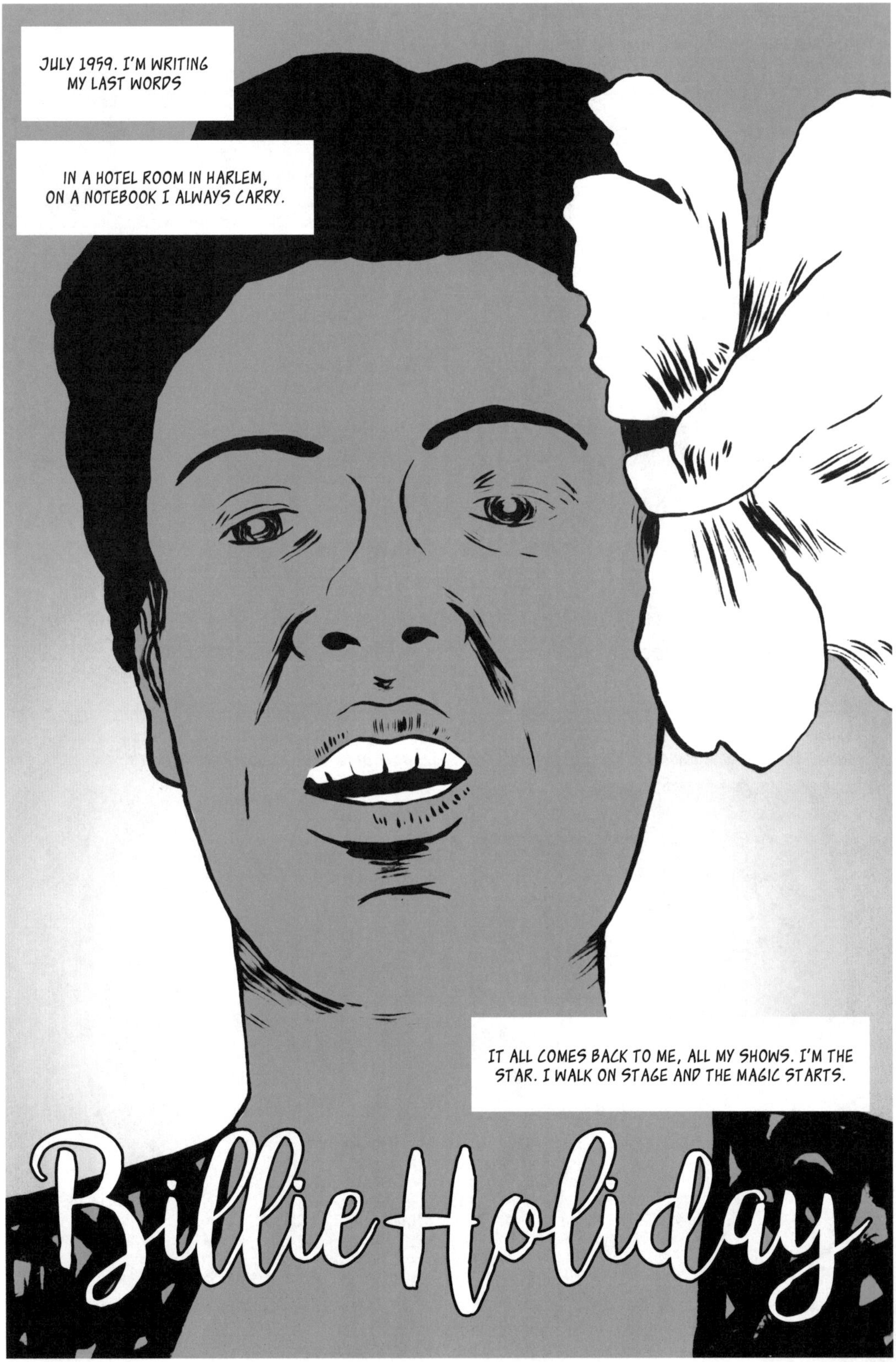
JULY 1959. I'M WRITING MY LAST WORDS
IN A HOTEL ROOM IN HARLEM, ON A NOTEBOOK I ALWAYS CARRY.
IT ALL COMES BACK TO ME, ALL MY SHOWS. I'M THE STAR. I WALK ON STAGE AND THE MAGIC STARTS.
Billie Holiday

THAT EVENING AT CARNEGIE HALL WAS UNFORGETTABLE. ALL THE GREATEST STARS WERE THERE TOGETHER.

I WAS BEING CONSUMED BY DRUGS AND BOOZE. I COULDN'T STOP. BACK THEN I EARNED A LOT AND I SPENT A LOT. HALF MY SALARY ENDED UP ON HEROIN AND OPIUM.

ELLINGTON
AND HIS ORCHESTRA

THE ONE AND ONLY
"LADY DAY"
Billie **HOLIDAY**

"YARD BIRD"
CHARLIE PARKER
AND HIS STRINGS

"THE KING OF BE BOP"
DIZZY GILLESPIE

"LONG ISLAND SOUND"
STAN GETZ

MY HEALTH ISSUES WERE SERIOUSLY JEOPARDIZING MY CAREER.

AND INTRODUCING
THE AMAD JAMAL TRIO

AT THE TIME, JOHN LEVY, MY MANAGER AND PARTNER, WOULDN'T GET OFF MY BACK. HE TOOK TOTAL CONTROL OF EVERYTHING.

FRIDAY-NOVEMBER 14. 1952-FRIDAY

CARNEGIE

"JUST FOCUS ON SINGING," HE WOULD SAY. BUT I HAD TOO MUCH MONEY AND DIDN'T KNOW HOW TO MANAGE IT ANYMORE. THEN ONE NIGHT, THE COPS BUSTED INTO OUR HOTEL ROOM IN SAN FRANCISCO AND CAUGHT US WITH DRUGS. IT WAS THE BEGINNING OF YET ANOTHER ORDEAL.

8:15 P.M. - (TWO) 2 PERFORMA
TICKETS SALE 3350 5200
ON SALE AT: CARNEGIE HALL BOX OFFICE

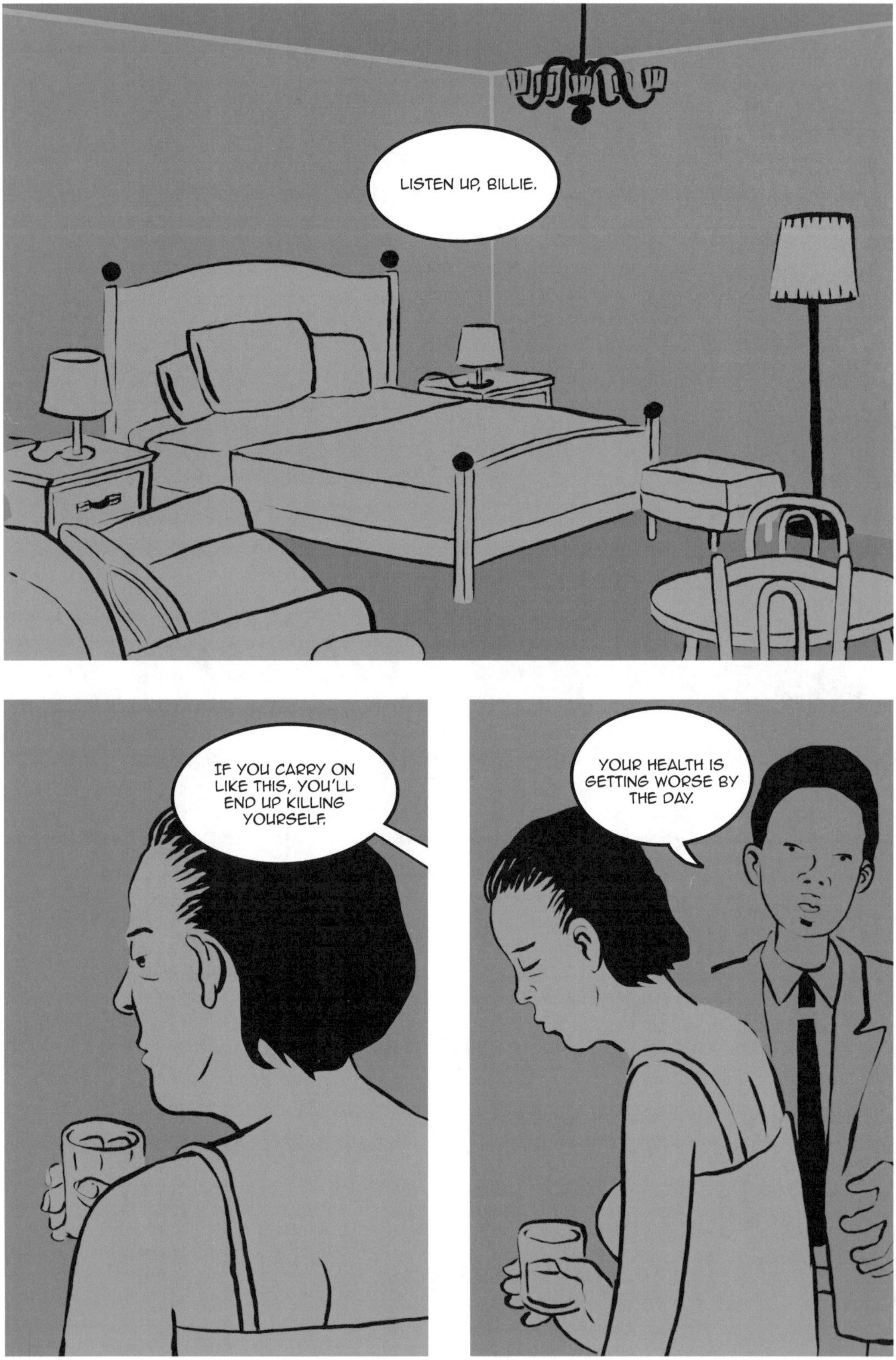
LISTEN UP, BILLIE.
IF YOU CARRY ON LIKE THIS, YOU'LL END UP KILLING YOURSELF.
YOUR HEALTH IS GETTING WORSE BY THE DAY.

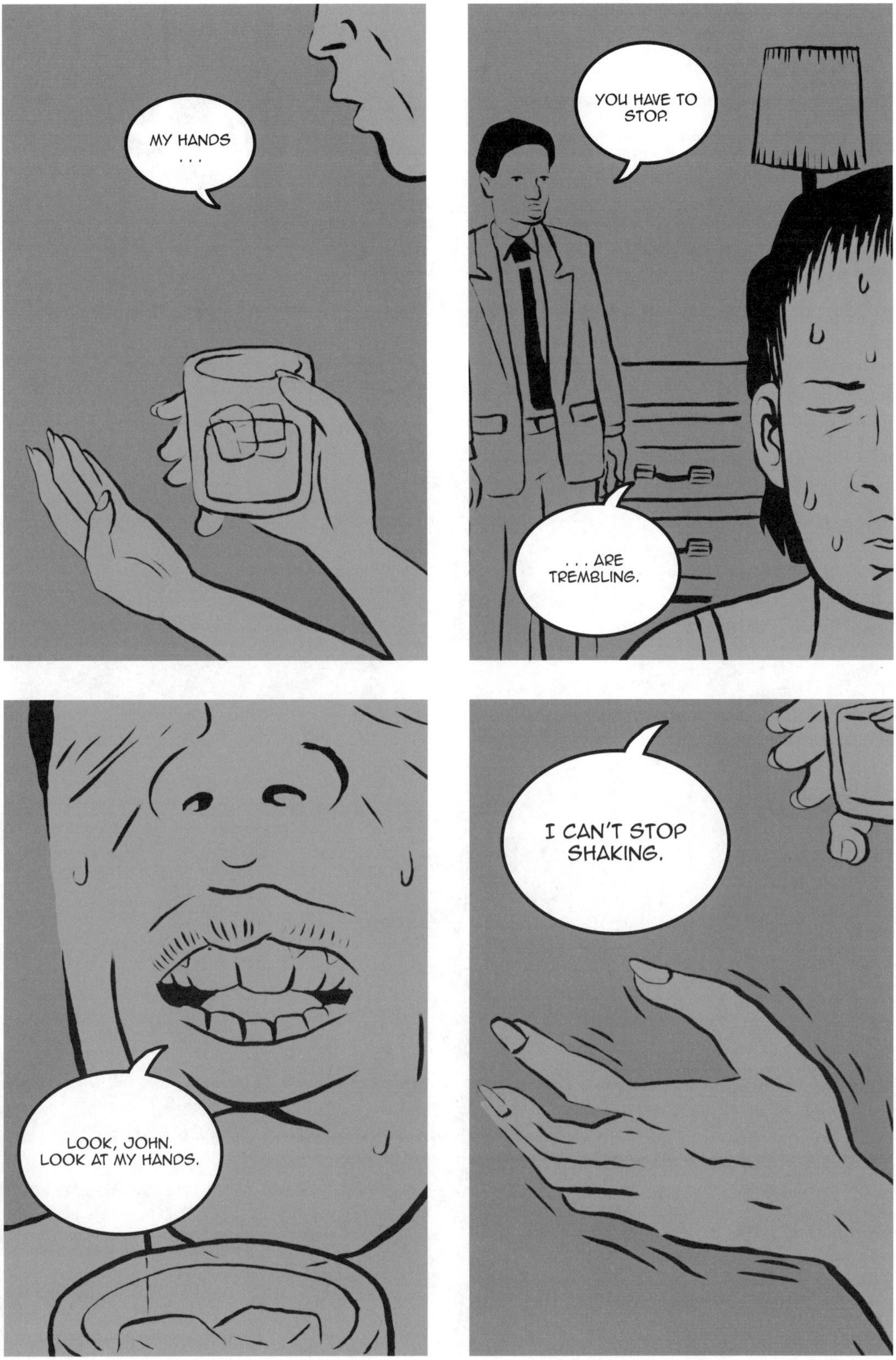
MY HANDS . . .
YOU HAVE TO STOP.
. . . ARE TREMBLING.
LOOK, JOHN. LOOK AT MY HANDS.
I CAN'T STOP SHAKING.

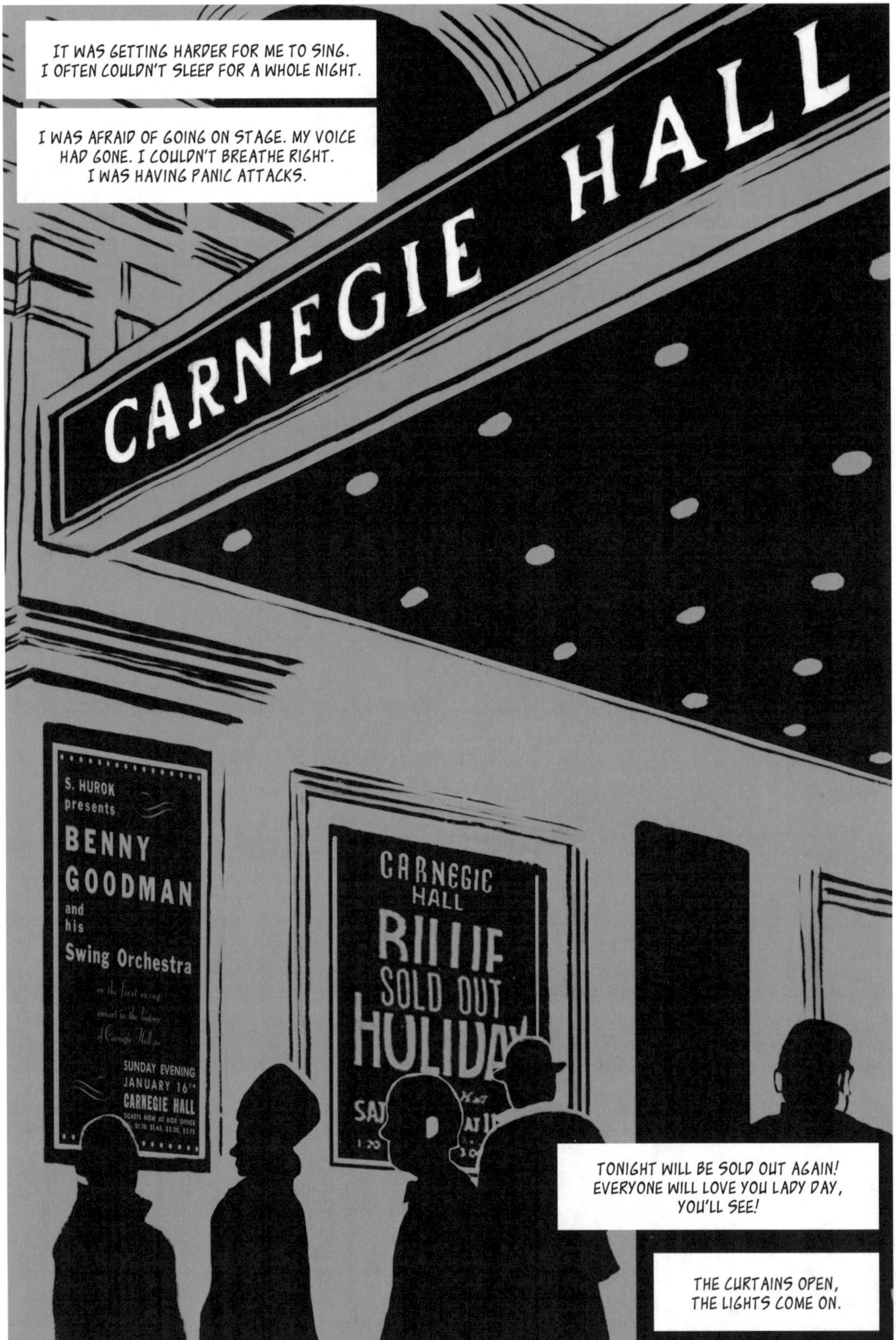
IT WAS GETTING HARDER FOR ME TO SING. I OFTEN COULDN'T SLEEP FOR A WHOLE NIGHT.
I WAS AFRAID OF GOING ON STAGE. MY VOICE HAD GONE. I COULDN'T BREATHE RIGHT. I WAS HAVING PANIC ATTACKS.
CARNEGIE HALL
S. HUROK presents
BENNY GOODMAN and his Swing Orchestra
SUNDAY EVENING JANUARY 16th
CARNEGIE HALL
CARNEGIE HALL
SOLD OUT
TONIGHT WILL BE SOLD OUT AGAIN! EVERYONE WILL LOVE YOU LADY DAY, YOU'LL SEE!
THE CURTAINS OPEN, THE LIGHTS COME ON.

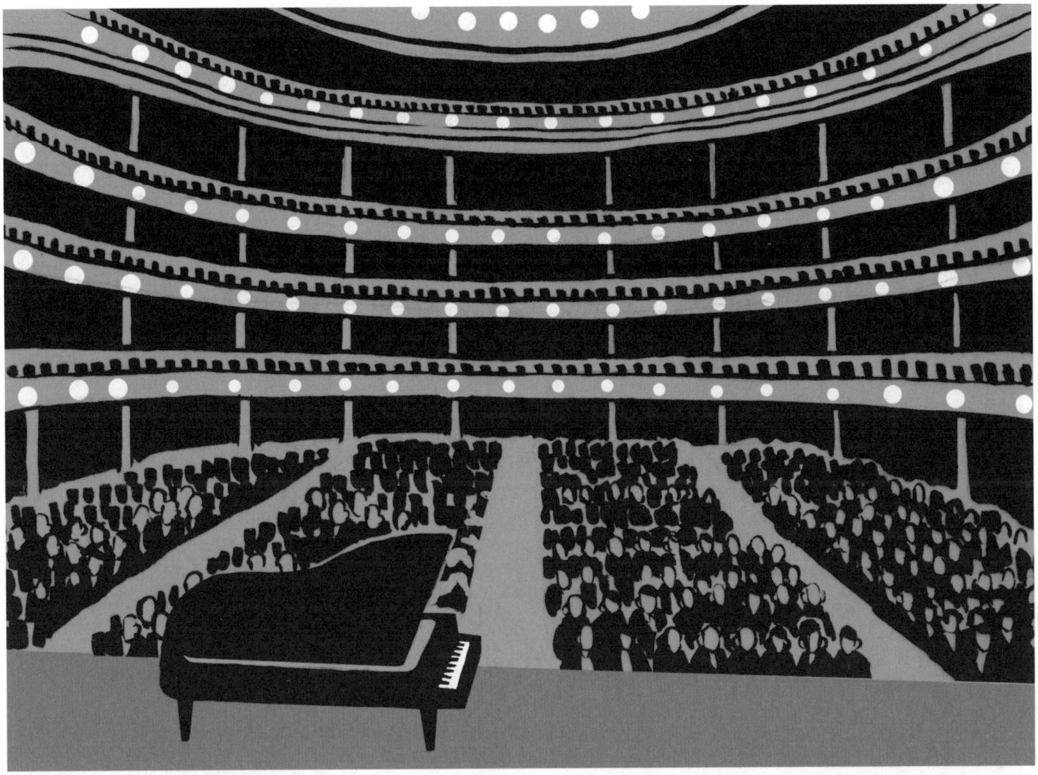

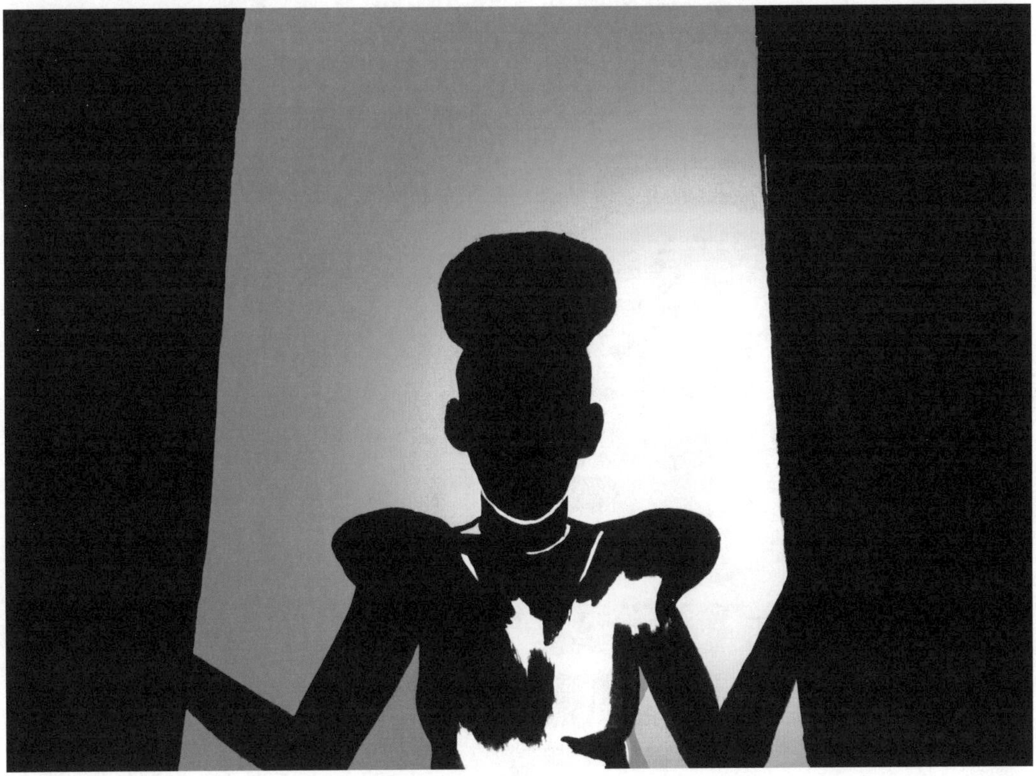

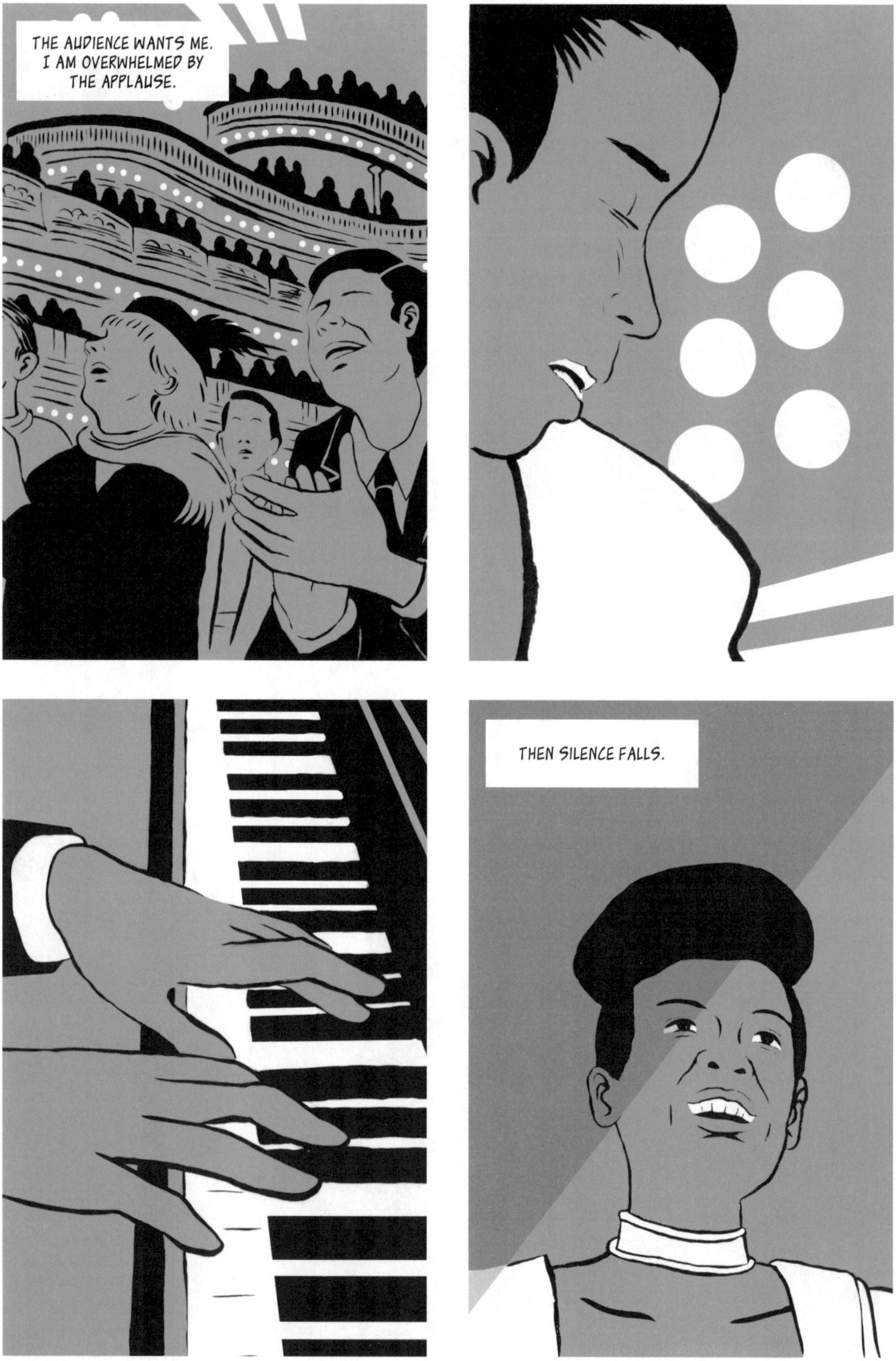
THE AUDIENCE WANTS ME. I AM OVERWHELMED BY THE APPLAUSE.
THEN SILENCE FALLS.

"Good Morning Heartache"

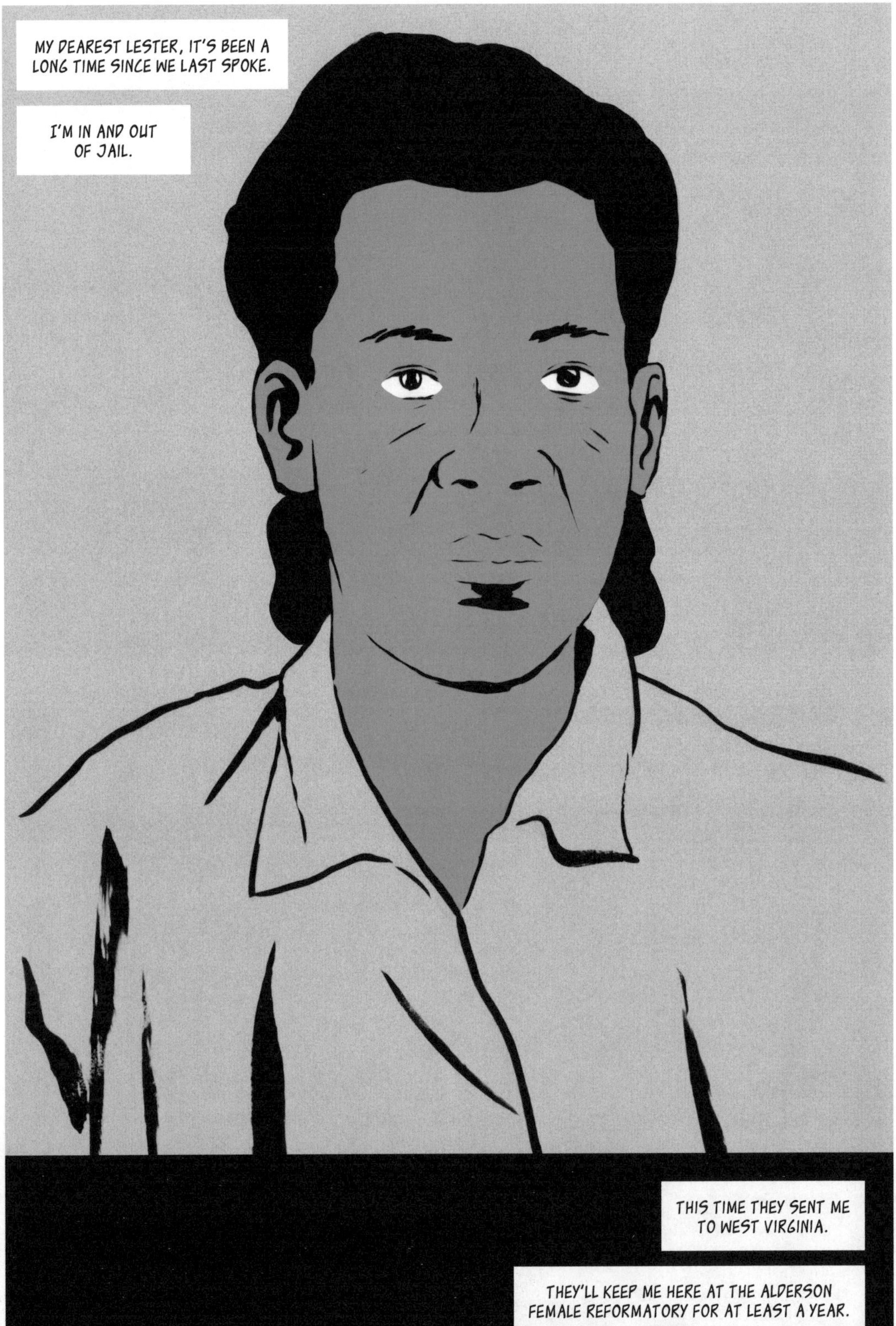
MY DEAREST LESTER, IT'S BEEN A LONG TIME SINCE WE LAST SPOKE.
I'M IN AND OUT OF JAIL.
THIS TIME THEY SENT ME TO WEST VIRGINIA.
THEY'LL KEEP ME HERE AT THE ALDERSON FEMALE REFORMATORY FOR AT LEAST A YEAR.

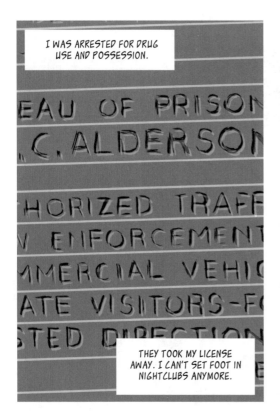

I WAS ARRESTED FOR DRUG USE AND POSSESSION.
EAU OF PRISON
.C. ALDERSON
HORIZED TRAFF
V ENFORCEMENT
MMERCIAL VEHIC
ATE VISITORS-F
STED DIRECTION
THEY TOOK MY LICENSE AWAY. I CAN'T SET FOOT IN NIGHTCLUBS ANYMORE.
THE FEDERAL BUREAU OF NARCOTICS HAS A RECORD ON ME.
THEY LOCKED ME UP AND THREW AWAY THE KEY.
MOST OF THE PRISONERS ARE BLACKS, AND KEPT SEPARATE FROM THE WHITES.
AT DAWN I WORK IN THE FIELDS AROUND THE REFORMATORY, THEN GO STRAIGHT TO CLEAN THE KITCHENS.
WORK IS EXHAUSTING AND I FEEL SO WEAK. I FEEL SICK. I DON'T KNOW HOW MUCH LONGER I CAN GO ON.

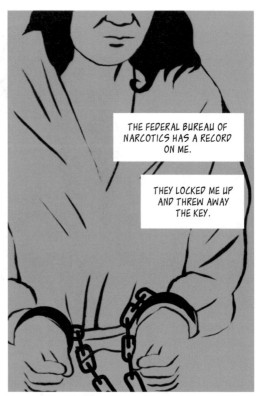

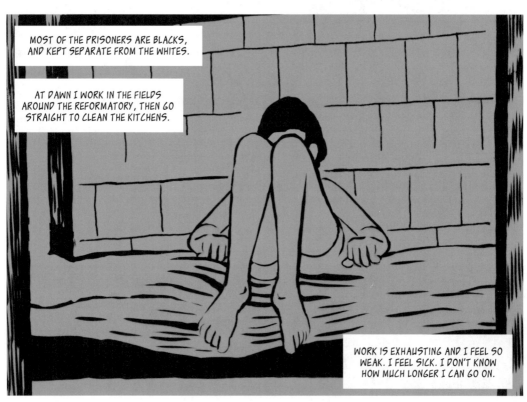

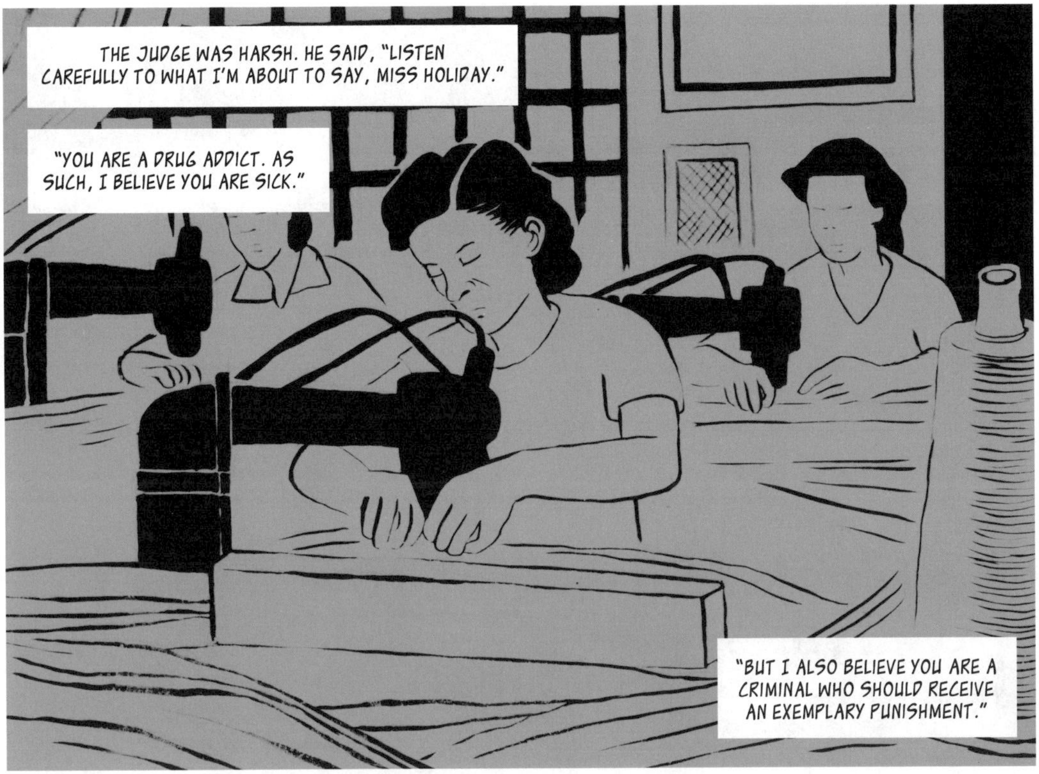
THE JUDGE WAS HARSH. HE SAID, "LISTEN CAREFULLY TO WHAT I'M ABOUT TO SAY, MISS HOLIDAY."
"YOU ARE A DRUG ADDICT. AS SUCH, I BELIEVE YOU ARE SICK."
"BUT I ALSO BELIEVE YOU ARE A CRIMINAL WHO SHOULD RECEIVE AN EXEMPLARY PUNISHMENT."

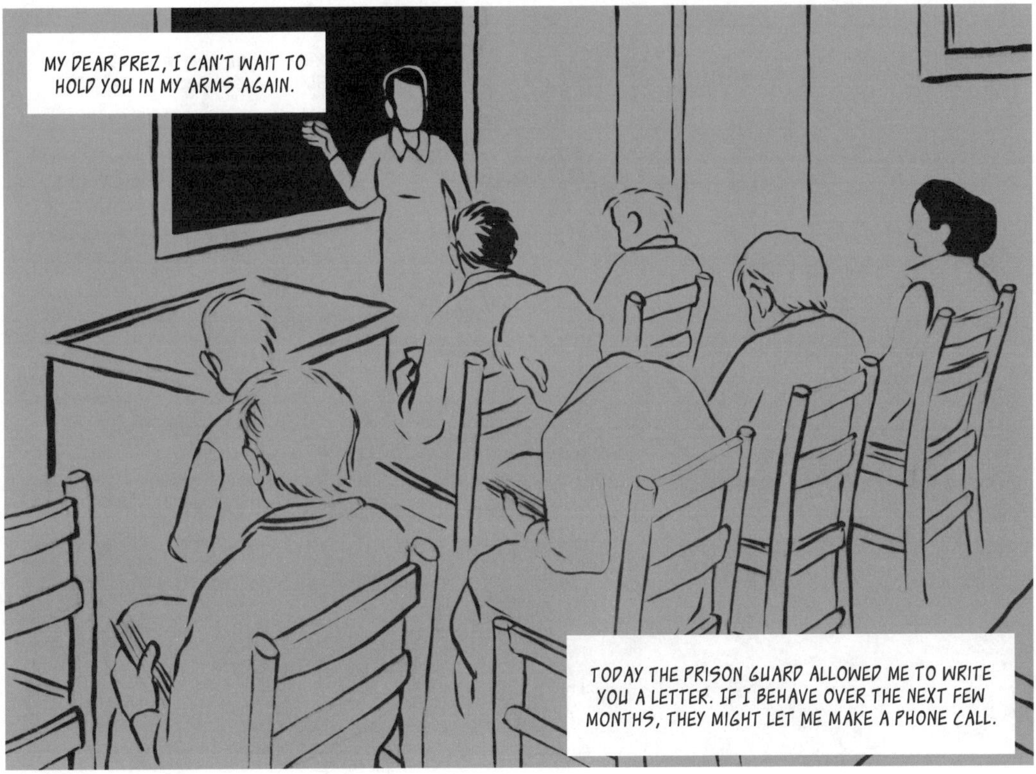
MY DEAR PREZ, I CAN'T WAIT TO HOLD YOU IN MY ARMS AGAIN.
TODAY THE PRISON GUARD ALLOWED ME TO WRITE YOU A LETTER. IF I BEHAVE OVER THE NEXT FEW MONTHS, THEY MIGHT LET ME MAKE A PHONE CALL.

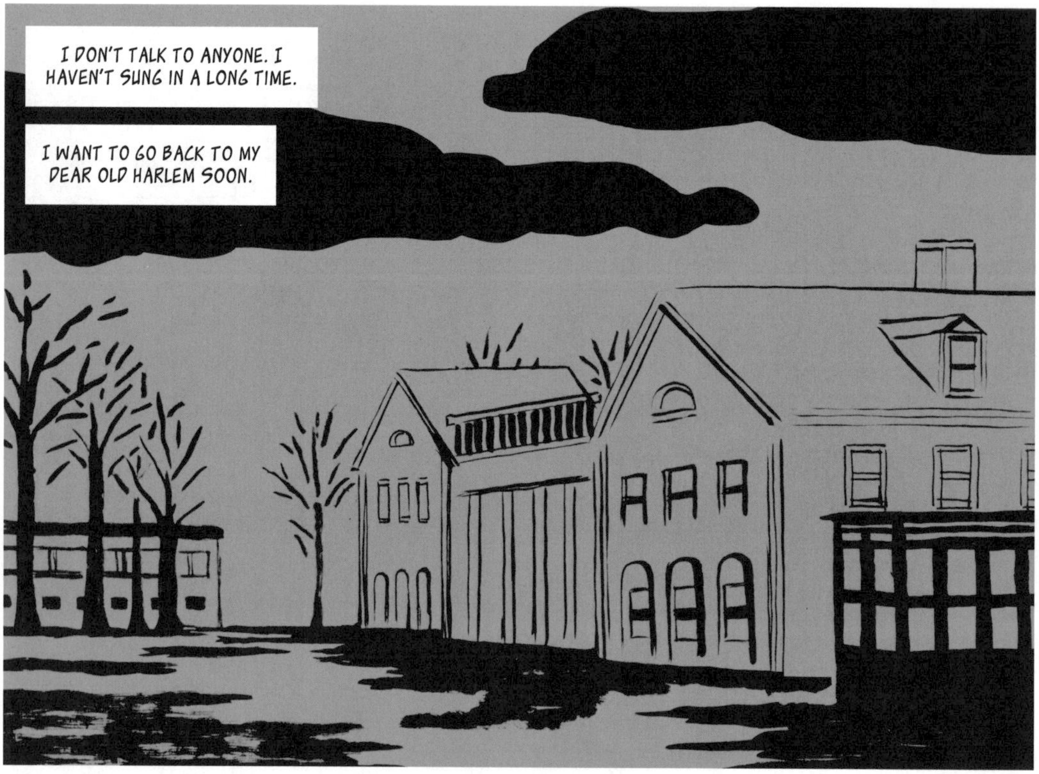
I DON'T TALK TO ANYONE. I HAVEN'T SUNG IN A LONG TIME.
I WANT TO GO BACK TO MY DEAR OLD HARLEM SOON.

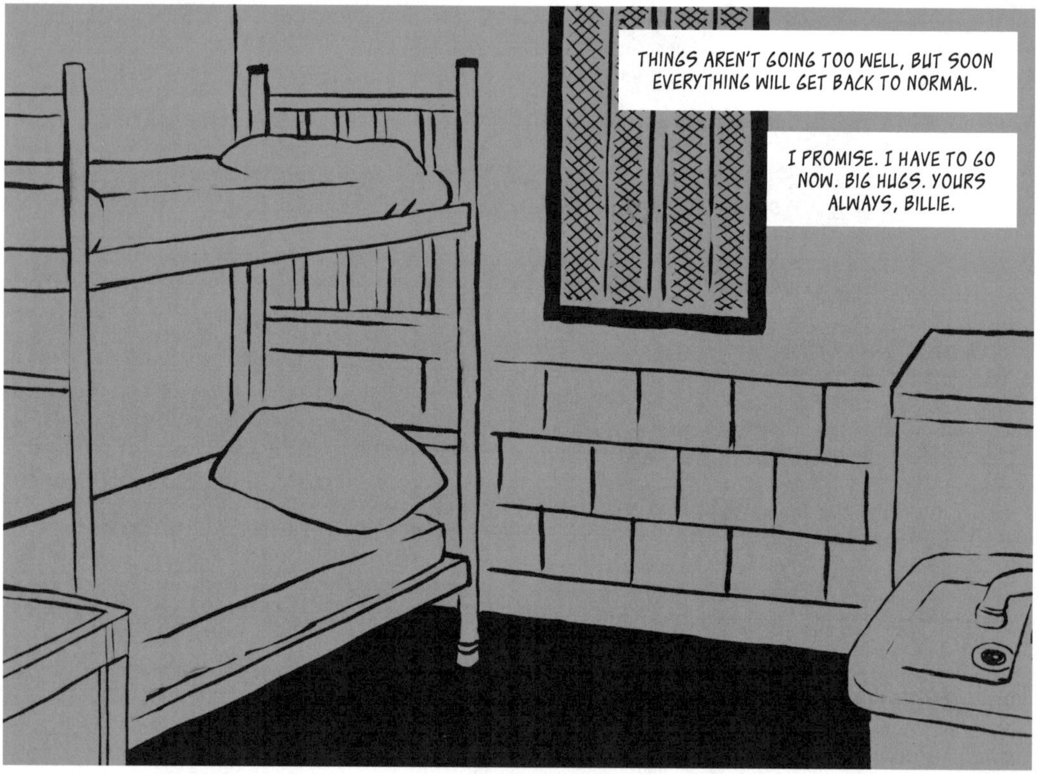
THINGS AREN'T GOING TOO WELL, BUT SOON EVERYTHING WILL GET BACK TO NORMAL.
I PROMISE. I HAVE TO GO NOW. BIG HUGS. YOURS ALWAYS, BILLIE.

"Willow Weep For Me"

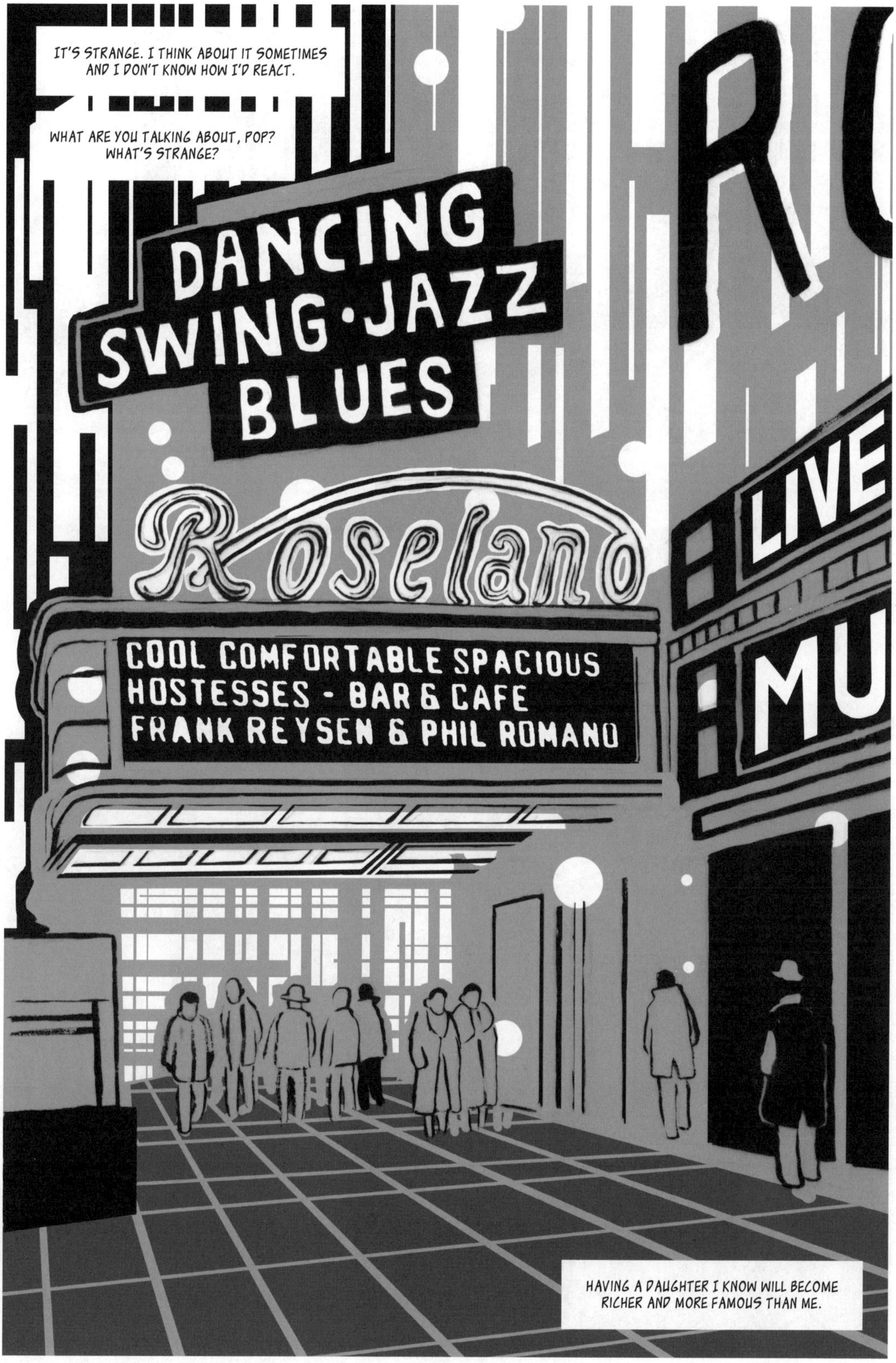

IT'S STRANGE. I THINK ABOUT IT SOMETIMES AND I DON'T KNOW HOW I'D REACT.
WHAT ARE YOU TALKING ABOUT, POP? WHAT'S STRANGE?
RO
DANCING SWING·JAZZ BLUES
Roseland
COOL COMFORTABLE SPACIOUS
HOSTESSES - BAR & CAFE
FRANK REYSEN & PHIL ROMANO
LIVE
MU
HAVING A DAUGHTER I KNOW WILL BECOME RICHER AND MORE FAMOUS THAN ME.

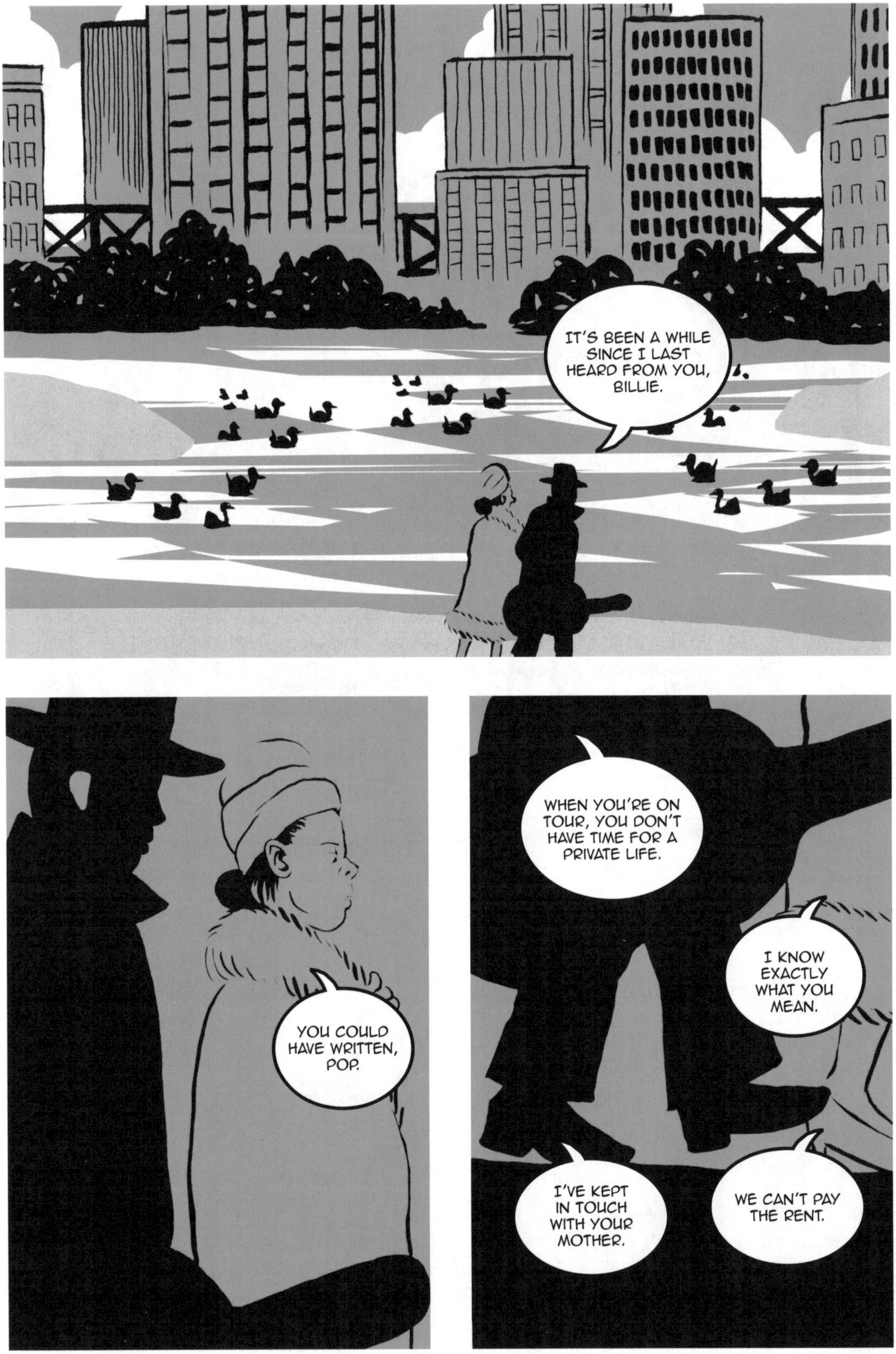
IT'S BEEN A WHILE SINCE I LAST HEARD FROM YOU, BILLIE.
YOU COULD HAVE WRITTEN, POP.
WHEN YOU'RE ON TOUR, YOU DON'T HAVE TIME FOR A PRIVATE LIFE.
I KNOW EXACTLY WHAT YOU MEAN.
I'VE KEPT IN TOUCH WITH YOUR MOTHER.
WE CAN'T PAY THE RENT.

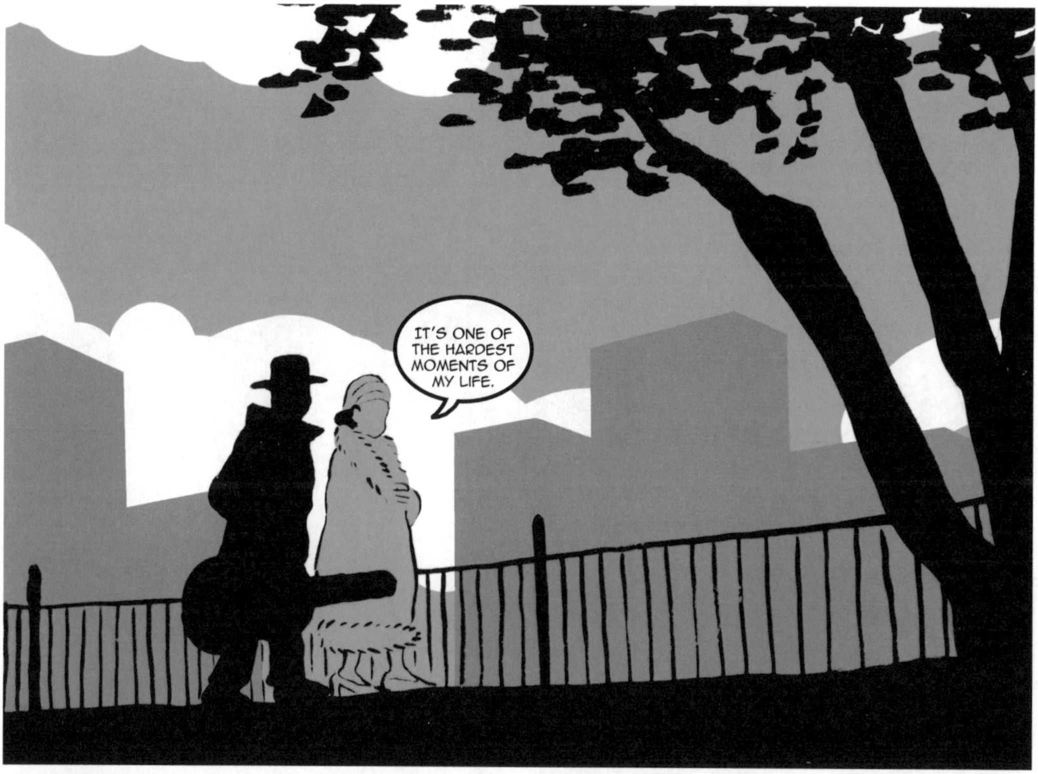
IT'S ONE OF THE HARDEST MOMENTS OF MY LIFE.

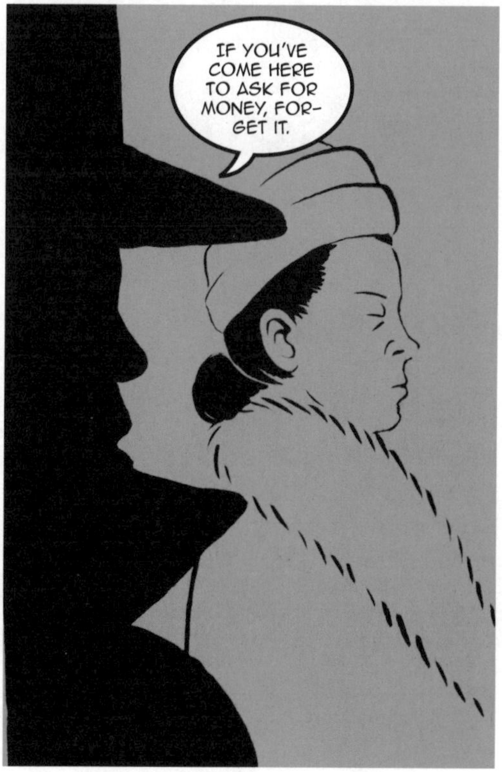
IF YOU'VE COME HERE TO ASK FOR MONEY, FOR-GET IT.

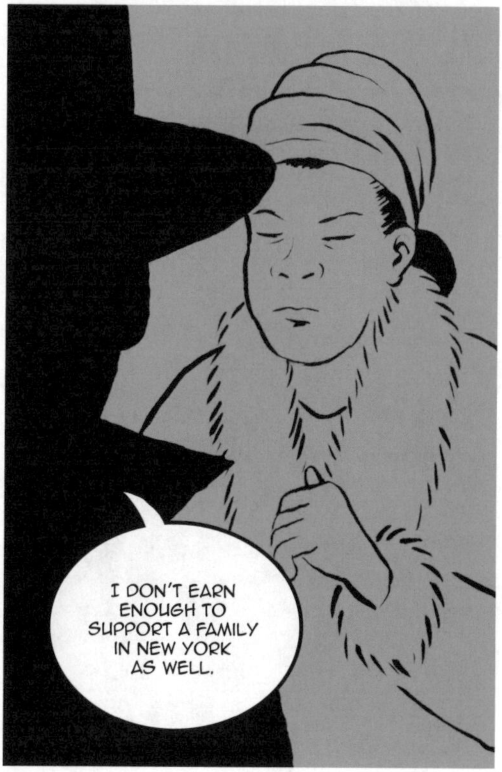
I DON'T EARN ENOUGH TO SUPPORT A FAMILY IN NEW YORK AS WELL.

CLARENCE HOLIDAY WAS A GUITARIST, ARRANGER, AND SESSION MUSICIAN. HE WAS MY FATHER. HE PASSED AWAY ONE NIGHT IN MARCH 1937 IN A HOSPITAL ROOM IN DALLAS, TEXAS. AFTER FIGHTING IN EUROPE DURING WORLD WAR I, HIS LUNGS WEREN'T FUNCTIONING PROPERLY ANYMORE.

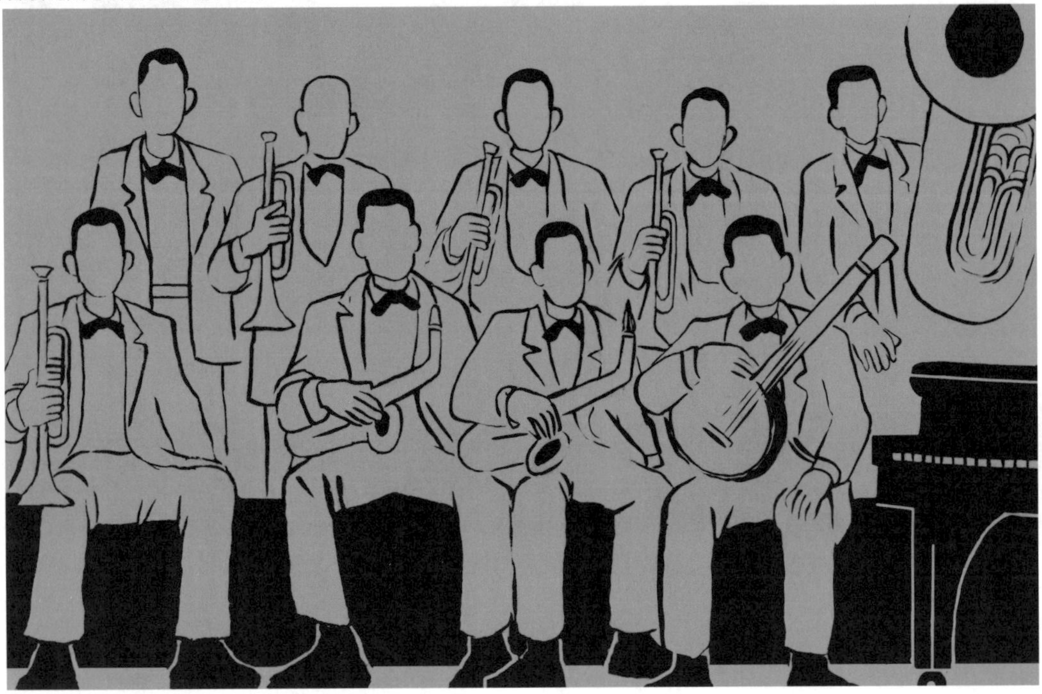

HE PLAYED WITH FLETCHER HENDERSON. I RECEIVED A TELEGRAM SAYING THAT HE WAS GONE.

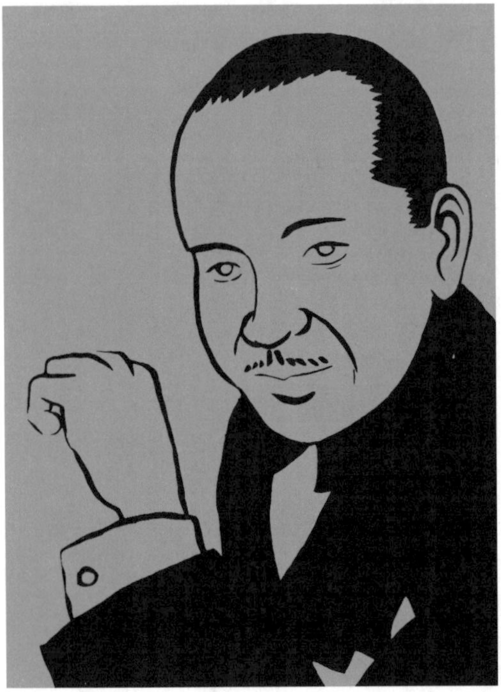

I DIDN'T GET THE CHANCE TO SEE HIM ONE LAST TIME. BACK THEN, I COULDN'T AFFORD A PLANE TICKET TO REACH THE OTHER SIDE OF THE COUNTRY.

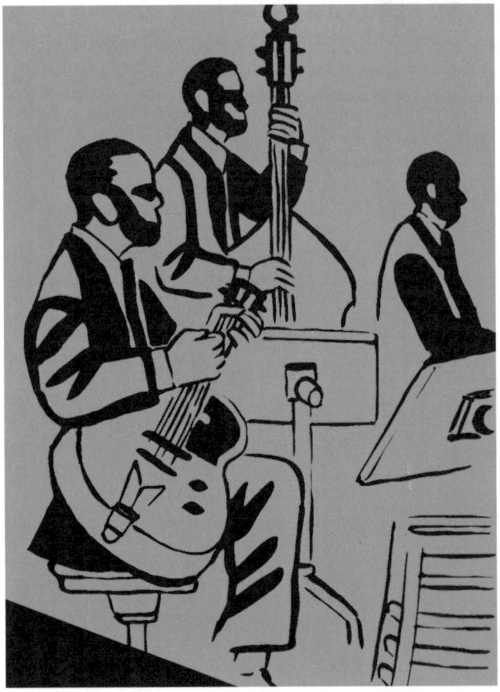

IT HIT ME HARD. I WAS IN A DARK PLACE, BUT I TRIED TO GET UP ON MY FEET AGAIN AND FACE UP TO THE SITUATION ON MY OWN. IT WAS HELL, BUT THAT WAS MY LIFE AT THE TIME.

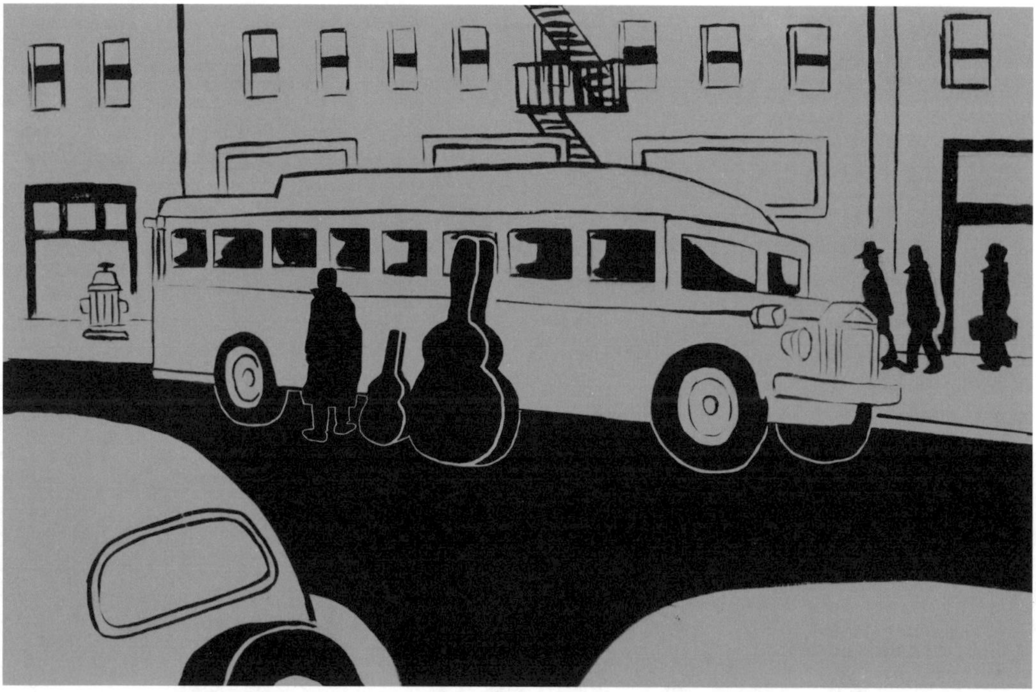

YOU DON'T REALIZE HOW MUCH YOU'LL MISS SOMEBODY OR SOMETHING UNTIL YOU'VE LOST IT.

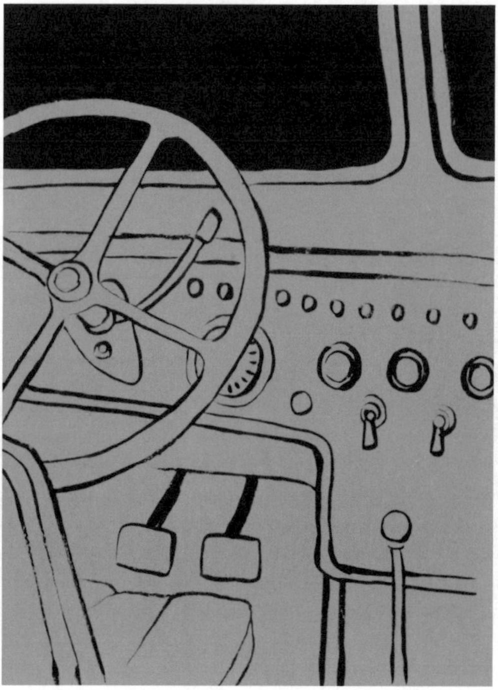

. . . UNTIL IT LEAVES YOU OR DISAPPEARS FROM YOUR LIFE FOREVER.

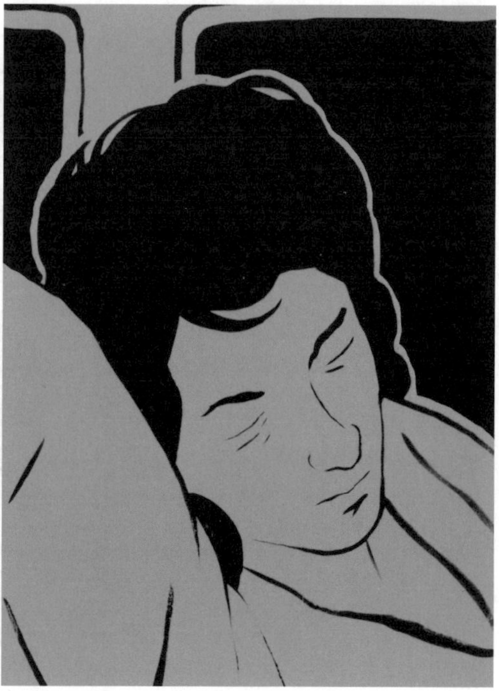

I ALWAYS THOUGHT OF HIM AND HIS WORDS WHEN I WAS ON TOUR WITH THE BAND. YOU NEVER HAVE A BREAK, YOU'RE ALWAYS ON THE MOVE. AT NIGHT YOU PLAY A GIG, GET THREE HOURS OF SLEEP, AND THEN HIT THE ROAD AGAIN TOWARDS A NEW DESTINATION.

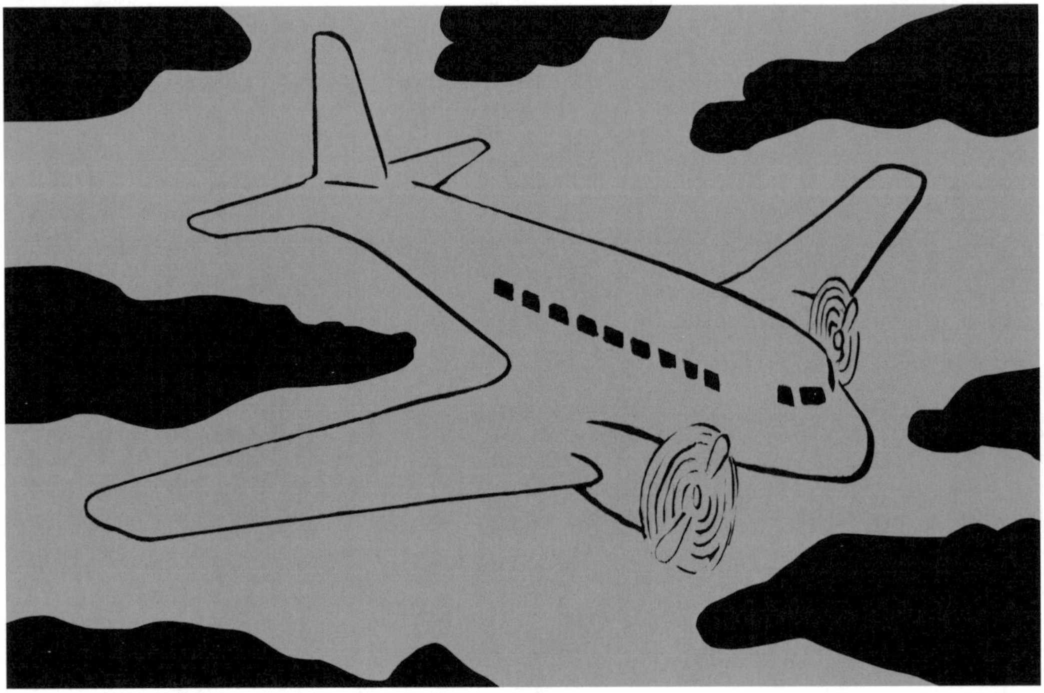

THE TOUR IN EUROPE WAS UNFORGETTABLE. IT WAS 1954 AND A DREAM WAS BECOMING REALITY. THERE WASN'T A SINGLE MUSICIAN WHO DIDN'T DREAM ABOUT LIVING AND PLAYING IN EUROPE ONE DAY.

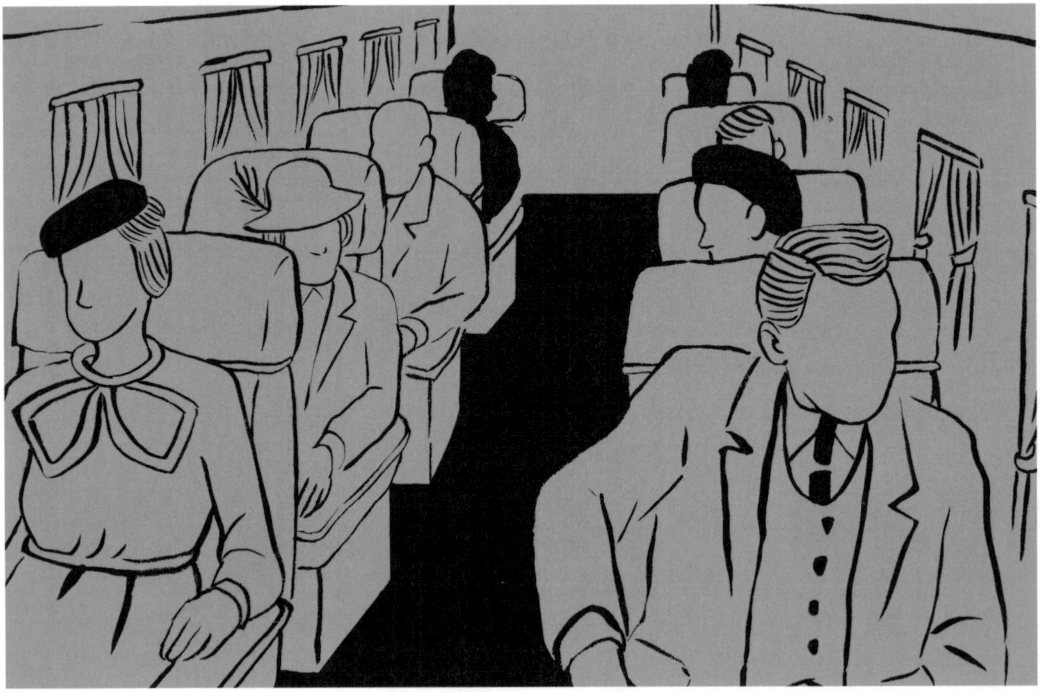

THERE'S A DIFFERENT BUZZ OVER THERE. PEOPLE ACKNOWLEDGE YOUR TALENT RIGHT AWAY. YOU'RE WELL PAID AND WORSHIPPED. IN THE STATES, YEARS CAN OFTEN GO BY BEFORE SOMEONE NOTICES YOUR MUSIC.

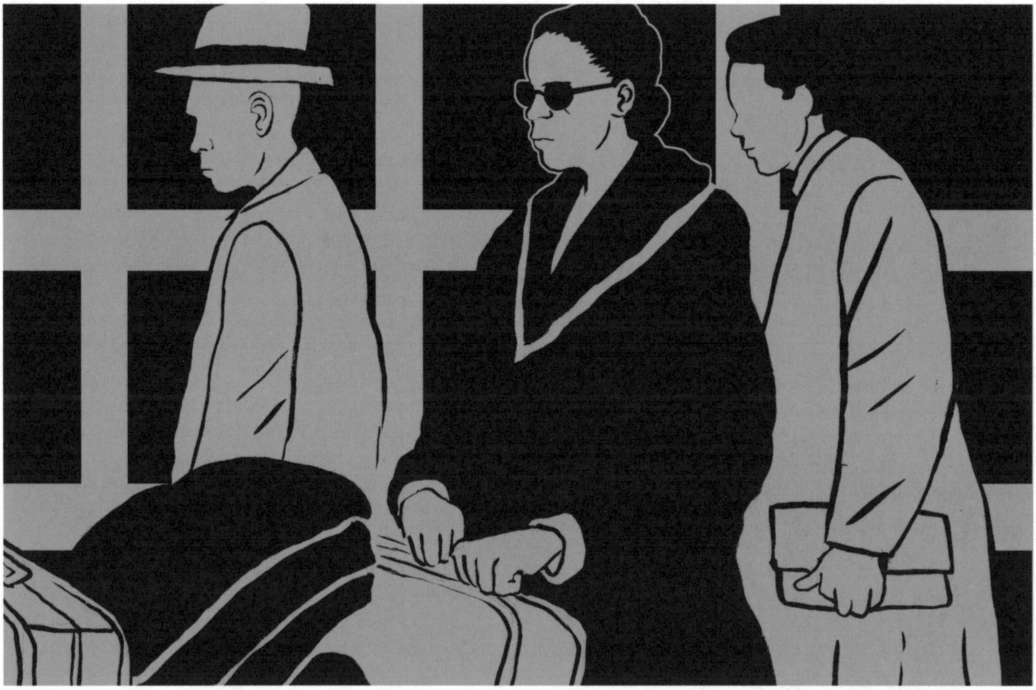

WE STARTED BY TOURING THE MOST NORTHERN CITIES. ALTHOUGH THE TEMPERATURES WERE BELOW ZERO, WE WERE VERY WARMLY RECEIVED.

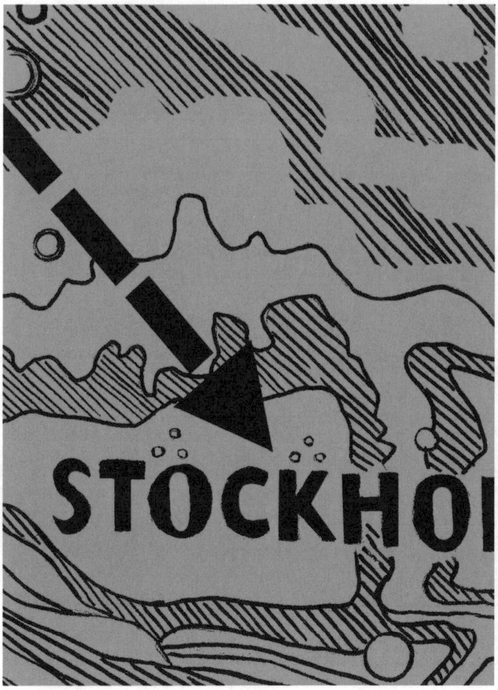
STOCKHO

THE ROYAL ALBERT HALL CONCERT IN LONDON WAS A TRIUMPH. AFTER THAT, WE TRAVELLED TO HOLLAND, SWITZERLAND, BELGIUM, BERLIN, AND PARIS.

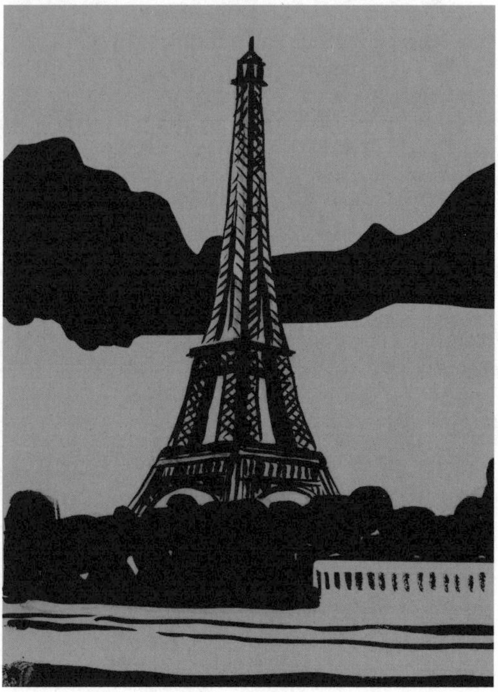

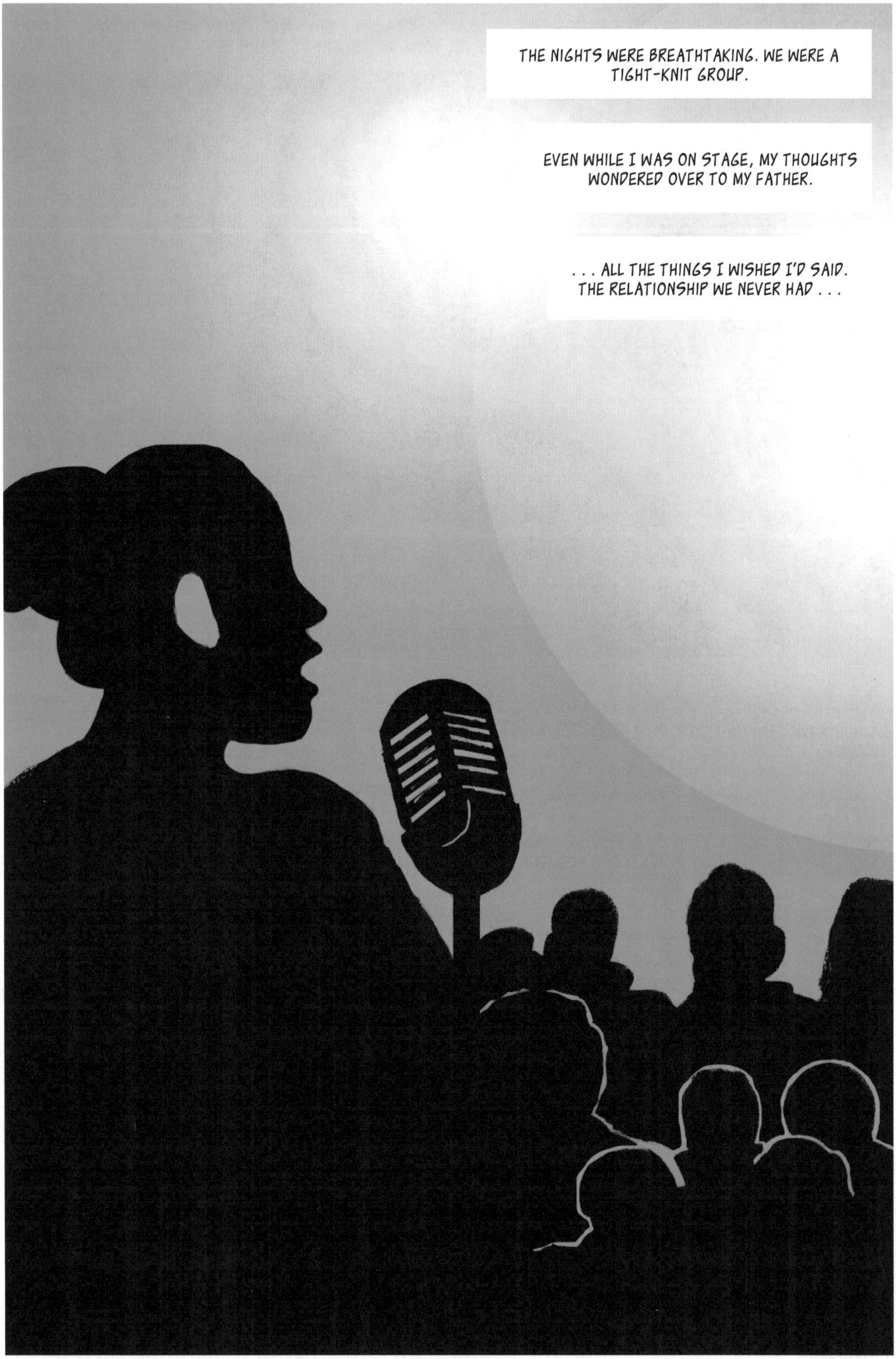
THE NIGHTS WERE BREATHTAKING. WE WERE A TIGHT-KNIT GROUP.
EVEN WHILE I WAS ON STAGE, MY THOUGHTS WONDERED OVER TO MY FATHER.
. . . ALL THE THINGS I WISHED I'D SAID. THE RELATIONSHIP WE NEVER HAD . . .

"Just One Of Those Things"

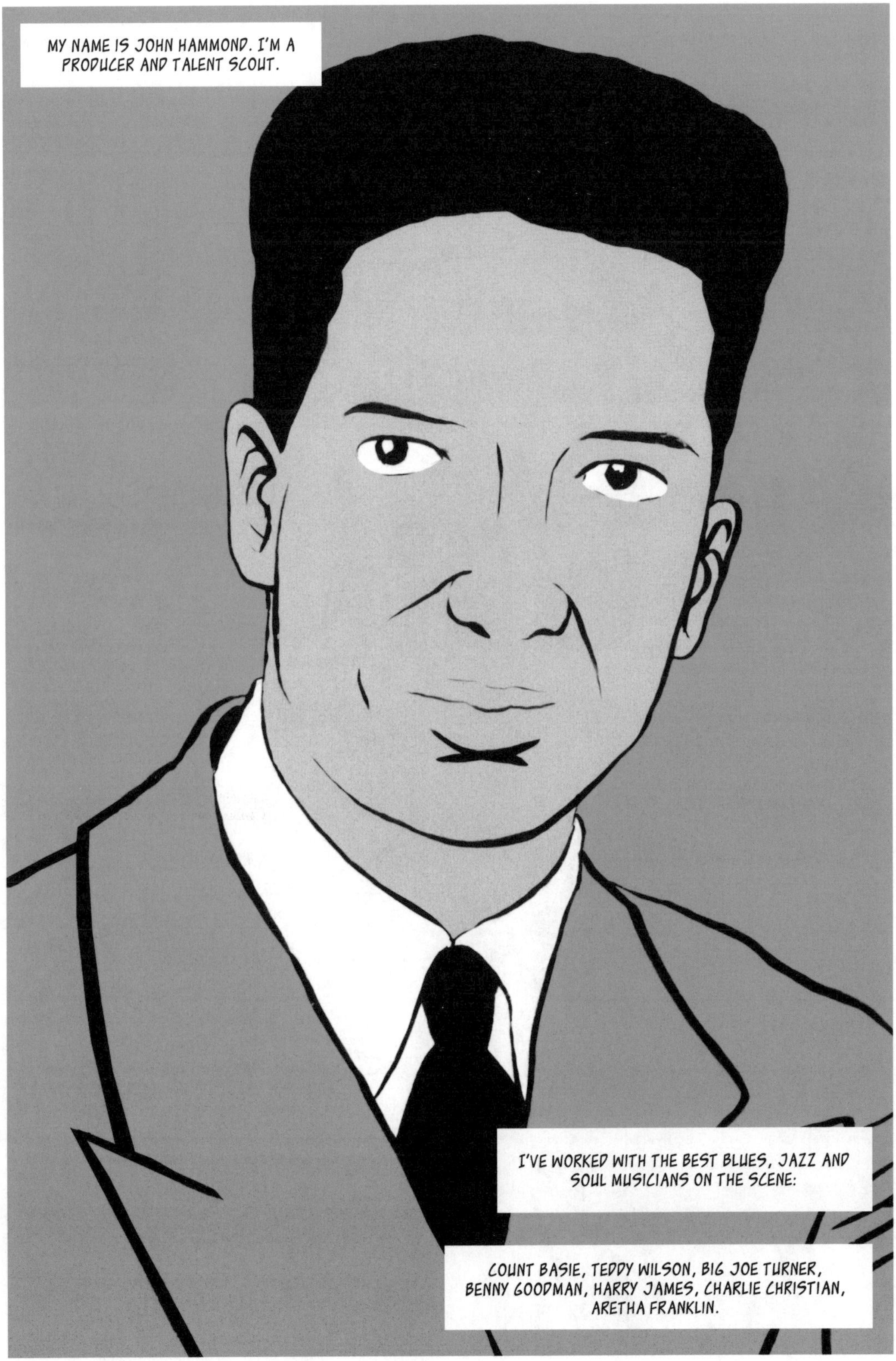
MY NAME IS JOHN HAMMOND. I'M A PRODUCER AND TALENT SCOUT.
I'VE WORKED WITH THE BEST BLUES, JAZZ AND SOUL MUSICIANS ON THE SCENE:
COUNT BASIE, TEDDY WILSON, BIG JOE TURNER, BENNY GOODMAN, HARRY JAMES, CHARLIE CHRISTIAN, ARETHA FRANKLIN.

BUT THE ONE PERFORMER I'LL NEVER FORGET IS MISS HOLIDAY, LADY DAY. I FIRST HEARD HER VOICE PURELY BY CHANCE, AND IT WAS ONE OF THOSE EVENTS THAT LEAVE A MARK. I STILL REMEMBER THAT FREEZING COLD NIGHT IN FEBRUARY 1933. I WAS WANDERING UP AND DOWN BROADWAY, GOING FROM ONE CLUB TO ANOTHER.

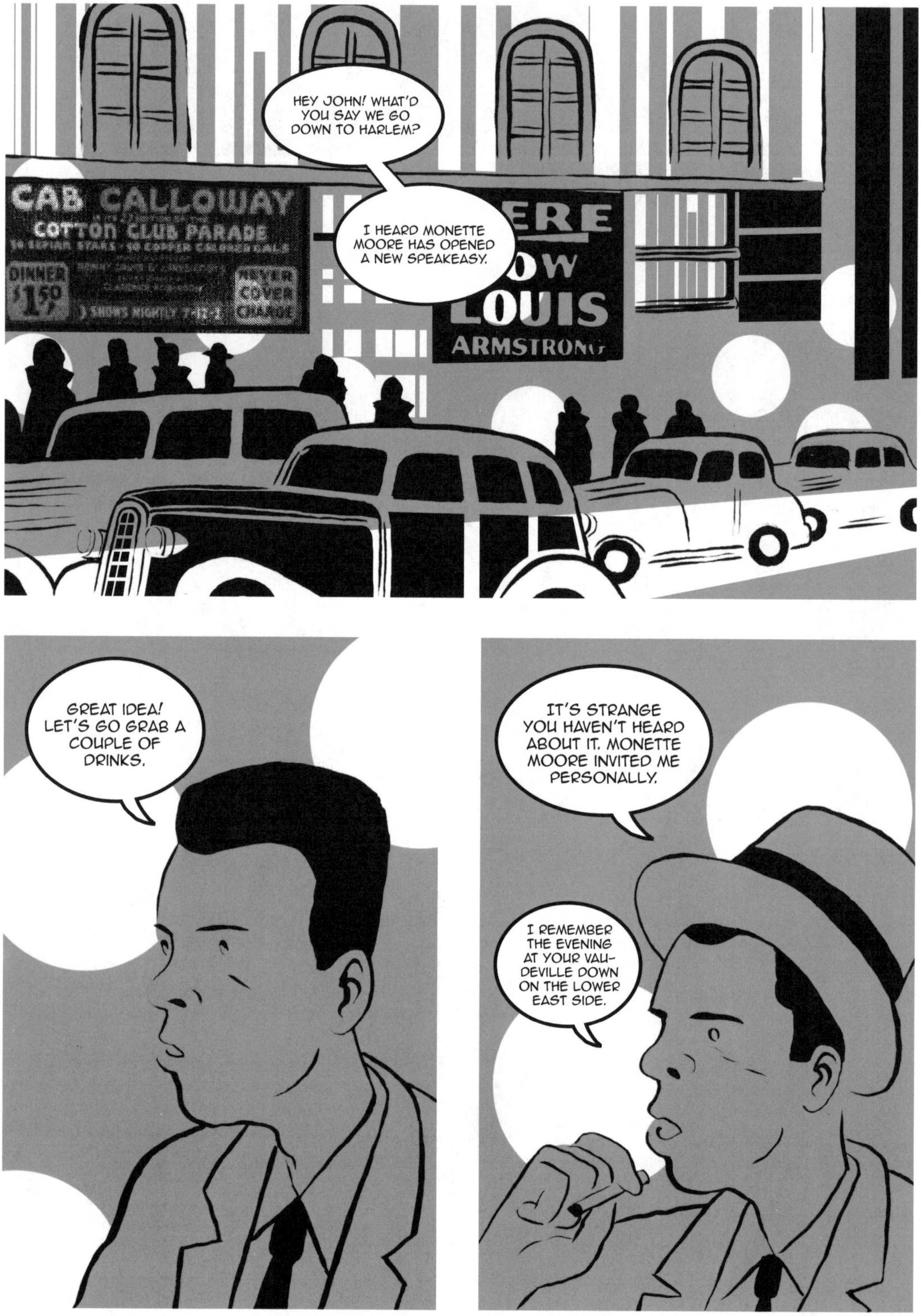

HEY JOHN! WHAT'D YOU SAY WE GO DOWN TO HARLEM?
I HEARD MONETTE MOORE HAS OPENED A NEW SPEAKEASY.
CAB CALLOWAY
COTTON CLUB PARADE
DINNER $1.50
NEVER COVER CHARGE
LOUIS ARMSTRONG
GREAT IDEA! LET'S GO GRAB A COUPLE OF DRINKS.
IT'S STRANGE YOU HAVEN'T HEARD ABOUT IT. MONETTE MOORE INVITED ME PERSONALLY.
I REMEMBER THE EVENING AT YOUR VAU-DEVILLE DOWN ON THE LOWER EAST SIDE.

IT WAS THE 1930s, A TIME WE ALL KNOW AS PROHIBITION, WHEN THE SALE AND TRANSPORTATION OF ALCOHOL WAS COMPLETELY BANNED IN THE UNITED STATES OF AMERICA. THE NIGHTS IN HARLEM, HOWEVER, WERE LAWLESS AND PULSATED WITH LIFE. SPEAKEASIES WERE CLUBS THAT OPENED AND CLOSED IN A WINK. BACK THEN, IF YOU DECIDED TO SELL CRATES OF BOURBON, WELL, YOU HAD TO BE QUICK ON YOUR FEET.

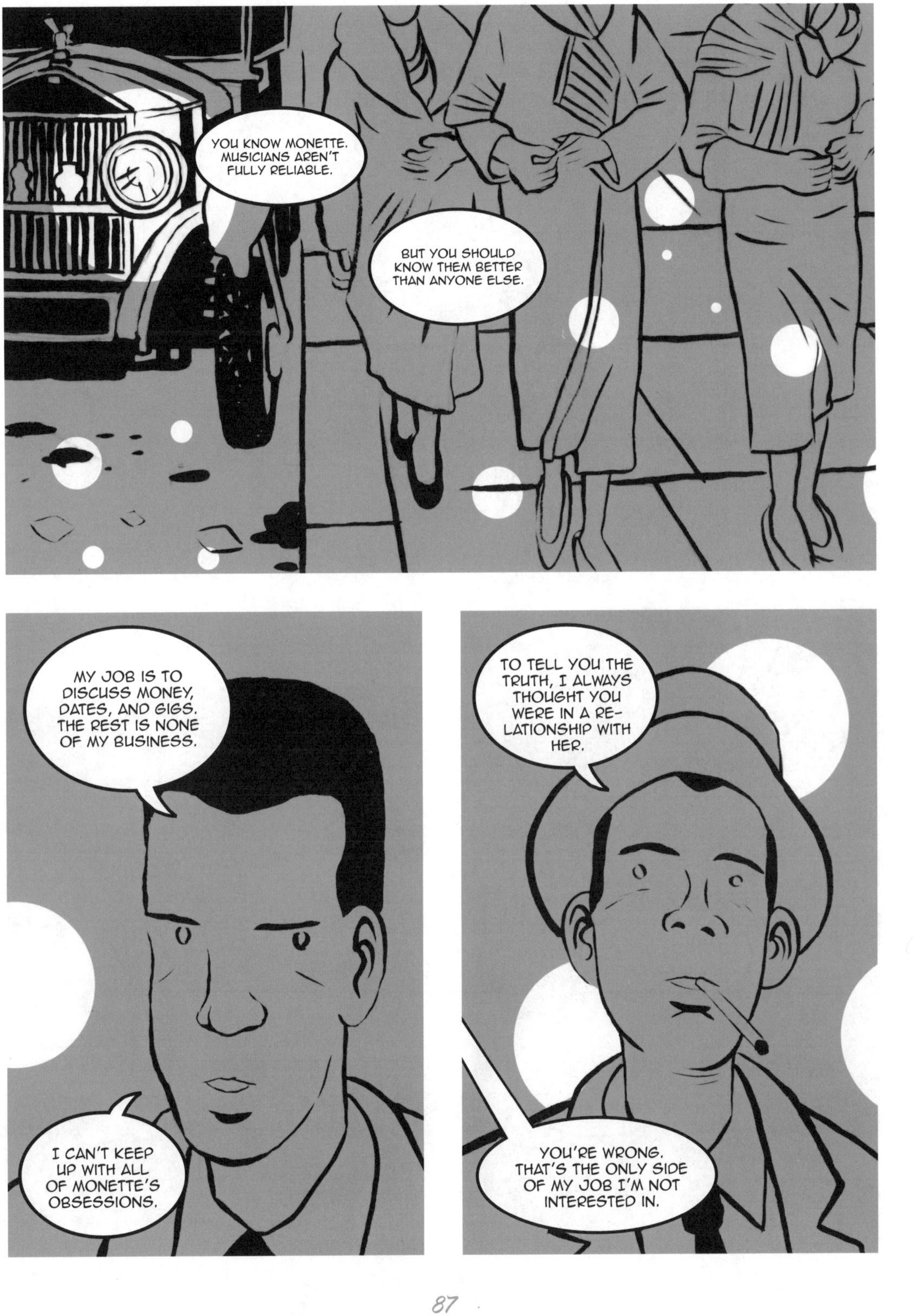
YOU KNOW MONETTE. MUSICIANS AREN'T FULLY RELIABLE.
BUT YOU SHOULD KNOW THEM BETTER THAN ANYONE ELSE.
MY JOB IS TO DISCUSS MONEY, DATES, AND GIGS. THE REST IS NONE OF MY BUSINESS.
I CAN'T KEEP UP WITH ALL OF MONETTE'S OBSESSIONS.
TO TELL YOU THE TRUTH, I ALWAYS THOUGHT YOU WERE IN A RE-LATIONSHIP WITH HER.
YOU'RE WRONG. THAT'S THE ONLY SIDE OF MY JOB I'M NOT INTERESTED IN.

THERE WAS A CONSTANT FLOW OF PEOPLE AND ALCOHOL. I REMEMBER A LOT OF CONFUSION AND A CONSTANT NOISE IN THE BACKGROUND. IT WAS HARD TO HEAR WHAT WAS HAPPENING ON STAGE.

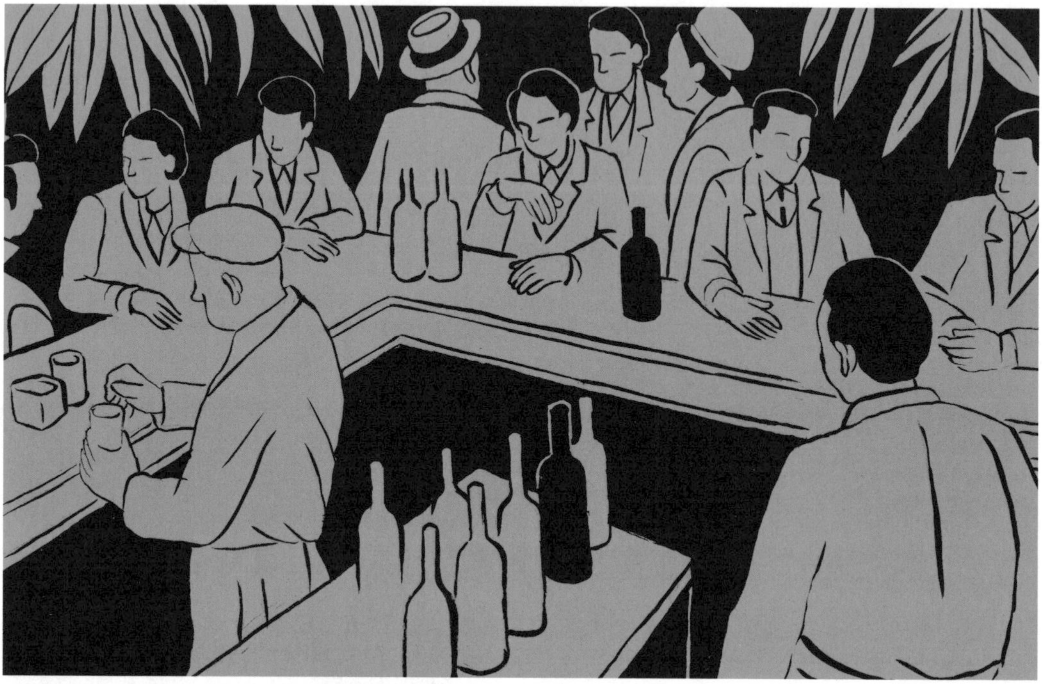

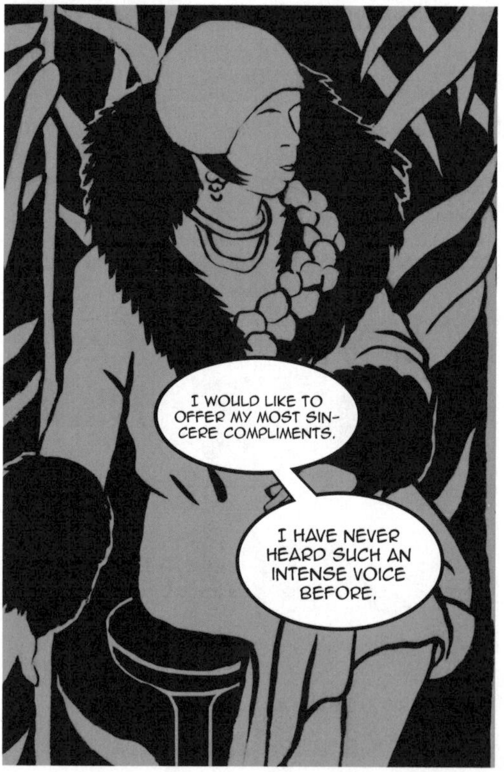
I WOULD LIKE TO OFFER MY MOST SINCERE COMPLIMENTS.
I HAVE NEVER HEARD SUCH AN INTENSE VOICE BEFORE.

IT WAS THE FIRST TIME I'D EVER HEARD A SINGER THAT WAS ABLE TO MODULATE THEIR VOICE LIKE AN ACTUAL MUSICAL INSTRUMENT.

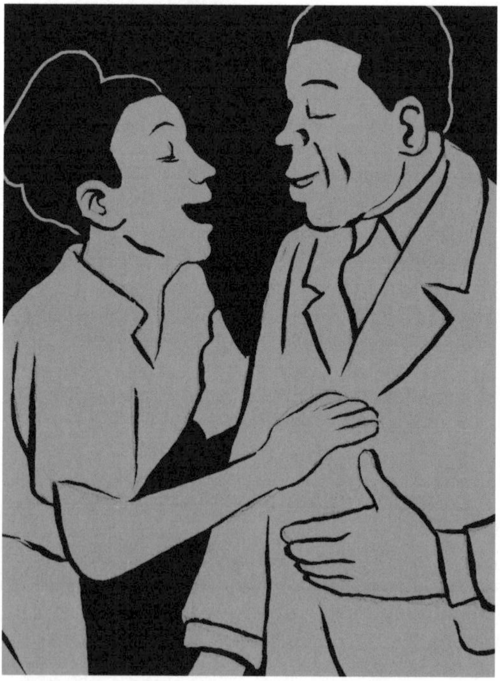

SHE COULDN'T READ MUSIC. SHE LISTENED TO IT AND LEARNED BY EAR, AS IF SHE WERE IMPROVISING SOMETHING PERSONAL. AT THE TIME SHE WAS VERY YOUNG, I BELIEVE SHE WAS STILL A MINOR, BUT SHE SHOWED MORE SELF-CONTROL THAN MOST EXPERIENCED PROFESSIONALS I'D SEEN. AND HER STAGE PRESENCE WAS CAPTIVATING, THE AUDIENCE WAS LEFT SPEECHLESS.

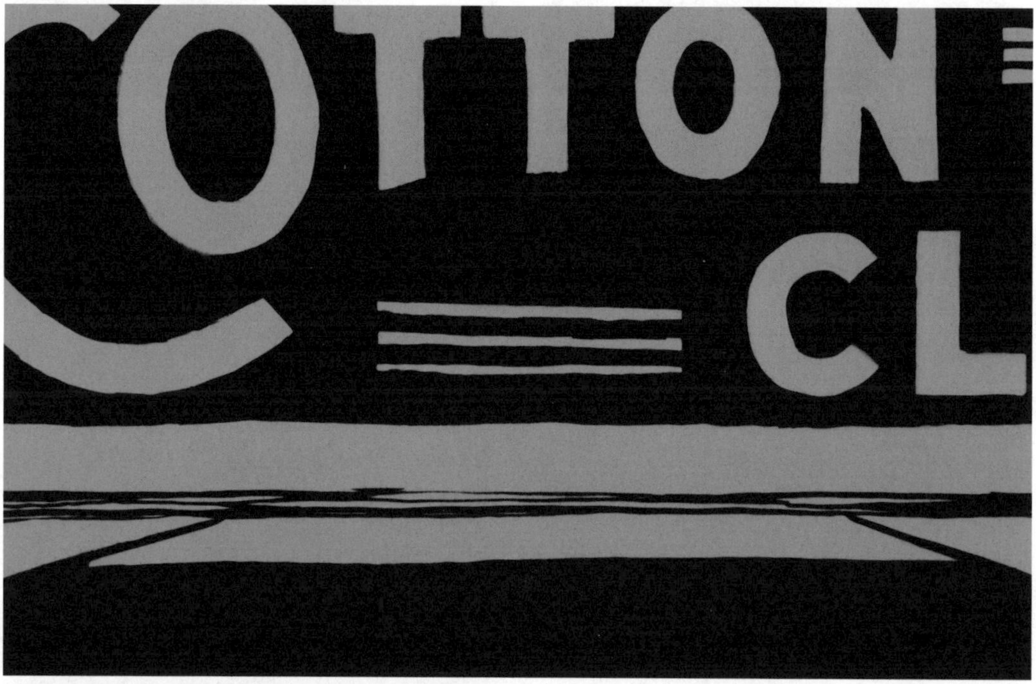
COTTON
CL

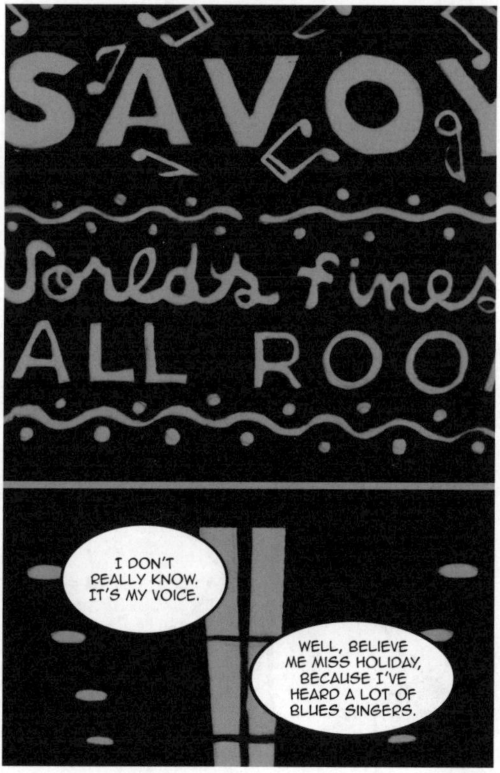
SAVOY
I DON'T REALLY KNOW. IT'S MY VOICE.
WELL, BELIEVE ME MISS HOLIDAY, BECAUSE I'VE HEARD A LOT OF BLUES SINGERS.

I COULDN'T BELIEVE IT. IT WAS EXTRAORDINARY. SHE DID WHAT SHE WANTED. SHE WOULD MODULATE WHEN AND HOW SHE PLEASED, THEN GO BACK TO THE CHORUS AND BACK TO IMPROVISING AGAIN.

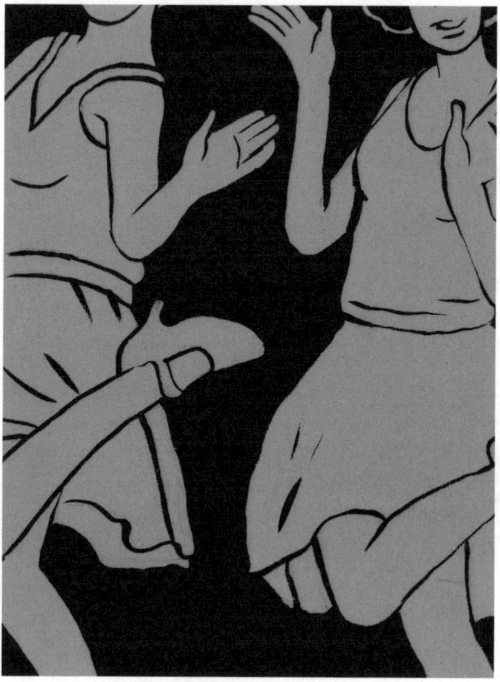

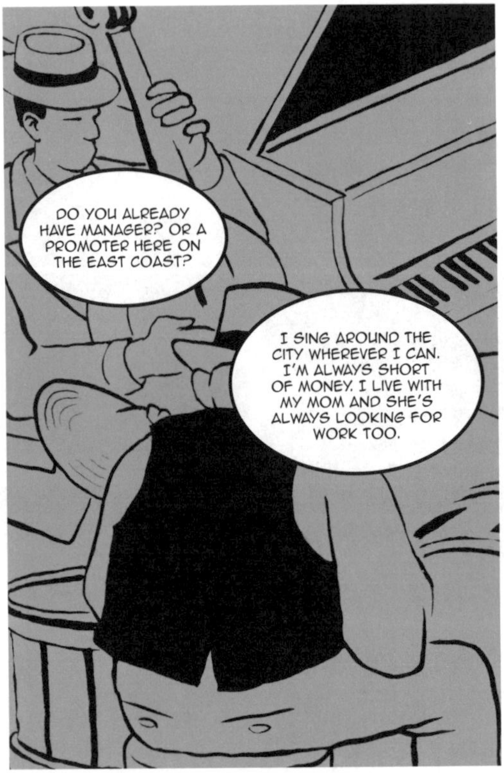
DO YOU ALREADY HAVE MANAGER? OR A PROMOTER HERE ON THE EAST COAST?
I SING AROUND THE CITY WHEREVER I CAN. I'M ALWAYS SHORT OF MONEY. I LIVE WITH MY MOM AND SHE'S ALWAYS LOOKING FOR WORK TOO.

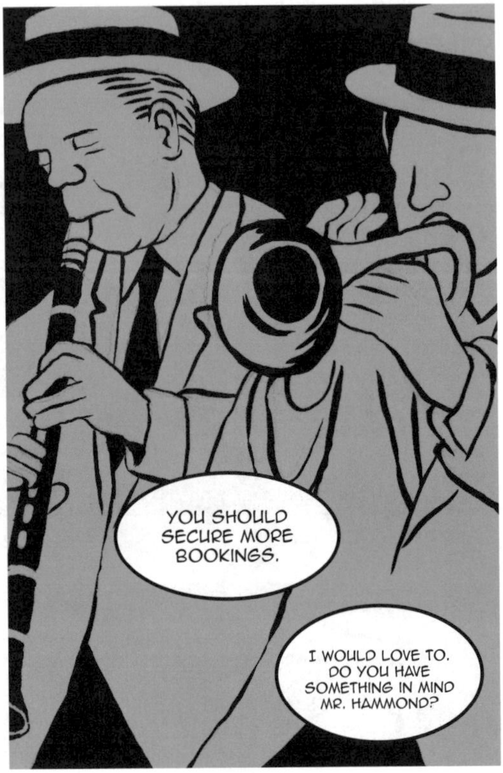
YOU SHOULD SECURE MORE BOOKINGS.
I WOULD LOVE TO. DO YOU HAVE SOMETHING IN MIND MR. HAMMOND?

HER BEAUTY WAS STRIKING. HER POSTURE WAS SPONTANEOUS AND ELEGANT. YOU COULD BE DAZZLED BY HER IN A HEARTBEAT.

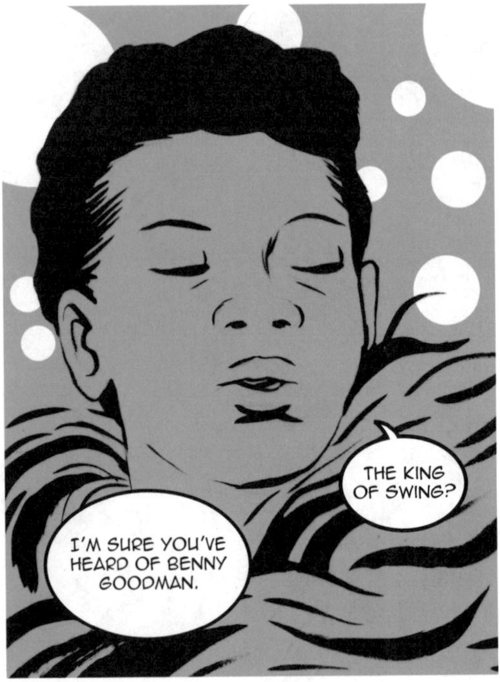
I'M SURE YOU'VE HEARD OF BENNY GOODMAN.
THE KING OF SWING?

SHE HAD MANY RELATIONSHIPS. EVERY TIME SHE WOULD BE ON CLOUD NINE AT FIRST, BUT THEN IT WOULD INEVITABLY GO DOWNHILL.

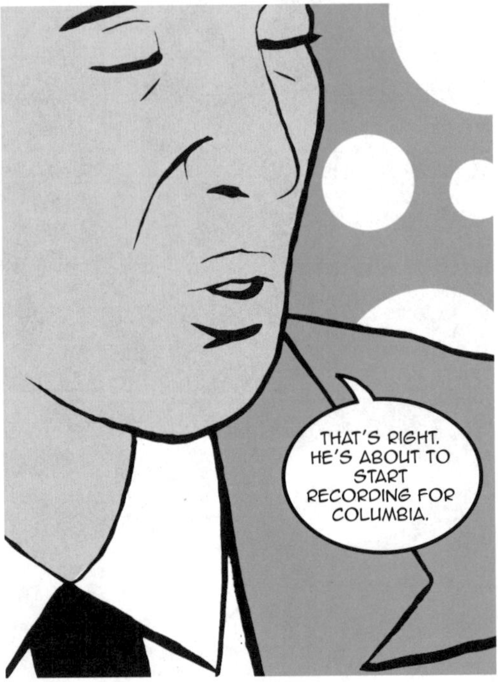
THAT'S RIGHT. HE'S ABOUT TO START RECORDING FOR COLUMBIA.

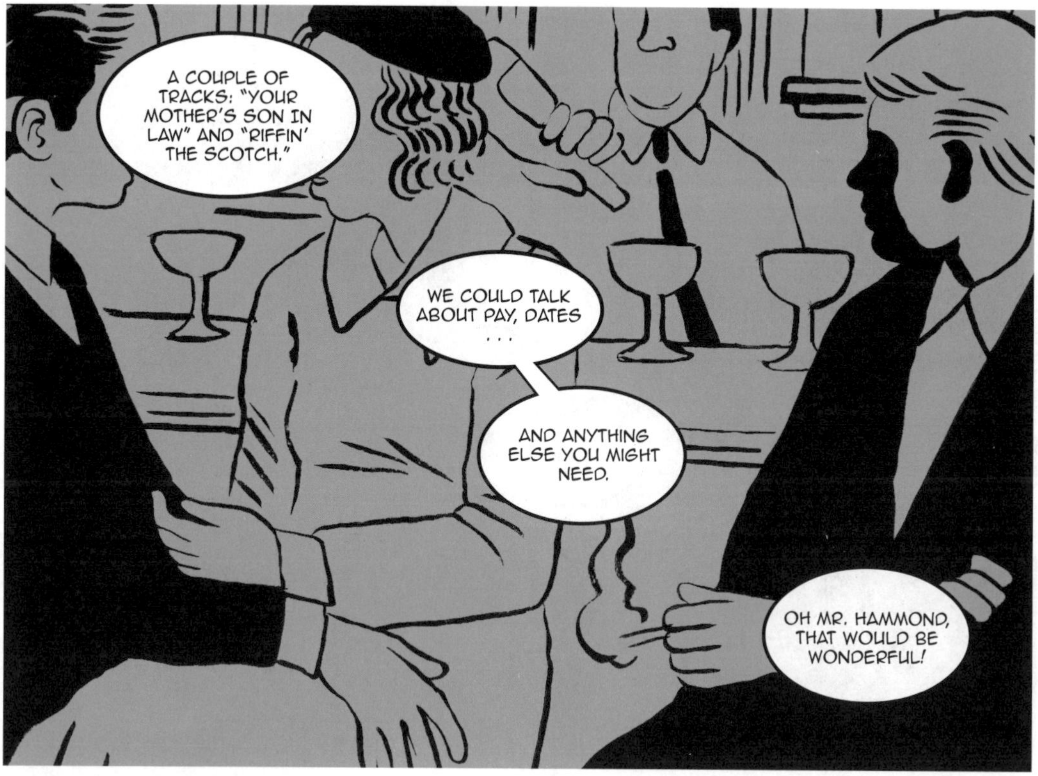
A COUPLE OF TRACKS: "YOUR MOTHER'S SON IN LAW" AND "RIFFIN' THE SCOTCH."
WE COULD TALK ABOUT PAY, DATES . . .
AND ANYTHING ELSE YOU MIGHT NEED.
OH MR. HAMMOND, THAT WOULD BE WONDERFUL!

IN THE FOLLOWING YEARS, I LEARNED ABOUT HER RELATIONSHIPS WITH HER HUSBANDS AND MANAGERS. JOHN LEVY WOULD COVER HER WITH MONEY AND JEWELRY. HE PROMOTED HER CAREER.

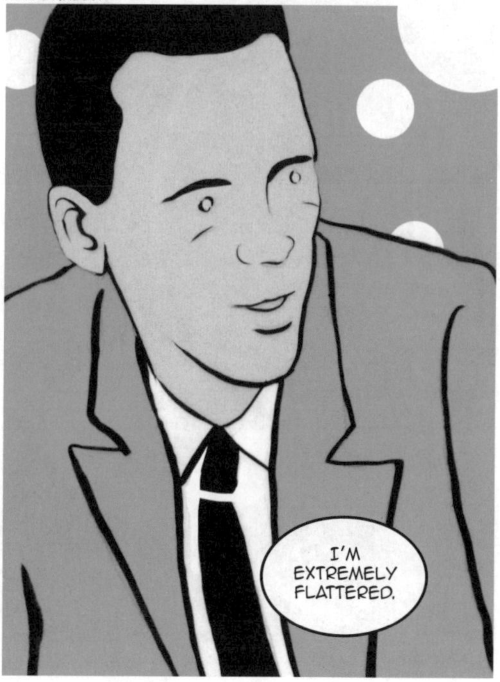
I'M EXTREMELY FLATTERED.

. . . OR HER TURBULENT MARRIAGE TO LOUIS MCKAY. IT WAS THE SAME MCKAY SHE WAS ARRESTED WITH AGAIN IN PHILADELPHIA IN 1956.

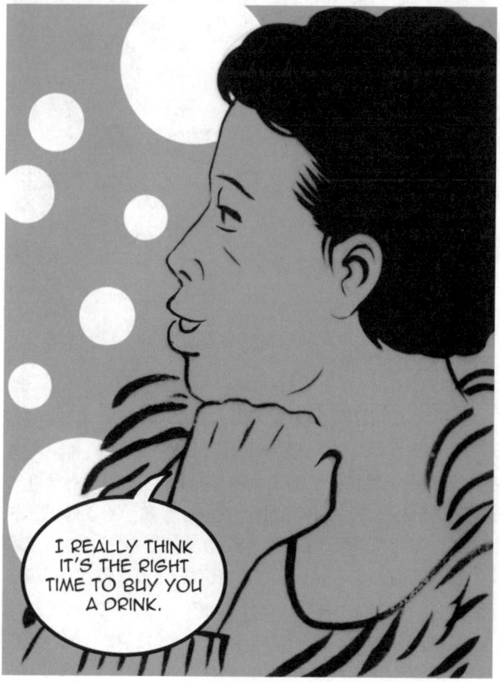
I REALLY THINK IT'S THE RIGHT TIME TO BUY YOU A DRINK.

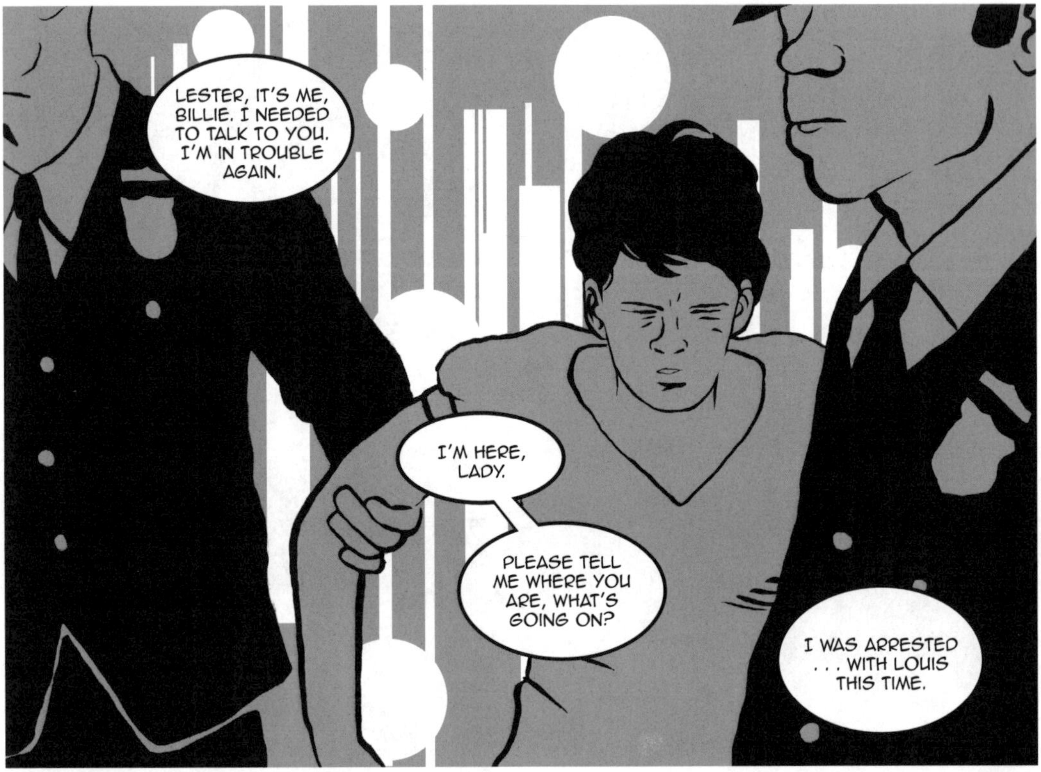
LESTER, IT'S ME, BILLIE. I NEEDED TO TALK TO YOU. I'M IN TROUBLE AGAIN.
I'M HERE, LADY.
PLEASE TELL ME WHERE YOU ARE, WHAT'S GOING ON?
I WAS ARRESTED . . . WITH LOUIS THIS TIME.

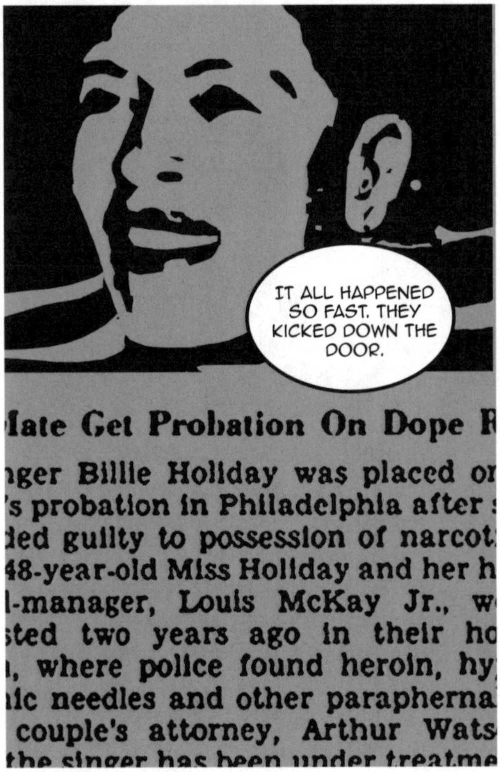
IT ALL HAPPENED SO FAST. THEY KICKED DOWN THE DOOR.
Mate Get Probation On Dope R
nger Billie Holliday was placed or
's probation in Philadelphia after s
ded guilty to possession of narcot
48-year-old Miss Holliday and her h
l-manager, Louis McKay Jr., w
sted two years ago in their ho
, where police found heroin, hy
ic needles and other paraphernal
couple's attorney, Arthur Wats
the singer has been under treatme

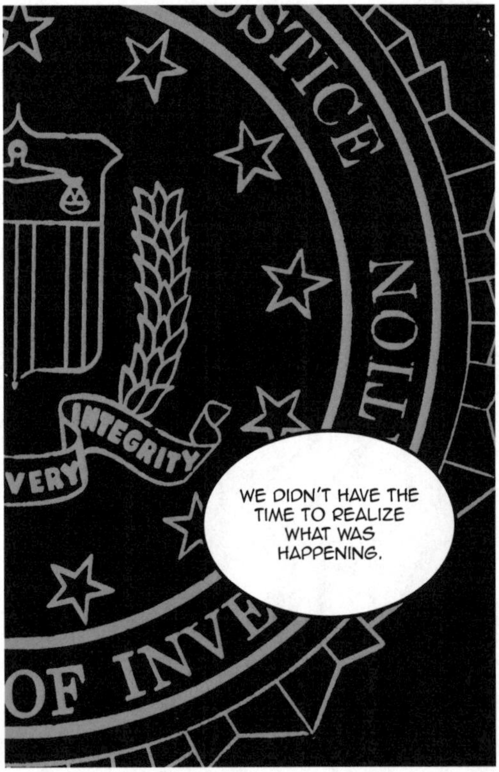
STICE
INTEGRITY
VERY
OF INVE
WE DIDN'T HAVE THE TIME TO REALIZE WHAT WAS HAPPENING.

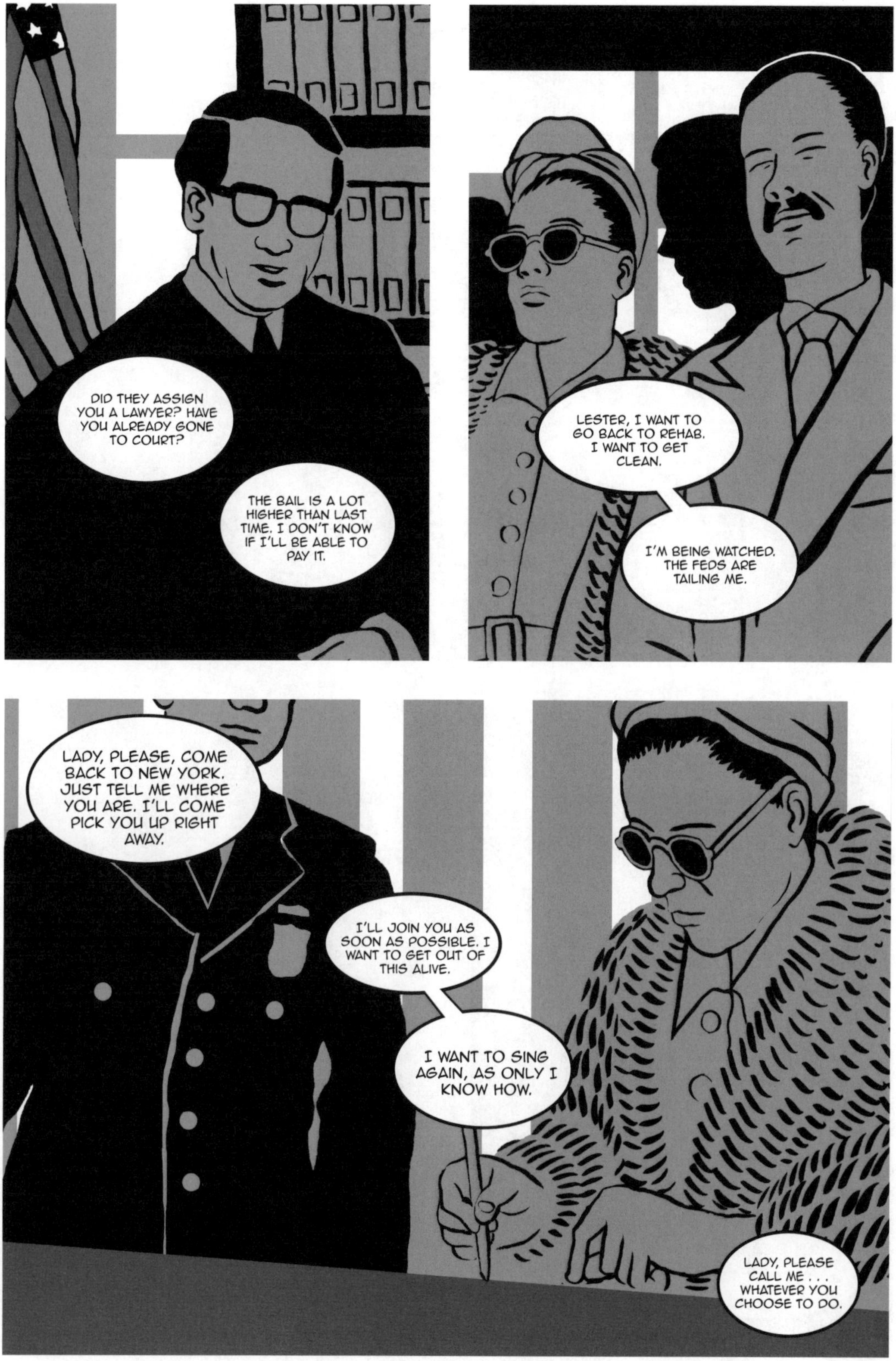
DID THEY ASSIGN YOU A LAWYER? HAVE YOU ALREADY GONE TO COURT?
THE BAIL IS A LOT HIGHER THAN LAST TIME. I DON'T KNOW IF I'LL BE ABLE TO PAY IT.
LESTER, I WANT TO GO BACK TO REHAB. I WANT TO GET CLEAN.
I'M BEING WATCHED. THE FEDS ARE TAILING ME.
LADY, PLEASE, COME BACK TO NEW YORK. JUST TELL ME WHERE YOU ARE. I'LL COME PICK YOU UP RIGHT AWAY.
I'LL JOIN YOU AS SOON AS POSSIBLE. I WANT TO GET OUT OF THIS ALIVE.
I WANT TO SING AGAIN, AS ONLY I KNOW HOW.
LADY, PLEASE CALL ME . . . WHATEVER YOU CHOOSE TO DO.

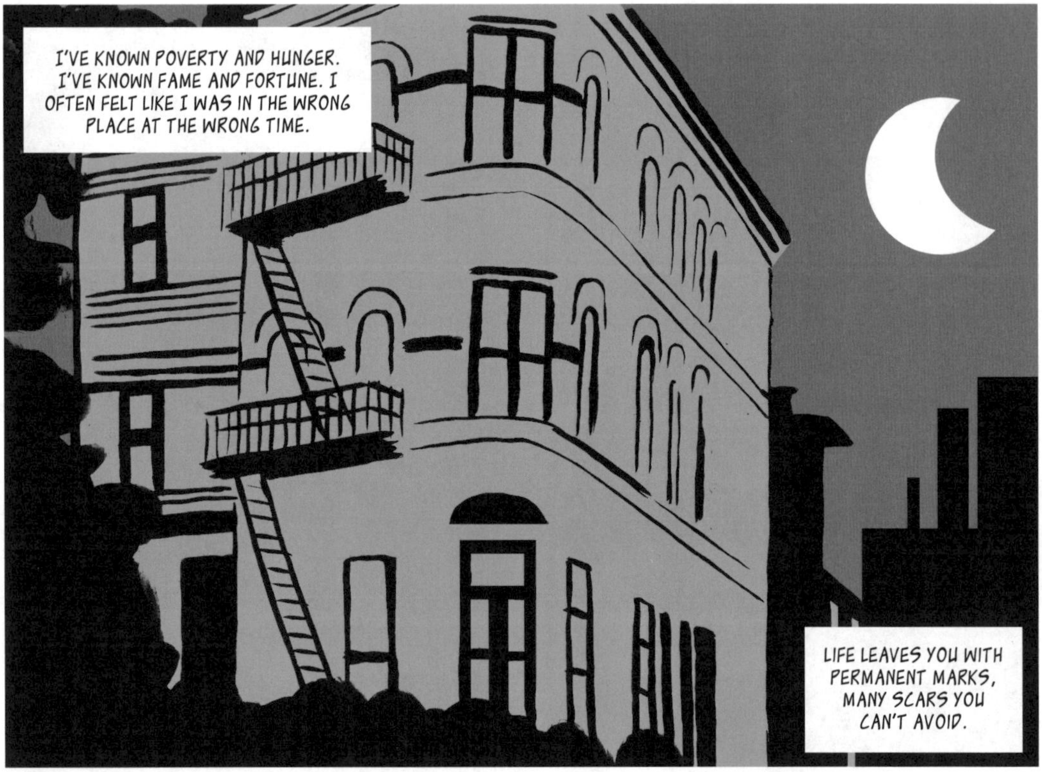
I'VE KNOWN POVERTY AND HUNGER. I'VE KNOWN FAME AND FORTUNE. I OFTEN FELT LIKE I WAS IN THE WRONG PLACE AT THE WRONG TIME.
LIFE LEAVES YOU WITH PERMANENT MARKS, MANY SCARS YOU CAN'T AVOID.

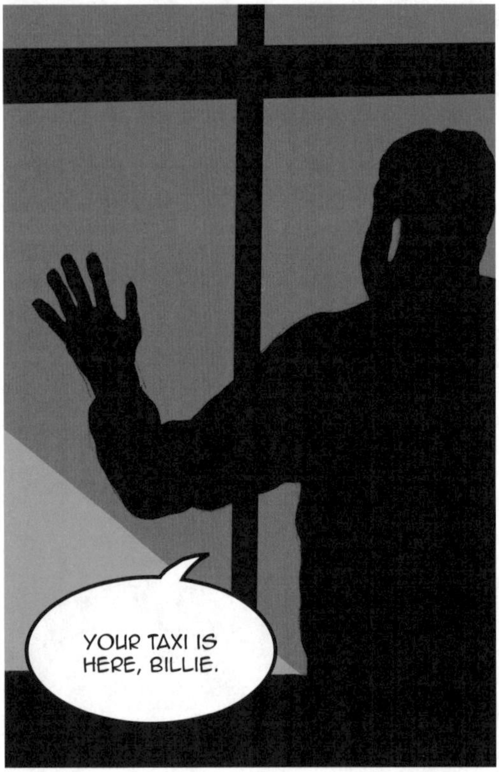
YOUR TAXI IS HERE, BILLIE.

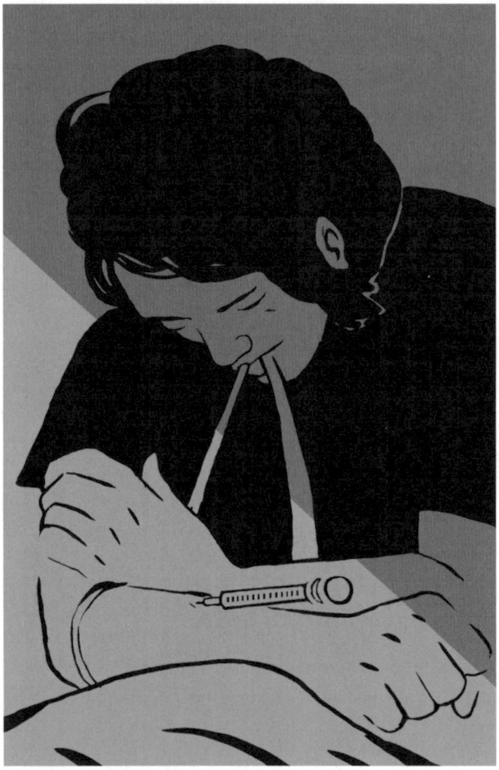

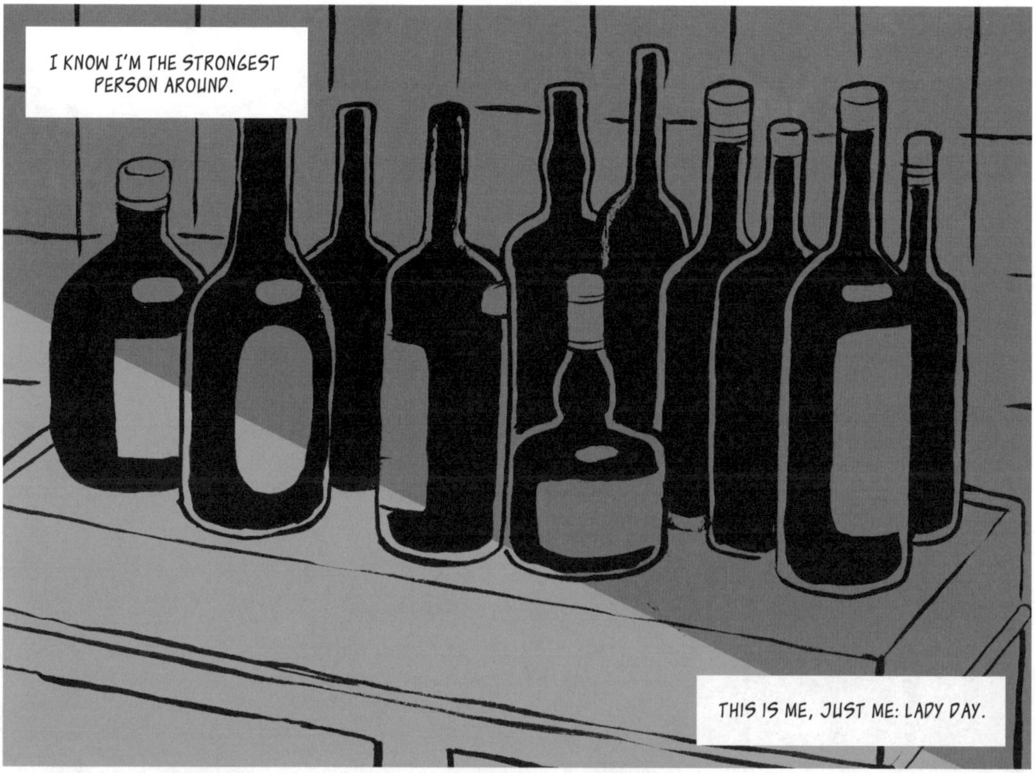
I KNOW I'M THE STRONGEST PERSON AROUND.
THIS IS ME, JUST ME: LADY DAY.

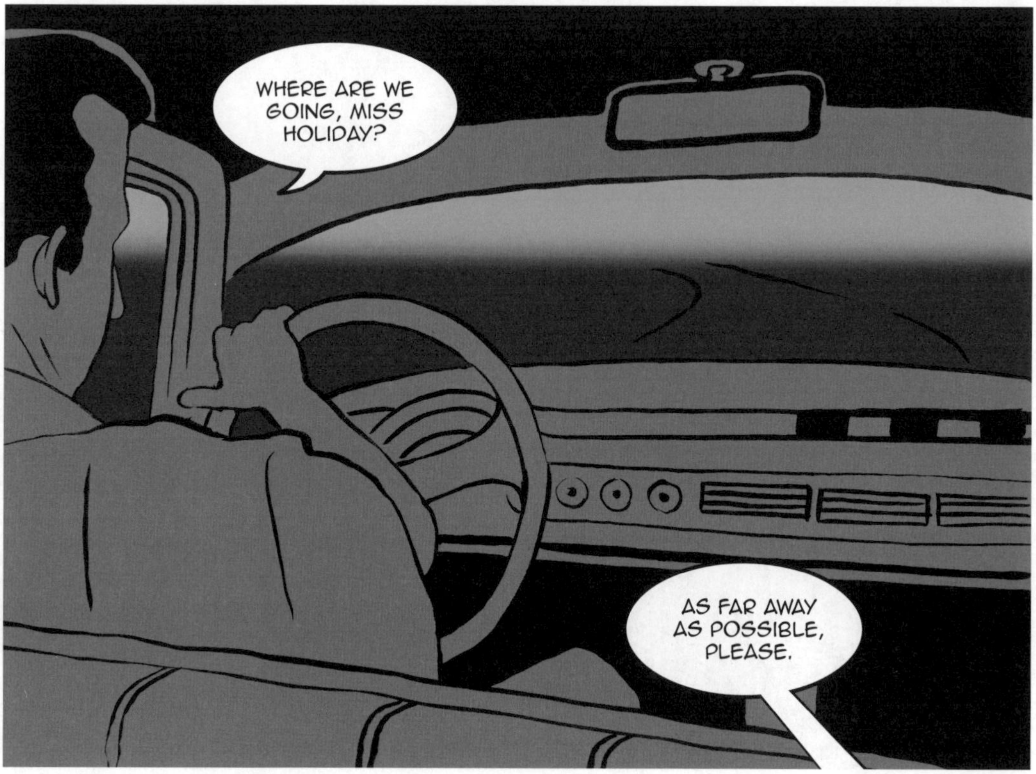
WHERE ARE WE GOING, MISS HOLIDAY?
AS FAR AWAY AS POSSIBLE, PLEASE.

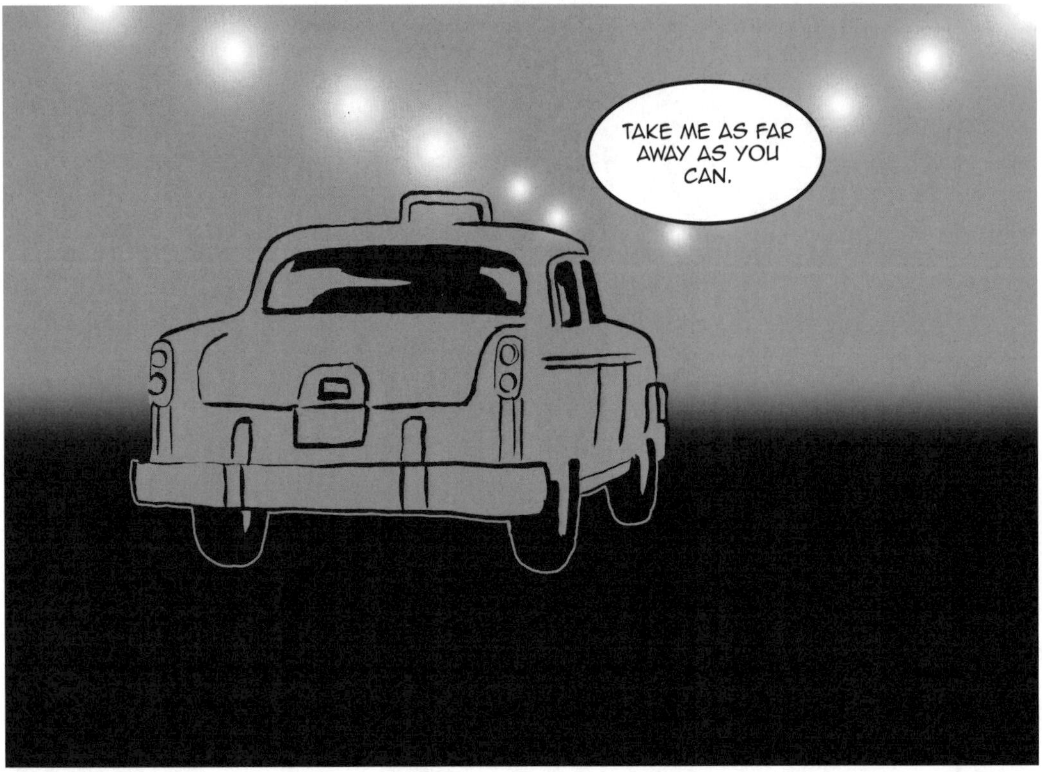
TAKE ME AS FAR AWAY AS YOU CAN.

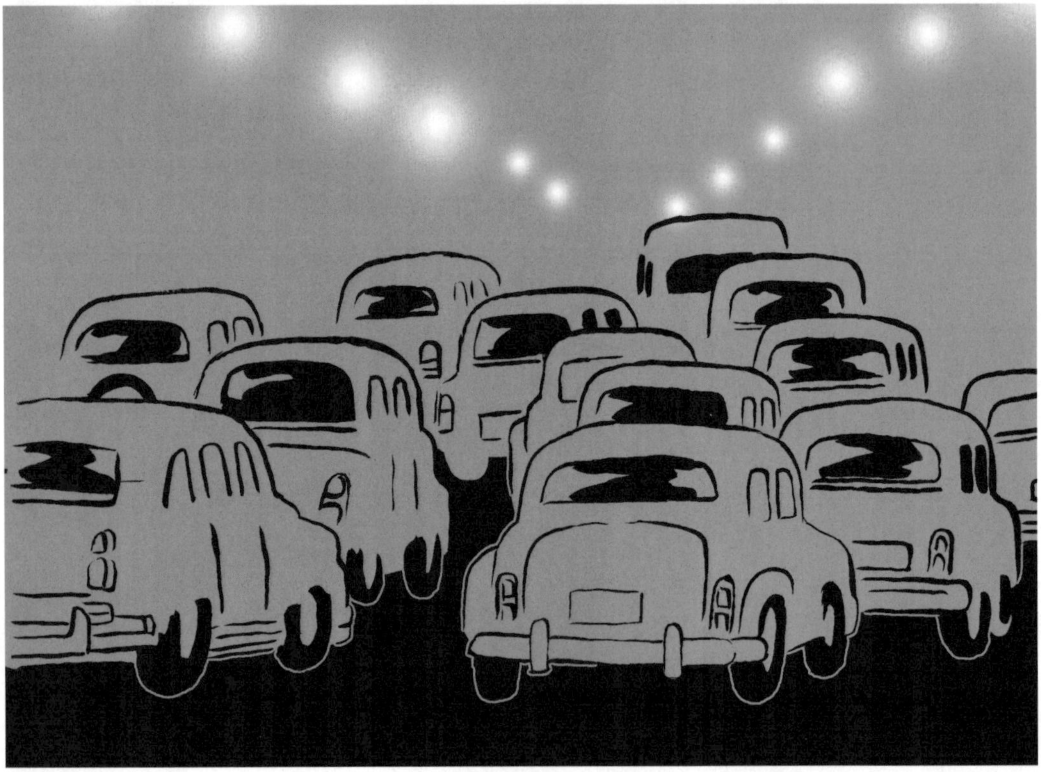

OUTRO

"Lady Sings The Blues"

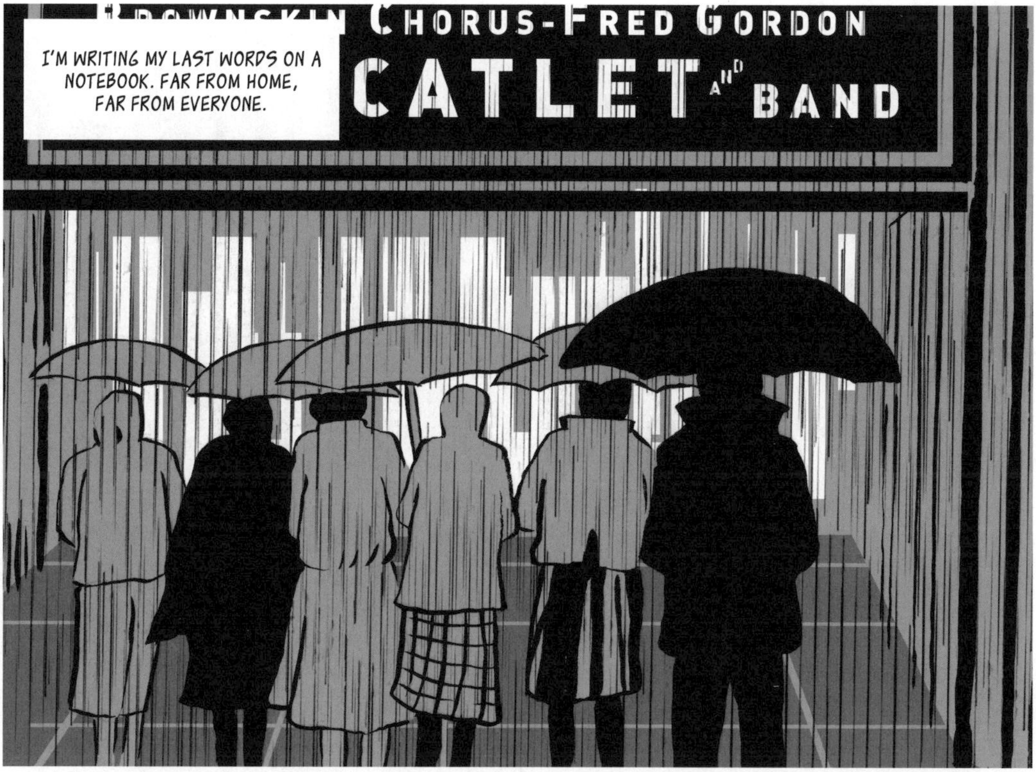
I'M WRITING MY LAST WORDS ON A NOTEBOOK. FAR FROM HOME, FAR FROM EVERYONE.
CHORUS-FRED GORDON
CATLET AND BAND

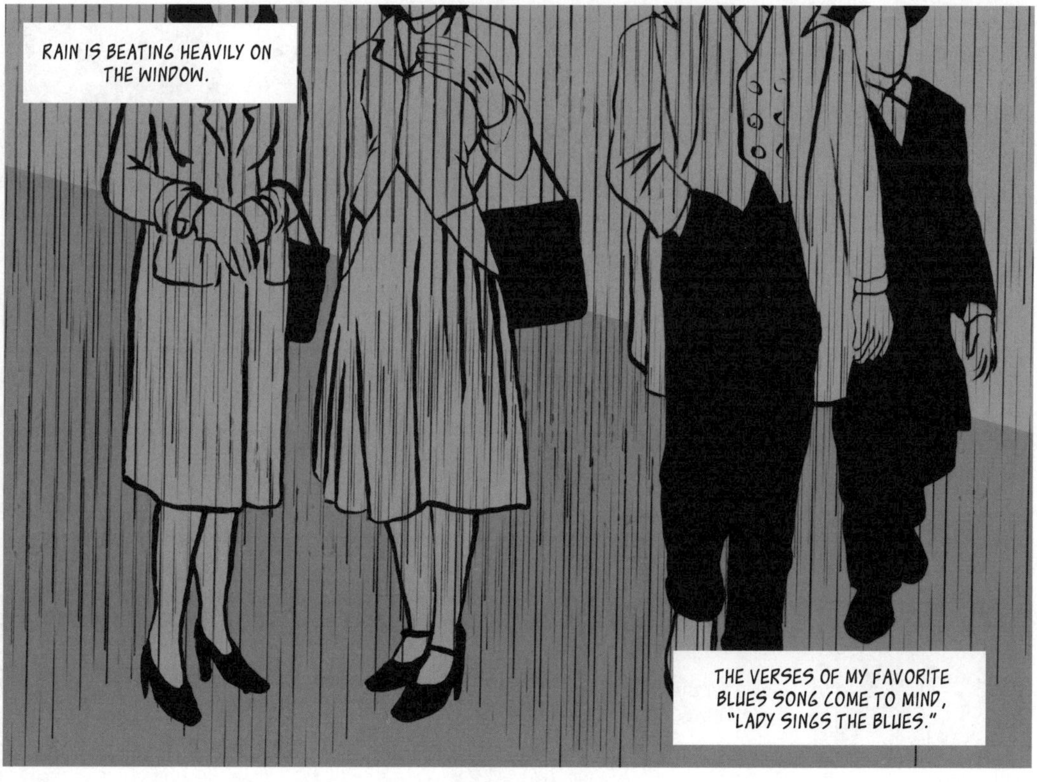
RAIN IS BEATING HEAVILY ON THE WINDOW.
THE VERSES OF MY FAVORITE BLUES SONG COME TO MIND, "LADY SINGS THE BLUES."

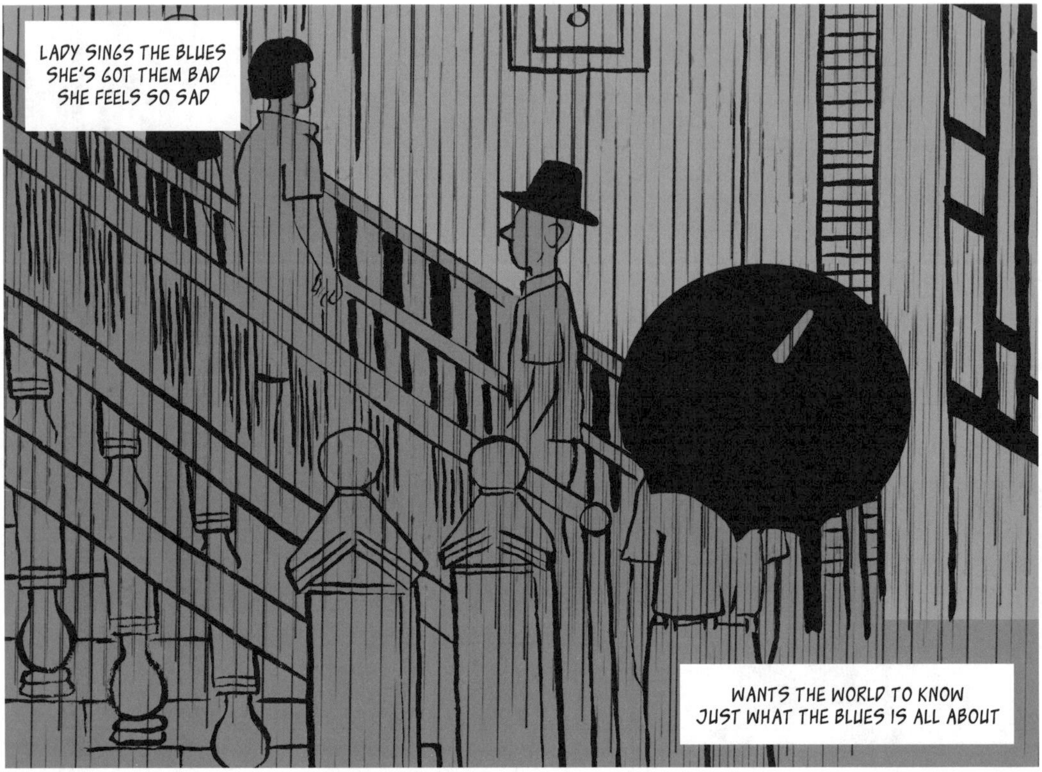
LADY SINGS THE BLUES
SHE'S GOT THEM BAD
SHE FEELS SO SAD
WANTS THE WORLD TO KNOW
JUST WHAT THE BLUES IS ALL ABOUT

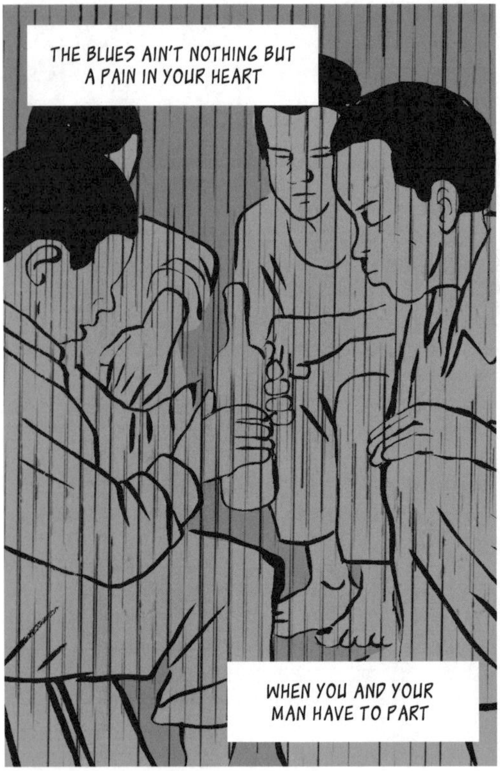
THE BLUES AIN'T NOTHING BUT
A PAIN IN YOUR HEART
WHEN YOU AND YOUR
MAN HAVE TO PART

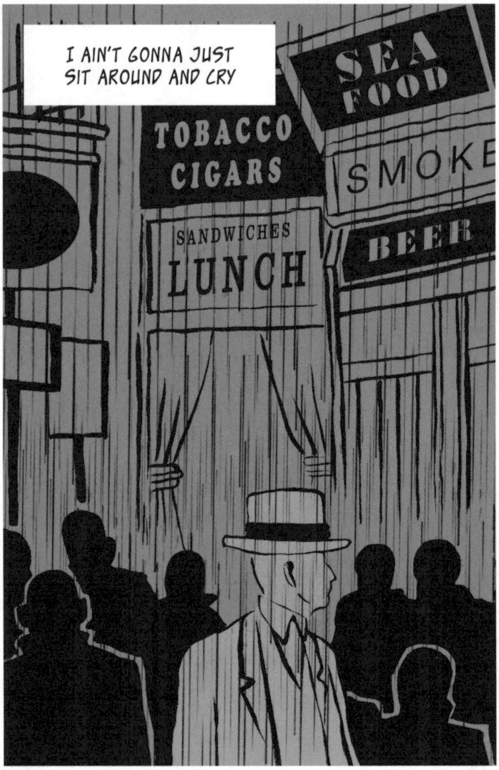
I AIN'T GONNA JUST
SIT AROUND AND CRY
SEA FOOD
TOBACCO
CIGARS
SMOKE
SANDWICHES
LUNCH
BEER

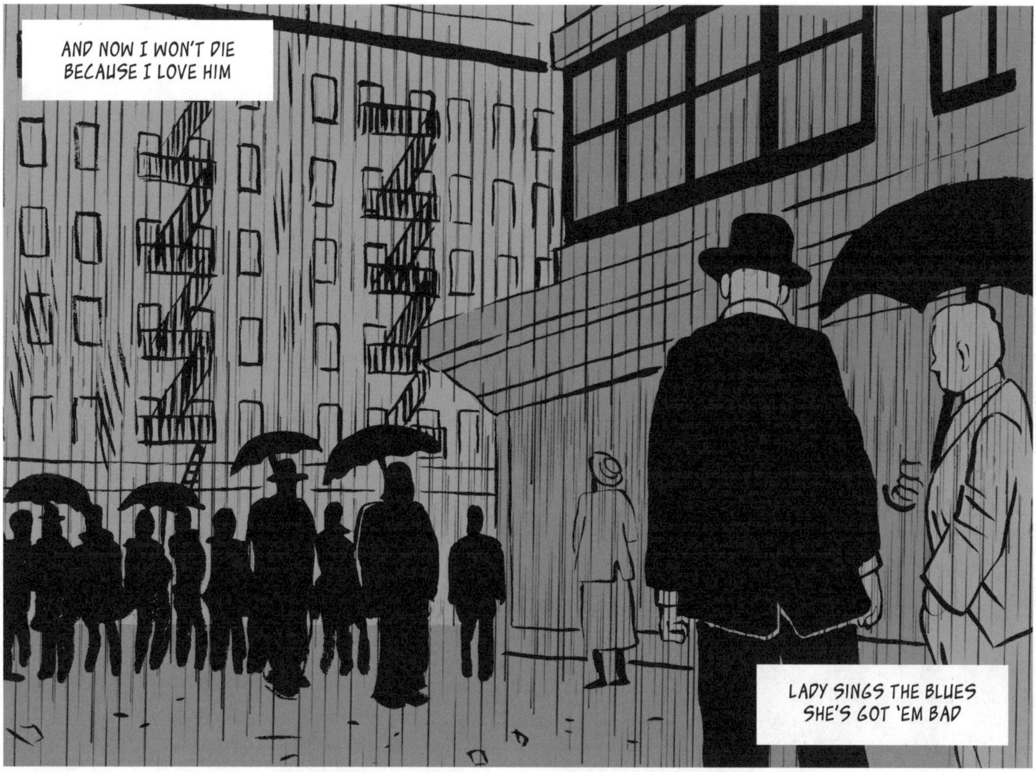
AND NOW I WON'T DIE
BECAUSE I LOVE HIM
LADY SINGS THE BLUES
SHE'S GOT 'EM BAD

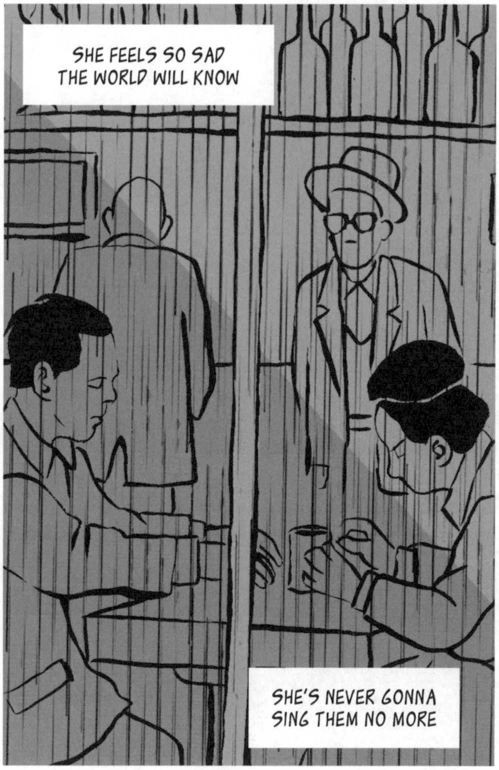
SHE FEELS SO SAD
THE WORLD WILL KNOW
SHE'S NEVER GONNA
SING THEM NO MORE

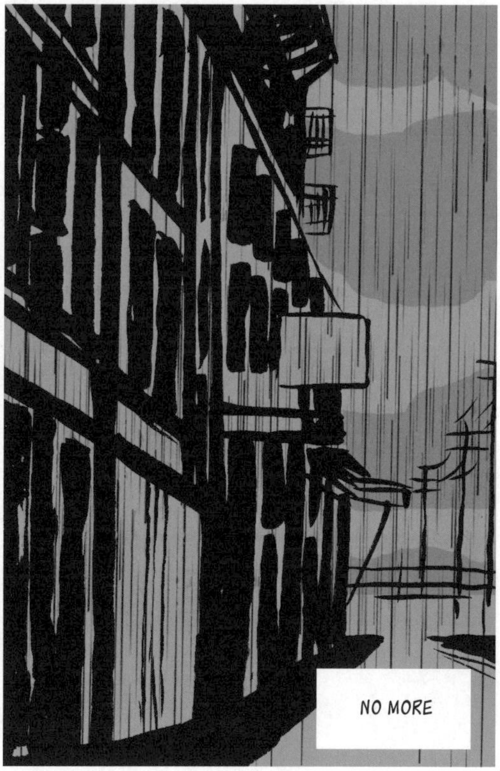
NO MORE

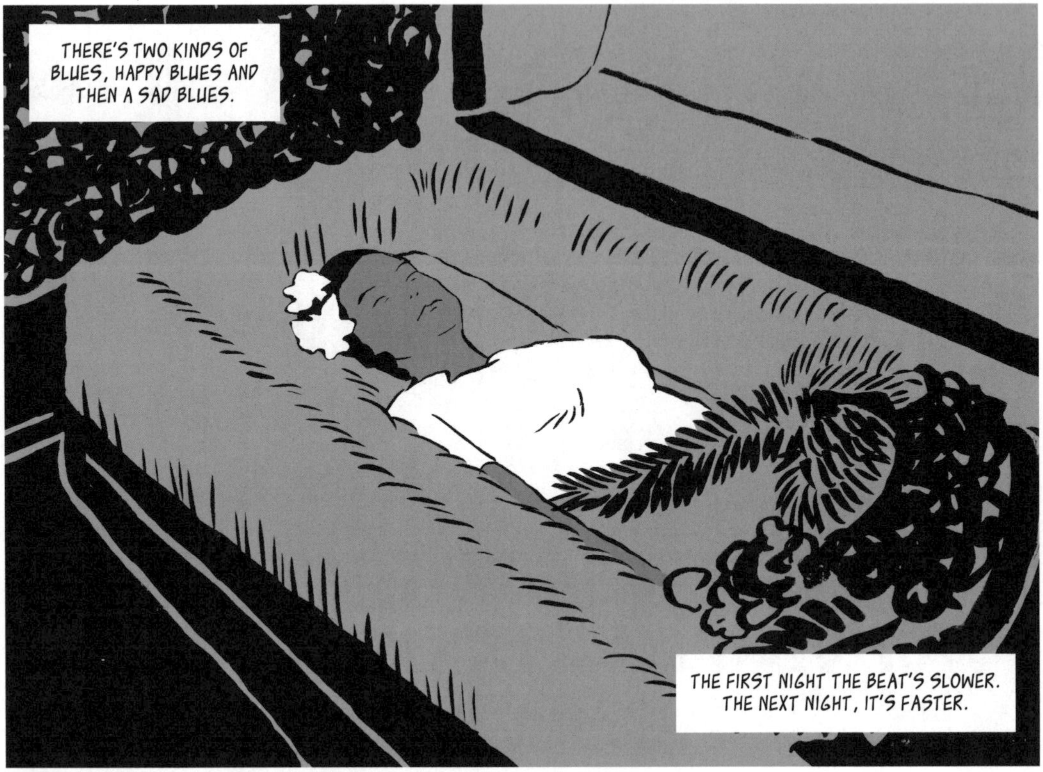
THERE'S TWO KINDS OF BLUES, HAPPY BLUES AND THEN A SAD BLUES.
THE FIRST NIGHT THE BEAT'S SLOWER. THE NEXT NIGHT, IT'S FASTER.

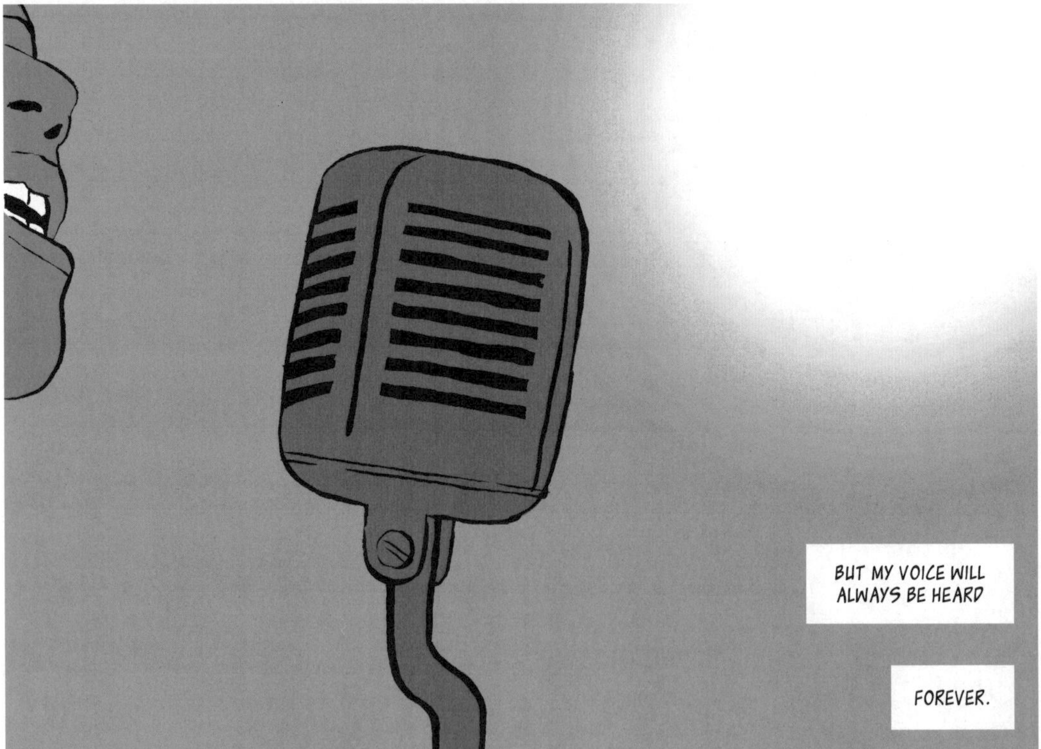
BUT MY VOICE WILL ALWAYS BE HEARD
FOREVER.

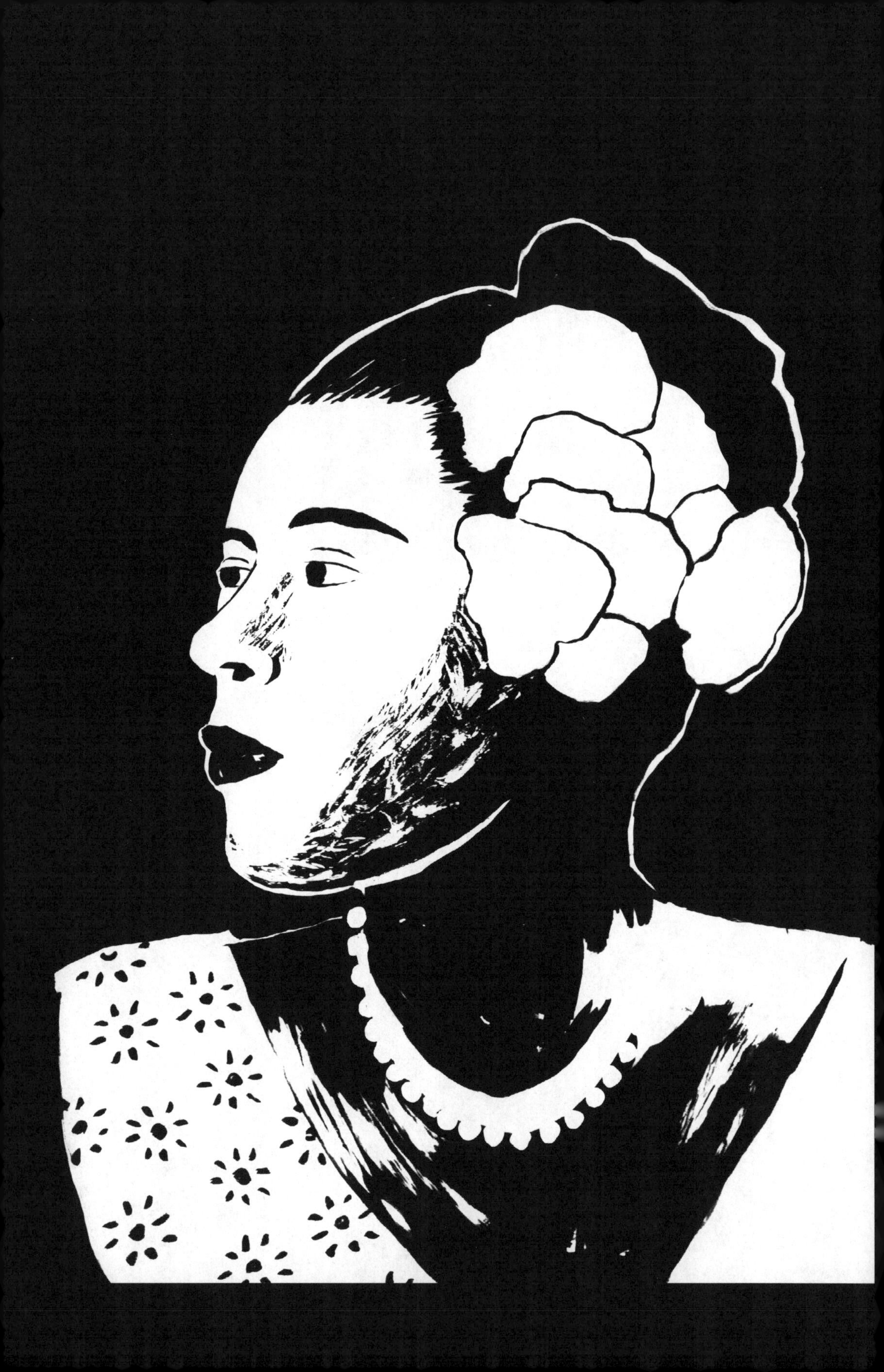

NOTES

This book is a blues song.
There is an intro and an outro.
The brief chapters bear the titles of some of my favorite Lady Day songs.

Talking about the blues means talking about events that happen around us, about fragments of life stories. Blues is life redemption, the will to be something different.
Blues is entertainment and storytelling.
Blues is a political statement.

I have always been fascinated by photos of Billy Holiday, especially the series taken in 1941 by the photographer Carl Van Vechten. They are specifically mentioned in pages 18 - 21. In this sequence of pictures, Lady Day appears with a melancholic expression, revealing one of the many aspects of her complex personality.

There is an additional mention on page 16, third panel, where I have included an excerpt of an interview with Van Vachten, featured in a 1962 issue of Esquire. The portrait of Lester Young on page 24 is based on a photo by Ojon Mili, which was featured in a 1944 issue of Life. The dialogue in speech bubble 3 and 4 on page 49 is taken from David Margolick's book *Strange Fruit: Billie Holiday, Cafe Society, And An Early Cry For Civil Rights*, published in 2000 by Running Press.

Unforgettable voice, key figure, legend, idol.

Born in total poverty, former prostitute and drug addict, Lady Day is immortal, but also an icon of a star system long gone.
Lay Day is a way perceiving life, taking on its challenges and recounting its stories. It means talking about entertainment, a word which alludes to a temporarily relief from the struggles of everyday life. Let us entertain ourselves and live another day.

Billy Holiday is all this. A strong woman who lived passionately until the very end.

Lady Day is the people's voice.

As usual, I should write an endless list of names of friends, colleagues, and contributors. But it is a fact that all the above people have contributed, more or less directly, to help piece together the structure of this story.

I would like to thank those who have shown me love, patience, and support throughout the years.

While awaiting for new paths, thank you.

P.
Rome, May 2017

BIBLIOGRAPHY

Billie Holiday & William Dufty, *Lady Sings the Blues*, Doubleday (1956)

Julia Blackburn, *With Billie: A New Look at the Unforgettable Lady Day*, Vintage Books (2006)

John Szwed, *Billie Holiday: The Musician and the Myth*, Viking (2015)

David Margolick, *Strange Fruit: Billie Holiday, Cafe Society, And An Early Cry For Civil Rights*, Running Press (2000)

Paola Boncompagni, *Lady Day. La vita e le canzoni di Billie Holiday*, Stampa Alternativa (2002)

Arrigo Polillo, *Jazz – La vicenda e i protagonisti della musica afro-americana*, Mondadori (1975)

John Chilton, *Billie's Blues: The Billie Holiday Story 1933–1959*, Stein & Day Pub (1975)

DISCOGRAPHY

Billie Holiday - Commodore, 1946

Lover Man - Decca, 1951

Billie Holiday Sings - Clef Records, 1952

An Evening with Billie Holiday - Clef Records, 1953

Lady Day - Columbia, 1954

Music for Torching - Clef Records, 1955

Lady Sings the Blues - Clef Records / Verve, 1956

Body and Soul - Verve, 1957

Songs for Distingué Lovers - Verve 1957

Lady in Satin - Columbia, 1958

Stay with Me - Verve, 1958

Last Recordings - MGM, 1959

INTRO   3

   "Stormy Blues"   5

BLUES FOR LADY DAY   9

   "Me, Myself And I"   11
   "Body And Soul"   33
   "Strange Fruit"   43
   "Love Me Or Leave Me"   57
   "Goodmorning Heartache"   67
   "Willow Weep For Me"   73
   "Just One Of Those Things"   83

OUTRO   97

   "Lady Sings The Blues"   99

NOTES   107

BIBLIOGRAPHY   109

DISCOGRAPHY   110

Blues for Lady Day: The Story of Billie Holiday
Text and Images © Paolo Parisi 2017

ISBN: 978-1-64273-021-0

Written and illustrated by Paolo Parisi
Translated by Denise Tripodi
English Edition First Published by One Peace Books 2019

Printed in Canada
2 3 4 5 6 7 8 9 10

One Peace Books
43-32 22nd Street STE 204 Long Island City New York 11101
www.onepeacebooks.com